Measuring
and Improving
Organizational
Productivity

MEASURING AND IMPROVING ORGANIZATIONAL PRODUCTIVITY

_____*A Practical Guide*

ROBERT D. PRITCHARD

New York
Westport, Connecticut
London

Library of Congress Cataloging-in-Publication Data

Pritchard, Robert D.
    Measuring and improving organizational productivity : a practical
guide / by Robert D. Pritchard.
        p.   cm.
    Includes bibliographical references (p.).
    ISBN 0-275-93668-6
    1. Industrial productivity—Measurement.   I. Title.
HD56.25.P68   1990
658.5′036—dc20   90-34680

British Library Cataloguing in Publication Data is available.

Library of Congress Catalog Card Number: 90-34680
ISBN: 0-275-93668-6

First published in 1990

Praeger Publishers, One Madison Avenue, New York, NY 10010
An imprint of Greenwood Publishing Group, Inc.

Printed in the United States of America

∞™

The paper used in this book complies with the
Permanent Paper Standard issued by the National
Information Standards Organization (Z39.48-1984).

10 9 8 7 6 5 4 3 2

To my parents,
George and Marge Pritchard.
Thanks for all the gifts you gave me.

Contents

Tables and Figures

FIGURES

TABLES

Acknowledgments

A book like this is a product of many forces and the influence of many people. The original research to evaluate the productivity measurement system was funded by the Air Force Human Resources Laboratory. Eindhoven Technical University in the Netherlands and Texas A&M University here in the United States provided financial support for my visit to the Netherlands where the first draft of the book was written. My colleagues at Eindhoven, Jen Algera, Harrie van Tuijl, and Paul Janssen were an invaluable source of ideas and encouragement. They also provided excellent comments on an earlier draft. Members of my research group, Margaret Watson, Patricia Galgay Roth, Lawrence Weiss, Amie Hedley Goode, Philip Roth, and Amy Price aided substantially in the process. They suggested things to be included and made valuable comments on earlier drafts. They also worked many hours on the production tasks needed to put this book together. Special thanks goes to Larry, who put together a very useful list of issues to be included in the book and to Amie, who did the figures. My wife Sandy gave me many valuable suggestions for making the book more understandable and, as always, was a great source of support and encouragement. Finally, my appreciation goes to Mayla Riley, who helped me find the energy. Thank you all.

Introduction

In the last ten years, productivity has received a great deal of attention because of its ties to important issues such as international competitive position, the success of industries, the survival of specific organizations, and the quality of life of individuals. Productivity growth has been tied to prosperity of national economies, decreased inflation, success of individual organizations, increases in our quality of life, and better use of natural and human resources.

Productivity improvement is also important for the individual organization. To make these improvements, however, tools are needed that help organizational personnel improve the productivity of their organizations. This book is intended as an information source for implementing a tool that should help in that process. It describes the use of the Productivity Measurement and Enhancement System (ProMES) developed by Pritchard and his associates (Pritchard, Jones, Roth, Stuebing, & Ekeberg, 1988, 1989).

The book is intended for several audiences. It should be useful to behavioral science professionals who wish to learn more about practical methods of measuring and improving organizational productivity. In addition, managers who want to learn more about ways to improve productivity in organizations should find it a source of helpful information. It will also be of benefit in teaching. It can be used as a source book in classes stressing practical methods of productivity improvement and for workshops on productivity.

The book is divided into five major parts. Part I presents background on productivity and a description of ProMES. Part II describes how to develop ProMES in an organization in very concrete terms. Part III covers more issues of how to implement a ProMES type system and discusses questions and answers about using the system. In Part IV, using the system with other productivity improvement systems is discussed and Part V describes how to evaluate the effects of a productivity improvement system.

PART I

Background and Description of the Productivity Measurement and Enhancement System (ProMES)

This first major section of the book has seven chapters. Chapter 1 presents information on the importance of productivity measurement and improvement. Chapter 2 is a discussion of the concept of organizational productivity. Desirable characteristics of a productivity measurement system are covered in Chapter 3. Chapter 4 is a description of how ProMES works and Chapter 5 compares ProMES with the desirable characteristics outlined in Chapter 3. Chapter 6 presents the results of past research evaluating ProMES. The final chapter is a discussion of why ProMES is effective in improving productivity.

The Importance of Productivity Measurement and Improvement

Productivity has received so much attention in recent years that it is now a household word. We talk with our spouse about how productive our day was. Computer software is advertised as being an aid to productivity. The national news contrasts the productivity of one country with another. Companies search for programs to improve productivity.

Productivity has become so important that it has been formally identified as a national priority. Tuttle and Weaver (1986a) note a 1985 message from then President Reagan asking for congressional support for a government-wide program to improve productivity in the federal government and requesting that they pass a joint resolution establishing improved productivity as a national goal. A White House Conference on Productivity (1984) was also held. The purpose of this chapter is to explore the reasons why productivity and productivity improvement have become so important.

PRODUCTIVITY: WHY SO IMPORTANT

In order to be fully understood, this great attention to productivity must be put into its historical context. Data on labor productivity have been collected since the early 1900s (Riggs & Felix, 1983). For many decades, these data were largely the concern of labor economists and were not of much interest to many others. By the 1950s and 1960s, the United States was the most productive country in the world and there was little doubt that this state of affairs would continue.

However, by the early 1970s it was clear that this superiority was threatened, especially by Japan and some western European countries. While the U.S. was still the most productive country, its rate of productivity growth was declining, and a number of other countries were improving their national productivity at a faster rate than the U.S. (Kendrick, 1984; Mahoney, 1988; Sink, 1985; Taira, 1988; Tuttle, 1983). During the '70s, the reality of this problem became clear to more than just the economists. The effects of these productivity changes started to be felt nationally. The success of the Japanese in U.S. automobile and steel markets led to plant closings and lost jobs. Major U.S. companies were in severe financial difficulties. Unemployment was rising. What had historically been a trade surplus became a trade deficit and the deficit was increasing. While many causes were responsible for these problems (e.g., Kopelman, 1986), loss of clear U.S. superiority in productivity was seen as one of the major causes.

The productivity issue became a hot topic in groups ranging from the media to labor unions and was presented as a very serious issue. In a special report on productivity, NBC concluded that, "Unless we solve the problem of productivity, our children will be the first generation in the history of the United States to live worse than their parents" (NBC White Paper, 1980). Productivity had become a national issue.

THE EFFECTS OF PRODUCTIVITY GROWTH

There are good reasons for this concern about productivity. Productivity has a major impact on our lives. Its effects can be broken down into effects at the national level, the industry and firm level, and the individual level.

At the national level, productivity is related to important economic outcomes. Productivity growth is an important factor in controlling inflation (Kendrick, 1984; Mahoney, 1988; Riggs & Felix, 1983; Tuttle, 1983). In a market economy, the prices paid for goods are determined largely by the costs of the inputs used to produce the goods (such as the costs of labor, energy, raw materials, etc.) and the profit margin of the producer. There is a constant upward pressure on the cost of these inputs. For example, the price of labor regularly increases due to the pay raises we get each year. If profit margins are roughly constant over time, then increases in the cost of the inputs must be offset by increases in productivity if the prices of the goods are to be kept constant. More output must be produced with the same, more expensive input. If the increases in the costs of inputs are not offset, the prices of the same goods must go up and inflation occurs.

Another way to look at this same process is to focus on wages. We all want higher wages. If higher wages are achieved without increased productivity, the cost of the goods goes up, helping increase inflation

(Kendrick, 1984; Kopelman, 1986). If wages increase with a cor-responding increase in productivity, no inflationary pressure is produced. This is confirmed when economists study growth in real income, that is, change in income relative to change in inflation. Studied over time, productivity growth appears to be responsible for the increase in real income (Kendrick, 1984).

Productivity also influences the real cost of goods (Kendrick, 1984; Mali, 1978). Productivity growth results in producing the same goods for lower costs. Again assuming a roughly constant profit margin, the real cost of goods decreases as productivity increases (Fleishman, 1982; Mahoney, 1988).

Productivity growth also influences some very important non-economic factors (Fleishman, 1982; Kendrick, 1984; Kopelman, 1986; Mali, 1978; Riggs & Felix, 1983). Increased productivity means generating the same goods and services with fewer inputs. Thus, it is a way of conserving societal resources ranging from oil to human labor. Looked at another way, increased productivity allows for more available outputs for the same inputs. Thus, we can be closer to a society of plenty while using fewer of our societal resources.

Productivity growth can also increase the quality of our lives. One can think of the financial resources to be distributed as a pie, with different interests getting a piece of that pie (Kopelman, 1986). Without productivity growth, the economic pie that is divided is constant in size. This means that one demand cannot be met without sacrificing another. For example, with a fixed-sized economic pie, if Social Security or Medicaid is increased, the money must come from somewhere else, such as education or defense. A fixed-sized pie results in battles between factions fighting over the resources, such as environmentalists vs. manufacturers, workers vs. retirees, majority vs. minorities, etc. Productivity growth creates the money to continue to increase the size of the pie. Thus, the size of each slice can increase without taking resources from someone else.

Productivity and productivity growth are also important at the level of the industry and the individual firm. If productivity growth of an industry or a firm is higher than its competitors, that industry or firm survives better (Craig & Harris, 1973; Kendrick, 1984; Tuttle, 1983). If the productivity growth of an industry or firm is higher than the average of its competitors, this leads to lower costs and prices, thus making those products and services more competitive. This leads to higher sales, higher profits, and more job opportunities. The reverse is true for below average productivity growth. Another way to look at the relationships is from the cost of inputs. When increases in wages or increases in the costs of other inputs exceed gains in production efficiencies, the goods produced from labor and capital become more expensive. Competitiveness is then decreased in the world or national marketplace (Riggs & Felix, 1983).

Finally, productivity and productivity growth have important effects on individuals. Aside from the quality-of-life issues raised above, productivity gains will lead to better use of our time, more leisure time, and is a key to advancement in organizations (Kendrick, 1984). Equally importantly, people like to be productive. It is a central aspect of self-fulfillment and self-respect.

THE IMPORTANCE OF MEASURING PRODUCTIVITY

To improve productivity, it is necessary to measure it. Only then can an organization effectively deal with it. Measuring productivity has a whole host of benefits. In addition to the general benefits of improving productivity such as inflation control, industry financial health, competitiveness of individual firms, and improvements in our quality of life, there are a number of specific reasons for measuring productivity in an organization with a system like the one described in this book. These can be broken down into (1) general reasons why productivity measurement is important, (2) advantages that occur through the process of developing the productivity measurement, and (3) beneficial uses of the resulting productivity measurement. These points are presented in list form below.

GENERAL REASONS FOR THE IMPORTANCE OF PRODUCTIVITY MEASUREMENT

Formal productivity measurement:
1. Takes the guesswork out of observations about productivity.
2. Assists in the efficient conduct of operations.
3. Facilitates communication between members of the organization.
4. Aids in evaluating progress toward improving productivity.
5. Is perceived as being more accurate than informal productivity judgments by all members of the organization.
6. Allows independent verification of level of productivity and productivity gains.
7. Makes it much easier to assess changes in productivity over time.
8. Defines and clarifies expected results and activities better than qualitative descriptions.
9. Helps the image of the organization with a parent organization, with clients, and with external funding sources.

ADVANTAGES OCCURRING THROUGH THE PROCESS OF DEVELOPING PRODUCTIVITY MEASURES

The process of developing productivity measures:

1. Serves as a way to review existing assumptions, practices, and measures.
2. Brings into the open the issues that are most central to organizational productivity.
3. Reveals potential problems and identifies productivity improvement opportunities.
4. Serves as a way to clarify roles and help with team building.
5. Helps heighten the awareness of all employees of the need to improve productivity.

BENEFICIAL USES OF THE RESULTING PRODUCTIVITY MEASUREMENT

The resulting measurement from a productivity measurement system can be useful for:

1. A source of feedback to personnel.
2. A source of motivation for increasing productivity.
3. Promoting renewal of professional pride and enhancing employee involvement.
4. Helping set priorities.
5. Comparing the productivity of different units.
6. Identifying problems before they become serious.
7. Helping diagnose reasons for increases or decreases in productivity.
8. Helping diagnose reasons for problems so that better decisions can be made about their solutions.
9. Providing for statistical and mathematical analyses of productivity.
10. The basis for evaluating the effects of any organizational change on productivity.
11. The basis for many other productivity improving interventions such as goal setting, incentives, gainsharing, etc.
12. Helping with long term planning.
13. A basis for wage negotiations.
14. Helping with decisions to continue or discontinue an organization, a function, or a program.
15. Helping with decisions to allocate resources among competing organizations, functions, or programs.

2

Understanding Organizational Productivity

While there is agreement that productivity is important, there is little agreement on what the term *productivity* means (e.g., Bullock & Batten, 1983; Campbell & Campbell, 1988a&b; Craig & Harris, 1973; Kopelman, 1986; Tuttle, 1983). It has been used to mean the efficiency or effectiveness of individuals, groups, organizational units, entire organizations, industries, and nations. It is sometimes used interchangeably with such concepts as output, motivation, individual performance, organizational effectiveness, production, profitability, cost/effectiveness, competitiveness, work quality, and what a new product will enable you to increase if you buy it. Productivity measurement is used to refer to performance appraisal, management information systems, production capability assessment, quality control measurement, and the engineering throughput of a system.

Most productivity authors agree, however, that the term productivity should be limited to efficiency or to efficiency and effectiveness (cf. Tuttle, 1981). *Efficiency* means a measure of outputs divided by inputs. For example, monthly output of a production unit divided by the number of personnel-hours used to generate that output would be an *efficiency measure*. *Effectiveness* is the relationship of outputs to some standard or expectation. For example, monthly production output expressed as a percentage of the goal for that month would be an *effectiveness measure*. Thus, efficiency is how well the organization uses its resources to produce its products or services. Effectiveness is how well the organization is reaching its goals.

It is also important to understand some specific issues about productivity measurement. The first issue is that different disciplines define productivity differently. To an industrial engineer, productivity is the outputs of a system divided by the inputs into that system. Thus, productivity is the efficiency of system throughput. To the typical industrial engineer, the system is a machine, a series of machines, or a series of processes. To an economist, productivity is the outputs of the entire organization or organizational unit divided by the inputs used to create those outputs, where both inputs and outputs are expressed in their dollar value. To the accountant, productivity is a series of ratios of financial information, such as dollars of gross profit divided by labor costs. To the organizational psychologist or organizational behavior specialist, productivity includes efficiency (outputs divided by inputs), but also includes effectiveness (outputs relative to goals or expectations). To such professionals, productivity might also include such things as individual performance, turnover, and accidents.

It is not necessary that one become an expert on the topic of productivity and how others view it to be able to measure and improve it in an organization. It is, however, very important to understand that if a group of people are talking about productivity they may not be using the same definition of the term. Thus, it is important to make sure the people you are working with are all using the same definition or at least know that they are using different ones. Otherwise, misunderstandings will be sure to occur, followed by much wasted time.

PURPOSES IN MEASURING PRODUCTIVITY

There are a number of different purposes for measuring productivity that result in quite different measurement approaches. Pritchard (1990) identifies five different approaches:

The first purpose of measuring productivity is to *compare large groups of organizations to each other*. Comparing national economies, such as France with Japan, or comparing the electronics industry to the health care industry are examples of this purpose. The goal is to see which groups of organizations are more productive and which are less. Economists typically specialize in such measurement.

The second major purpose for productivity measurement is to evaluate the *overall productivity of individual organizations for comparison with each other or with some standard*. Assessing the productivity of individual organizations in order to decide whether a specific firm would be a good financial investment would be an example of this application. Another example would be where organizations compare themselves to similar organizations to assess their competitive position. Both economists and accountants would typically be involved in such measurement.

The third purpose is as a *management information system*. Here the focus is on a single organization and productivity deals with the functioning of the human/technological system. Such measurement is used by top management for strategic planning and policy making. The main question is how well the entire organization or major parts of it are functioning and whether this functioning is improving or declining. Decisions that will be made have to do with allocation of resources to the various organizational functions and with the growth or reduction of these functions. A variety of disciplines might be involved with such measurement.

The fourth purpose is to *control parts of the organization*. The basic objective is to control the movement and timing of both material resources and output products. Industrial engineering and related disciplines typically deal with this type of measurement. Under this heading would be included such activities as production engineering, quality control, production scheduling, physical distribution, materials management, logistics, and inventory control. The intent of such a productivity measurement system is to assess the quality of functioning of a part of the organization by monitoring that functioning. The goal is to identify whether problems are developing or to assess the effect of changes made in the operations.

The management information system and the control function are similar, but there is a difference. The management information system is done on a much larger part of the organization and typically deals with measures which are much more broad in nature. The control function is typically done on a single, identifiable function using very specific measures unique to that function. The information from a management information system is used by higher management while information from a control system is used by lower level management.

The last purpose for measuring productivity is for *use as a motivational tool*. This approach is typically done by industrial-organizational psychologists or organizational behavior specialists. The objective is to improve productivity and the assumption is that if individuals change their behavior appropriately, productivity will increase. The assumption in this approach is that the personnel in the organization have a great impact on productivity. While the technical subsystem is also important, the focus is not on that part of the system directly, but rather on how the technical subsystem is used by the personnel. Therefore, to increase productivity one needs to increase the productivity of the personnel in the organization.

This productivity increase would occur through changes in motivation. Personnel would work more efficiently; their efforts would be more directly related to organizational objectives. They would also improve their work strategies and would use their own and others' time and efforts with less waste. The foundation of this approach is measuring productivity and feeding the productivity data back to unit personnel with the assumption that this will produce the appropriate behavior change that will lead to the increase in productivity.

The Purpose Influences the Measurement System

Each of these different purposes requires a productivity measurement system that is quite different and frequently incompatible with the others. For example, if one wants to compare national economies, the economic approach is the only really practical method. This means using outputs divided by inputs where both are expressed in dollars. In addition, because of the practical constraints, only very broad measures of inputs and outputs can be used, such as gross national product divided by total labor hours used to produce it. Because such measures are so broad, they are not useful for management information systems or for day-to-day management. In addition, these broad measures will not be useful for guiding resource allocation within an organizational unit or for providing information useful for motivational purposes. This purpose also requires that any measures used be common across all the organizations that are to be compared. This limits measures to partial productivity measures, typically focusing on labor productivity. Such measures will not give a complete picture of organizational functioning since they measure only some of the inputs and outputs.

One main difference between measuring productivity for use as a motivational tool and the other purposes is the issue of separating out the effects of factors that personnel can control from those that personnel cannot control (Algera, 1989). In the other four applications, it is desirable to assess the combined effects of the personnel and the technology or the combined effects of the personnel, the technology, and the environment. Measuring productivity for motivational purposes implies measuring those aspects of the organization's productivity that the personnel can control. The principle is that to be maximally effective, feedback should be limited to aspects of the work that personnel can change.

There are a number of other differences between the motivational purpose and the other purposes. One difference is that for motivational purposes all aspects of the work should be measured. This is because there is a tendency for personnel to direct more energy toward tasks that are being measured, giving less attention to tasks which are not being measured. For example, both quantity and quality should be measured if they are both important. The other approaches must frequently be satisfied with incomplete measures of productivity since measuring all important functions is not feasible. Another difference in the motivational approach is that the productivity measurement system should be applicable to all units of the organization, not just production or areas where outputs are easily measured. Finally, both effectiveness and efficiency are typically measured in the motivational approach since both are frequently important.

THE INTENT OF ProMES

It is important to understand that ProMES, the productivity measurement system described in this book, is primarily designed as a productivity measurement system for the last of the purposes identified above: improving productivity through the activities of the personnel in the organization. While it can be adapted to function as a management information system or for the control function, it is primarily designed as a motivational tool where feedback about productivity is given to personnel to help them do their work better and more effectively.

It is also important to be sensitive to the fact that different people in the organization may well have different purposes in mind for starting a productivity measurement project. It is very important that all agree on the purpose of doing the measurement. If all agree that the purpose is to improve productivity of the organization or some unit(s) in the organization by having personnel work more effectively, then this manual will be very useful in accomplishing that purpose.

3

Desirable Characteristics of a Productivity Measurement System

With some of the conceptual background about productivity summarized, we now turn to a discussion of the criteria for a good measurement system. Numerous authors have discussed such criteria (e.g., Kendrick, 1977; Kopelman, 1986; Mahoney, 1988; Mali, 1978; Muckler, 1982; Pritchard, 1990; Tuttle, 1981). These serve as comparison points for evaluating a productivity measurement system, and will be used in a later chapter as the basis for evaluating ProMES.

A productivity measurement system should produce an *overall index of productivity*. One reason a single index is important is its motivational value. A single index provides personnel with a sense of improvement or decrement. It allows them to see the results of their efforts and strengthens the ties between their actions and their productivity. A single index is also beneficial for its information value. A large number of pieces of information about organizational functioning can be very difficult to assimilate and use for making decisions.

A single index is also useful for attempts at organizational change. It is valuable for designing interventions, such as goal setting and incentives, because the single index can readily be used for setting the goal and as the basis for awarding the incentives. Multiple measures require multiple goals and make awarding incentives difficult. Having a single index also makes it fairly easy to evaluate the effects of behavioral, structural, or technological change efforts. Many approaches to measuring productivity use a single index (e.g., Riggs & Felix, 1983; Joint Financial Management Improvement Program, 1976; Kim, 1980; Peeples, 1978; Pritchard, et al., 1989; Rowe, 1981; Tuttle & Weaver, 1986a, 1986b; Tuttle, Wilkinson, & Matthews, 1985).

In addition to an overall index of productivity, a productivity measurement system should also have *subindices of productivity*, which deal with multiple tasks and activities. Since the vast majority of organizational units do multiple activities, it is important to use multiple indices of productivity that provide information on the separate functions of the unit. Personnel can then see how they are doing on the different functions and change their behavior accordingly. Information on subindices is also useful for identifying problem areas and determining strategies to increase productivity.

It is also desirable for a system to give information on *how much as well as how good* the output of the unit is. That is, personnel need to know how much was done, for example that 240 units were done this week. This is purely descriptive information that helps to judge the functioning of the unit. However, it is also important that they know how good or bad that level of output is. In other words, is finishing 240 units good or bad? Does it meet expectations, is it slightly above expectations, well above, or what? This type of information is evaluative rather than descriptive. Both kinds of information are important to provide personnel with a complete picture of their functioning and to maximally motivate.

A productivity measurement system must be *valid*. In this context, validity means several things. The first thing it means is that the system be complete. That is, all important aspects of the productivity of the organization must be measured by the system, not just a subset of the important functions. Second, the system should be accurate in the sense that the things measured are accurate reflections of what the organization is supposed to be doing.

Validity also means maintaining differences in importance. The various things an organizational unit does are not of equal importance and this differing importance must be preserved in the measurement system. Measures of quantity, quality, extent to which preventative maintenance is done on schedule, and timeliness of paperwork may all be aspects of the work of a manufacturing unit, but these activities would vary considerably in importance. Thus, some method of importance weighting must be used so differing importance is communicated to personnel. For example, the individual measures such as quantity, quality, extent to which preventative maintenance is done on schedule, and timeliness of paperwork should be combined into the single index in such a way that the differing importance is maintained.

Another issue in the validity of a productivity measurement system is that the system must account for the principle that more is not always better. Improving quantity of production, for example, is not always a good thing. Quantity of output is very important and must be kept high. However, going beyond some level of output may have some negative consequences. At some point, quality may suffer or the equipment may be more easily damaged. In other words, improving quantity is very important, but only up to a point. Beyond that point, further improvements in quantity are not as important since a point of diminishing returns is reached. Another example would be in the area of training. Training may be a crucial function in the organization, but training more people than needed to do the work becomes counterproductive.

Pritchard, et al. (1989) refer to this as the *non-linearity issue*. The idea is that the function relating amount of output to value or effectiveness of that output is not linear. This can be seen more clearly in Figure 3–1. The figure uses the quantity example discussed above. Suppose a unit is making aluminum cans. The figure shows the relationship between number of cans produced and the contribution or *effectiveness* of that number of cans for the functioning of the unit. The horizontal axis shows number of cans going from a low of 700 per hour to a high of 1300 per hour. Effectiveness increases steadily from 700 cans per hour to 1100. However, after 1100 the line begins to level off. This shows that increases beyond 1100 are not as valuable as increases below 1100. A point of diminishing returns is reached at 1100.

The figure is a good example of where the line or function relating amount of output to the contribution of that output is not a straight line, it is non-linear. The point is that such non-linearities are very common and must be accounted for in a valid productivity measurement system.

The problem is not solved by weighting the different types of output the unit does by how important each is. This does not account for non-linearities. Importance weights assume that the importance is constant no matter how much is actually being done. This is not an accurate assumption because the importance of a measure changes as a function of the level of the output. This is precisely what non-linearities are saying. This can be seen by comparing two unit activities. Suppose a unit manufactures a product and must also maintain its equipment. Overall, the amount of output is more important than doing preventative maintenance on the equipment. However, if the number of units produced is already high and many pieces of equipment are overdue for maintenance, it might be more important to do the maintenance than to further improve the number of units produced. Importance weighting would indicate that improving amount of output is always more important than doing maintenance; non-linearities would indicate that sometimes improving on maintenance is more important than more output.

This problem has been recognized before. Campbell (1977), Campbell and Campbell (1988c), Kahn (1977), and Seashore (1972) have made similar arguments that more is not always better. A solution to the problem is offered by ProMES. It incorporates a method of accounting for non-linearities in measures of performance and

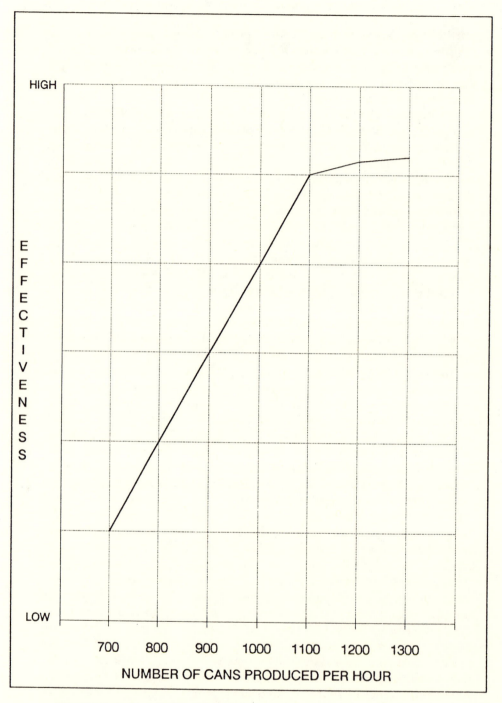

Figure 3-1 Example of Non-Linearity

productivity. Pritchard and Roth (1989) and Galgay and Pritchard (1989) compared the ProMES approach with one based on a linear system and found that the non-linear system produced information leading to very different decisions on how to improve productivity than did the linear system.

The next criterion is that the system be *flexible*. By this we mean two things. In any organization there will be changes over time in what the organization's goals and policies are. There may be a change, for example, from an emphasis on quantity to an emphasis on quality. The productivity measurement system must be able to accommodate these changes when they occur.

The second type of flexibility is that an ideal productivity measurement system should also be able to accommodate both efficiency and effectiveness measures, since both have advantages. A system that could only accommodate one or the other would not be as useful.

Another desirable feature of a productivity measurement system is the ability to *aggregate the measurement systems of different units* into a single broader measurement system. For example, suppose one department of a community mental health organization had six sections. It would be desirable to develop a measurement system for each section and then be able to aggregate those systems to produce a single measure for the department and then a single measure for the multiple departments.

Such aggregation requires that the separate functions of the smallest units be measured and that the measurement for the separate units be expressed in a common metric. Next, since not all units are equal in their contribution to the broader organizational unit, a determination of the relative importance or contribution of each of the units must be made when doing the aggregation.

It would also be desirable to be able to *directly compare the productivity of units* doing quite different things. For example, it would be very informative to be able to compare a maintenance unit with a production unit in the same part of the organization. Such a comparison would be useful for resource allocation, producing competition between units, and for awarding outcomes such as incentives and forms of recognition to the units.

The next criterion is that the system be *accepted* by the organization. The best system that could be imagined would be ineffective if organizational personnel did not accept it and find it useful. This acceptance must include members of the unit and supervisors, as well as management.

Finally, a good system should have *positive motivational properties*. By this we mean that the system should have built into it the capability to increase productivity by increasing motivation. Its implementation and use should in and of itself be expected to enhance productivity.

These criteria are the main factors against which to evaluate a productivity measurement system. In the next two chapters, ProMES is described and how this system meets these criteria is discussed.

4

The ProMES Approach:
An Overview

The approach to be described here is termed the Productivity Measurement and Enhancement System, abbreviated ProMES (Pritchard et al., 1989). ProMES is a way of measuring productivity and feeding back productivity information to personnel. Its theoretical background stems from the theory of organizational behavior presented by Naylor, Pritchard, and Ilgen (1980).

In its most simple form, the idea behind ProMES can be seen in Figure 4–1. The process starts with the identification of the objectives of the organization. From these objectives, a productivity measurement system is developed that is consistent with the objectives. Next, the data resulting from measuring productivity is fed back to members of the organization in the form of regularly occurring formal feedback reports. These feedback reports are the basis of discussions about how to improve productivity. As productivity is increased, the organizational objectives are more fully achieved.

```
                              PRODUCTIVITY
ORGANIZATIONAL                                          FEEDBACK
                    ----->    MEASUREMENT    ----->                  ----->
OBJECTIVES                                              SYSTEM
                              SYSTEM


                                            MEETING
            INCREASED
  ------>                       ------>      ORGANIZATIONAL
            PRODUCTIVITY
                                            OBJECTIVES
```

Figure 4–1 Basic ProMES Approach

The basic process in ProMES is a bottom-up approach. After approval of the project by higher management, the development of the productivity measurement system is done at the bottom of the organizational hierarchy and brought up. Specifically, a design team composed of facilitators, representative members of the unit (incumbents) and supervisors have a series of meetings to go through the process of developing the measurement system. Once this design team agrees on the specifics of the measurement system, they bring it to higher management for discussion and final approval. Once it is approved by management, written feedback reports are developed and circulated.

STEPS IN THE DEVELOPMENT OF ProMES

The specific steps in developing the ProMES are to: (1) identify salient products; (2) develop indicators of these products; (3) establish contingencies; and (4) develop feedback reports.

To illustrate these four steps concretely, we shall use an extended example of a small production unit working for an electronics assembly plant. The plant is responsible for producing various kinds of printed circuit boards which are used in computer-related equipment. Boards are assembled and tested by a series of teams that work on the boards in a serial fashion. Thus, a given team cannot finish more boards than the previous team has ready for them.

The team in the example is composed of technicians who are responsible for the final steps in the production process. After the team has finished with a board it goes to inspection for a functional check and inspection of its construction. Some boards are identified as high priority because they are necessary to complete customer orders on time. These must be completed on schedule. The team is also responsible for a series of maintenance and housekeeping/safety procedures that are checked with a regular inspection.

This example is based on an actual unit for which the system was developed, but it is an abbreviation of the system developed for that unit. In addition, it is meant as an overview only. The specific steps in developing the system and the issues to be considered in development are the subject of the second and third sections of the book.

Step 1: Identify Products

Each unit in an organization has a set of objectives or results that it is expected to accomplish. In ProMES, these are called products. Since the productivity of an organization is a function of how well it generates these products, the first step in developing the productivity measurement system is to identify them.

The design team of supervisors, representative members of the unit, and one or more facilitators would first meet to develop a list of the salient products. Assume that the following products were identified:

1. Maintain High Production
2. Make Highest Quality Boards Possible
3. Maintain High Attendance
4. Correctly Follow Housekeeping and Maintenance Procedures

Step 2: Develop Indicators

Once the products have been identified, the next step is to develop indicators of these products. An indicator is a measure of how well the unit is generating the product in question. To identify the indicators, the members of the design team (facilitators, supervisors and members of the unit) are asked to think of measures they would use to show how well they are generating their products. There may be one or several indicators for a given product. Some indicators may already be available; some may have to be developed. After the indicators are discussed and refined, the products and indicators might look like this:

Product 1. Maintain High Production
> Indicator 1: Output—Percent of boards completed. Number of boards completed, divided by number received to work on.
> Indicator 2: Meeting Priorities—Number of high-priority boards completed, divided by number needed.

Product 2. Make Highest Quality Boards Possible
> Indicator: Inspections Passed—Percentage of boards passing inspection.

Product 3. Maintain High Attendance
> Indicator: Percent hours worked = Total hours worked divided by maximum hours possible to work.

Product 4. Correctly Follow Housekeeping and Maintenance Procedures
> Indicator: Audit Violations—Number of violations of a general audit of housekeeping and maintenance procedures.

Once the products and indicators are finalized by the design team, they are presented to higher management for review and approval. This can result in some discussion and modification of the products and indicators.

Step 3: Establish Contingencies

Once approval is obtained for the products and indicators, the next step is to establish the contingencies. A contingency is the relationship between the amount of the indicator and the effectiveness of that amount of the indicator. It is a way of expressing how much different amounts of the indicator contribute to the overall functioning of the unit. The top half of Figure 4–2 is a picture of the general form of a contingency. The horizontal axis is the amount of the indicator which ranges from its worst feasible level to the best level that is realistically possible. On the vertical axis of the figure are the effectiveness values of the various levels of the indicator. The scale ranges from +100, which is maximum effectiveness, to –100, minimum effectiveness. It also has a zero point which is defined as the expected, or neutral, level of effectiveness. It is the level that is seen as neither good nor bad, but the level that the unit is expected to generate.

For the example in the figure, we have chosen the quality indicator. Suppose that the best possible percentage of boards passing inspection is seen as 100 percent. In other words, it was seen as feasible to have all boards pass inspection. Let us assume they say that the worst realistically possible percentage passing inspection is 99 percent. Anything even close to a value as low as 99 percent would mean a major problem was occurring in production.

Once the best and worst levels of output have been established, the next task is to identify the actual function that relates the amount of the indicator to effectiveness. First, the zero point of the indicator is determined; the level that is neither good nor bad. Once this is decided, a point would be placed on the figure at the intersection of the zero point of the vertical axis and the level of the established neutral point on the horizontal axis. If the neutral point was identified as a return rate of 99.4 percent, it would be so indicated as shown in the bottom half of Figure 4–2 where the line passes through the value of 0 on the vertical axis directly above the value 99.4 on the horizontal axis.

Next, the effectiveness level of the maximum and minimum indicator levels would be established. The steps to do this are described in detail in Chapter 11. Assume that the personnel in the organization said that the lowest possible percent of boards passing inspection

GENERAL FORM

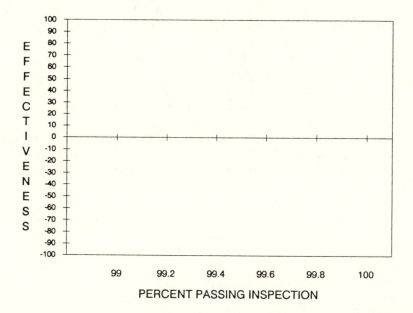

COMPLETED CONTINGENCY

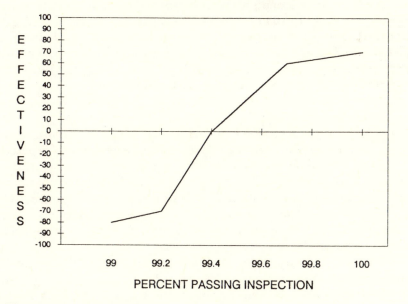

Figure 4-2 General Form of a Contingency

(99%) would correspond to an effectiveness of -80, and to be at the highest possible passing rate (100%) would be a +70.

Once the zero points are identified and the effectiveness values of the maximums and minimums are established, the remainder of the points in the function are discussed and agreed on by the group. Group discussion is continued until consensus is reached. Once these other points on the function are identified, this might result in a contingency like that in the bottom of Figure 4–2. It indicates that going above the neutral point of a 99.4 percent passing rate is positive, but this increase is not linear because once they get to a passing rate of 99.7 percent, further increases do not represent as great an increase in effectiveness. Likewise, at the low end, once the passing gets as bad as 99.2 percent, they are doing very badly and further decreases are proportionally not as bad.

This process would be done with each of the indicators and once they were all scaled and reviewed for accuracy, the contingency set would be complete. An example of what the set might look like is presented in Figure 4–3.

For each indicator there is a contingency. The contingency for the first production indicator, percent of boards completed, shows that it is expected for the team to finish almost all the boards they are given, since the zero point is at 97 percent. This contingency is very steep from 90 percent to 100 percent and much flatter after 100 percent. This means that improvements over 100 percent are not as valuable as improvements up to 100 percent. This is because the unit could get a score of over 100 percent only if they finished all the boards from the current month plus boards they had not finished from the past month. While it is good for the unit to make up this backlog, it would have been better for them to do it during the month the work was due. This is reflected by the less steep slope.

The second contingency is also for production and is the percent of high priority boards completed during the month. The contingency shows that a point of diminishing returns is reached at 97.5 percent since the slope becomes less steep there, although the change in slope is small. This change occurs because some high priority boards are delivered at the very end of the month and stopping the team activity to complete them is not necessary as long as they are completed at the beginning of the next month. Together these first two contingencies form the product Maintain High Production.

The third contingency, for the quality indicator, is a copy of the contingency in the lower part of Figure 4–2. The fourth contingency is for attendance. It shows that personnel are expected to work 97 percent of their scheduled hours and that after 98 percent, further increases are not as important. This was due to the belief that some

PRODUCTION #1

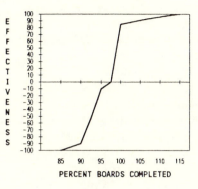

PRODUCTION #2

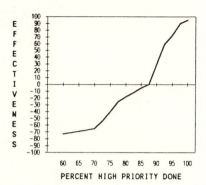

QUALITY

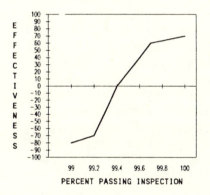

ATTENDANCE

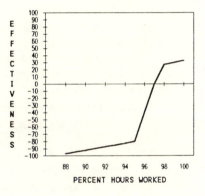

HOUSEKEEPING AND MAINTENANCE

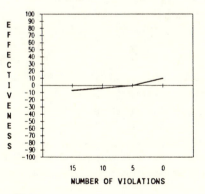

Figure 4–3 Contingency Set

illness is unavoidable and if personnel came in when truly ill, they could cause errors and accidents and could spread their illness to other employees. The last contingency is for violations of housekeeping and maintenance procedures. This contingency is quite flat, indicating that it is not nearly as important as the other indicators. Essentially it reflects keeping the work areas neat and doing the minimal maintenance needed to keep the equipment functional.

Two things are particularly important about the contingencies. First, the overall slope of the contingency expresses the relative importance of the indicator. Steep slopes such as in the first three indicators mean that they are very important to the functioning of the unit. Fairly shallow slopes like the one for housekeeping and maintenance mean the indicator is much less important. Those of intermediate slope, such as for attendance, are in the middle. A steep slope implies that variation in the indicator results in large variations in effectiveness; a less steep slope implies that variations in the indicator result in less variation in effectiveness. Second, the contingencies can be non-linear as can be seen from the fact that the lines do not form a straight line. As will be discussed below, this is necessary to accurately reflect the realities of an organization's functioning.

These properties of the contingencies are very important. Many productivity measurement systems, even if they attempt to measure all the important tasks of the unit and combine them into a single number, do so by some form of summing the measures. This amounts to assuming that all the functions of the organization are equally important. Clearly, this does not reflect organizational reality. Different things the organization does are not equally important. Another approach that could be used to incorporate differential importance into the measurement system is to weight each measure by its importance. The ProMES approach is superior to this technique because the simple weighting method assumes that there is a linear relationship between amount of the measure and productivity. That is, to improve a given amount at the low end of the measure is as good as improving that same amount at the high end. It would be very common, for example, for improvements in the middle range of an indicator to result in large improvements in effectiveness, but for improvements at the high end to result in very little increased effectiveness. In other words, a point of diminishing returns is reached. Once the organization gets to a fairly high level of productivity on one aspect of the work, it is frequently better to work on improving something they are not doing as well, rather than continue to improve something that is already at a high level.

For example, if the circuit board manufacturing unit was getting a very high percentage of its high priority boards completed it might be better to try to improve attendance rather than attempt to further improve its percentage of high-priority boards. Put another way, even though percentage of high-priority boards is more important overall than attendance, if percentage of high-priority boards is very good, improving low attendance can become more important to the overall effectiveness of the organization.

Simply weighting each measure by its importance ignores this non-linearity, because no matter where the organization is on the measure, it is always weighted by a constant amount. The contingencies in ProMES capture this non-linearity and thus provide a more accurate picture of the organization's functioning.

Step 4: Develop Feedback Reports

The last step is to put the system together by putting the measures into a formal feedback system. This would be accomplished by first collecting the indicator data for a given period of time. Assume that the time period selected was one month. The data for the five indicators would be collected at the end of the month. Then, based on the contingencies, effectiveness scores would be determined for each indicator. This is illustrated in Table 4–1. For example, if the maintenance unit completed 98 percent of its boards for the month of July, this value of the indicator is associated with an effectiveness value of +40 on the vertical axis of the contingency. Continuing this process would give an effectiveness value for each indicator, as shown in the table.

Once the effectiveness values are determined, they can be summed to get overall effectiveness for products with more than one indicator, as seen for the first product. The total effectiveness of the product Production would be the sum of the two indicators for that product: +40 for percent of boards completed and -5 for percent high priority boards completed, for a total of +35. Next, overall productivity can be calculated by summing the effectiveness scores for each product. In the example, this Overall Effectiveness score is +92.

These effectiveness scores have a specific meaning. A score of zero means that the unit overall is meeting expectations, their productivity is neither particularly good nor bad. As the score becomes positive, they are exceeding expectations. The more positive the score, the more they are exceeding expectations. As the score becomes negative, they are below expectations.

The ability to simply sum effectiveness scores is one of the major advantages of ProMES. Essentially, the different things the unit does and how much they are doing of each are being expressed on a

Table 4–1
Completed System
Circuit Board Manufacturing Unit

DATE: July, 19XX

	INDICATOR DATA: JULY	EFFECTIVENESS SCORE
I. Production		
A. Percent Boards Completed	98%	+40
B. Percent High Priority Boards Completed (Mix)	85%	-5
Total Effectiveness: Production = +35		
II. Quality		
A. Percent Passing Inspection	99.8%	+62
III. Attendance		
A. Percent of Max Hours	97%	0
IV. Housekeeping and Maintenance		
A. Number of Violations	10	-5
OVERALL EFFECTIVENESS =		+92

common measuring scale, which is the contribution to the organiza-tion as expressed by the overall effectiveness index. In addition, because the contingencies already reflect the relative importance and the non-linearity of the indicators, a simple summing reflects the overall effectiveness of the unit. As will be discussed later, this proper-ty also makes it possible for the system to be used to aggregate across individual units to get the productivity of larger and larger units of the organization.

Comparing Different Units

An additional feature of the system is that the productivity of units can be directly compared even if they do quite different functions. This is done by examining each unit's maximum possible overall effectiveness score. This is the overall effectiveness score the unit would receive if they were at the maximum possible value on each indicator. In our example, looking at the effectiveness values of the maximums in Figure 4–3 indicates that the unit would get the maximum possible overall effectiveness score if they completed 115 percent of their boards, 100 percent of their high priority boards, 100 percent of their boards passed inspection, had 100 percent attendance, and had 0 housekeeping and maintenance violations. If they did this they would obtain their maximum effectiveness score of 100 +95 +70 +35 +10 = 310. The unit's actual overall effectiveness can be expressed as a percentage of that maximum possible. In our example, since the unit's July productivity score as shown in Table 4–1 was +92, *their percent of maximum* was 92/310 = 29.7 percent. The closer they are to 100 percent, the closer they are to their best possible productivity. The productivity of units doing different things can then be compared by examining their percent of maximum score. The unit with the higher percent of maximum is higher in productivity.

Aggregation Across Units

One unique feature of the productivity measurement system is the ability to aggregate across units, and thereby aggregate the measurement system to larger and larger organizational units. For example, if a division was composed of five separate departments, it would be valuable to have a measure for each department and be able to combine those five measures into a single measure for the entire division. In most productivity measurement systems this is not possible since the measurement system varies from department to department. A feature of ProMES is that it is possible to do such across-department aggregation. Each department is measured on a common metric: overall effectiveness. This can be thought of as the overall amount of contribution that each department is making to the organization. Since each of the departments is measured on this common metric, it seems appropriate to simply add the overall effectiveness of each of the departments to get a measure of the overall effectiveness of the division. In fact, this is exactly what can be done as long as an additional step is taken in the process of contingency development. We shall explain how this is done in Chapter 13.

5

Comparison of ProMES to the Desirable Characteristics

Having presented the basics of ProMES, we can now compare it to the criteria we suggested in Chapter 3 for a good productivity measurement system. Each criterion will be noted and the way ProMES meets it will be discussed.

The first two criteria are that a system produce a *single index* of productivity as well as *subindices* of the important aspects of productivity. Clearly, the system does this. The important aspects are identified by the personnel in the organization and each is measured. These are then combined to the level of the products and again to the level of overall productivity by the Overall Effectiveness Index. The effectiveness values for the subindices and the overall index also show how well the organization is doing relative to expected levels of productivity.

A good system should provide information on *how much as well as how good* the output of the unit is. The "how much" is provided by the listing of indicator values. Information on "how good" is contained in the effectiveness scores. Since the effectiveness scores express the indicator level in terms of how it compares to expectations, personnel can immediately see how well they did for that period.

The *validity* of the system is the next criterion. Validity is composed of several factors. The first is completeness. Completeness is insured in the system by carefully exploring with the personnel what the unit is expected to do. These things then become the products on which the system is based. In addition, these are reviewed by the management of the organization to insure that nothing of importance is omitted.

Accuracy is another factor in validity. One aspect of accuracy is that the indicators are indeed good measures of the products. As with the products, the indicators are based on extensive input from the organizational personnel, and are reviewed by management. Another aspect of validity is maintaining the relative importance of the different functions in the unit. This is done by the contingencies. Their overall slope reflects relative importance, and this is carried through in the calculation of effectiveness. Finally, validity includes accounting for non-linearities. Non-linearity is maintained by the contingencies.

It is clear that the quality of the system is heavily dependent on the contingencies. However, the contingencies are judgments and thus introduce subjectivity into the system. This subjectivity is not necessarily a problem. The contingencies are really statements of policy. They say what level of output is expected (the zero point), how good other levels of output are, and the relative importance of the different activities of the unit. This is policy. However, policy is by its nature subjective. A manager's primary responsibility is to set policy in the sense that he/she must determine the priorities of the personnel in his/her unit. What ProMES does is to reduce the subjectivity in policy and priorities by formally discussing it, quantifying it, and subjecting it to formal review and approval by the management in the organization.

The next criterion for the system is that it be *flexible*. The first type of flexibility is the ability of the system to respond to changes in priorities in the organization. Such changes could come about, for example, from a change in the environment or in management. ProMES can deal with such changes readily. In most cases the only modification would be a change in some of the contingencies. In the circuit board example, if quality became more important, the contingency could be easily changed to reflect this. If a more extensive change occurred, the products and indicators could be changed.

The second type of flexibility is that it would be ideal if the system could accommodate both effectiveness (output relative to a standard) and efficiency (output divided by input) notions of productivity. ProMES can do this. Clearly effectiveness is included since output relative to standards is what the effectiveness scores are. However, efficiency can also be included in the system. One way is by including efficiency measures in the indicators. For example, the indicator of "percent of boards completed" could be expressed as the percentage divided by the number of personnel hours available that month. Another way for the system to deal with the efficiency notion is to weight overall effectiveness by a measure of inputs, such as operating budget, number of personnel hours, etc.

A good productivity measurement system should be able to *aggregate across units* doing different things. How ProMES does this was discussed briefly in the last chapter. The specific methodology for accomplishing this aggregation will be presented in Chapter 13.

A good system should also allow for *direct comparison of units* doing very different functions. This is done by comparing the actual overall effectiveness score with the maximum possible overall effectiveness score. The idea is that while overall effectiveness is an index of the contribution the unit is making to the organization, it is not directly interpretable as an index of how well the units compare to each other. This is because overall effectiveness partially depends on the number of tasks the unit is doing, and how many indicators are being measured. However, the ratio of actual effectiveness divided by maximum possible effectiveness is a measure that is comparable across units. With this methodology, for example, a maintenance unit working on engines could be compared with another maintenance unit working on electronics or even a totally different type of group, such as a supply unit.

The next criterion is that the system be *accepted* by organizational personnel. ProMES system would do well on this criterion since unit personnel are designing their own system. The unit's personnel determine the products, the indicators, and the contingencies. Because all levels of the organization, including management, are involved during each phase of the development of the system, acceptance should be very high. In addition, the data from the system should be very valuable to the organization's personnel since it indicates what is important, how well they are doing on all the important areas in their work, and how well they are doing overall. There are very few members of the unit, supervisors, and managers who would not welcome this information.

The final criterion of a good system is that it have *positive motivational properties* so that it not only measures productivity, but will help enhance productivity as well. ProMES does this in a variety of ways. First, the process of developing the system itself should have a positive effect. The development of the system calls for a series of meetings to identify products, indicators, and contingencies. By their very nature such meetings foster clarification of roles. It becomes clear what is important and what is not so important. Discrepancies in perceptions get exposed and worked out. In addition, communication within the unit and between units is facilitated by the very process of working out the system. Finally, the process promotes an examination of current activities, work practices, and the measurement of these activities and practices. Such an examination can easily lead to refinements in operations that will enhance productivity.

Aside from participation in the process itself, the output of the productivity measurement system should have motivational properties. The productivity data which is fed back to the personnel in the organization would be expected to enhance productivity directly (e.g.,

Algera, 1989; Dockstader, Nebeker, & Shumate, 1977; Ivancevich & McMahon, 1982; Pritchard, Bigby, Beiting, Coverdale, & Morgan, 1981; Pritchard & Montagno, 1978). In addition to the direct effect of the feedback, ProMES also gives information on the subparts of the unit's productivity. This would allow the personnel to see how well they are doing on all important aspects of their responsibilities. By examining the information over time they could assess what areas needed improvements.

ProMES also has the capability of providing information to establish a clear set of priorities for improving productivity. Recall from Table 4–1 that for a given time period, such as one month, the system presents the actual data for that period, and the effectiveness of those amounts of the indicators. It would be a simple matter to look at the data for each indicator and calculate the effectiveness gain that would occur if the unit went up one value on each of the indicators. For example, if the unit completed 98 percent of its boards in July as is indicated in Table 4–1, for them to go to the next level up in percent of boards completed, to a 100 percent completion rate, would mean an increase in effectiveness from +40 to +90 for a gain in effectiveness of +50 units. This could be calculated for each indicator. Once it was calculated, one could list each of the potential changes and the corresponding increase in effectiveness. Such a listing for our example would look like Table 5–1.

What this information communicates is exactly what should be changed to maximize productivity. In the example, the best thing the

Table 5–1
Priorities for Increasing Productivity
Circuit Board Manufacturing Unit

PRIORITIES FOR: AUGUST, 19XX

CHANGE	GAIN IN EFFECTIVENESS
Percent Boards Completed from 98% to 100%	+50
Percent High Priority Boards (Mix) from 85% to 90%	+35
Percent Boards Passing Inspection from 99.8% to 100%	+3
Percent of Maximum Hours from 97% to 99%	+33
Number of Housekeeping and Maintenance Violations from 10 to 5	+5

unit can do is to increase their percent of boards completed. That is where they should focus their efforts if they want to best increase their productivity. Once this is done, or if increasing this is not possible, the next best things they could do would be to improve the percent of high priority boards and improve attendance. Improving the percentage of boards passing inspection and decreasing the number of housekeeping and maintenance violations will not have much effect on their productivity. Thus, the system can generate a set of priorities that unit members can use to guide their efforts to increase productivity.

Finally, the system could facilitate productivity enhancement by serving as a measurement system for other productivity enhancement strategies. For example, it is very difficult to set up good goal setting and incentives programs because of the multiple activities a unit does. The problem is that one must choose between a system that considers all the different aspects of the unit's productivity, or simplify the system by just using the one most important aspect. Both solutions have problems. If all the responsibilities are used, goals are set in multiple areas and the system becomes cumbersome and confusing to the participants. If the single most important responsibility is used, the system is incomplete and those areas where goals are not set can show a decrease in productivity since attention is focused on the area where the goal is set. The same problem exists with incentives. With ProMES this problem is resolved since a single index of productivity is generated. Goals can be set and incentives awarded on the overall effectiveness index.

In summary, ProMES meets all the criteria for a good system. Thus, the system appears to be a sound method of measuring and improving productivity. The next question is how well it works in actual organizations. This question is addressed in the next chapter.

6

Past Experience with ProMES

ProMES was formally evaluated by developing the productivity measurement system in five units of an Air Force base in the southwest United States (Pritchard et al., 1987, 1988, 1989). One was a maintenance section called Communications and Navigation (Comm/Nav). This section repaired a variety of electronic equipment used for aircraft communication and navigation. The other four sections together comprised the Material Storage and Distribution Branch (MS&D). The four sections were Receiving, Storage and Issue, Pickup and Delivery, and Inspection. The MS&D branch was essentially the base warehouse. Property was delivered to the warehouse and checked in by the Receiving section. Storage and Issue shelved the property and retrieved it as it was ordered by sections on the base. The Delivery section delivered the property to sections on base that had ordered it. Inspection made sure the property was in good condition, and insured that regulations were being followed concerning packaging, storage, and identification.

The research approach consisted of first developing ProMES in each of the five units. Next, a baseline period was instituted where productivity data were collected but not fed back to unit personnel. This baseline period would serve as the source of comparison data against which the effects of ProMES could be evaluated. After this baseline period of 8–9 months, each of the units received monthly feedback from the system for five months. After the measurement and feedback phases of ProMES were completed, two additional interventions were added. A goal-setting condition was added to feedback for five months where units set group goals for their productivity. Finally, incentives in the form of time off from work were added to the feedback and goal-setting for five more months. This experimental design is shown graphically in Figure 6–1. (Details of the project can

TIME

DEVELOP PRODUCTIVITY MEASUREMENT SYSTEM	BASELINE	FEEDBACK	FEEDBACK + GOAL SETTING	FEEDBACK + GOAL SETTING + INCENTIVES

Figure 6–1 Experimental Design

be found in Pritchard et al., 1988, and 1989). The complete set of products and indicators for the Comm/Nav unit are presented in Appendix A, the actual contingencies in Appendix B, and an example of a feedback report is in Appendix D. Products and indicators for some of the MS&D units are presented in Appendix A.

PRODUCTIVITY RESULTS

Effects on productivity are summarized in Figure 6–2. This figure is the mean overall effectiveness across the five units for each month. In the figure, the period of baseline is indicated by the letter B, the five months of feedback by the letter F, goal setting by G, and incentives by I. These results indicate a major increase in productivity after the start of feedback from ProMES. For feedback alone, the average increase over baseline was 50 percent. The increase under ProMES plus goal setting and incentives was even stronger, 74 percent under ProMES with goal setting and 75 percent under ProMES with incentives. The strength and pattern of results were consistent for the five individual units. The effects were extremely large, much larger than those found in other research of this type (Guzzo, Jette, & Katzell, 1985).

The results above deal with the overall effectiveness scores. It is also instructive to examine the data for the indicators. Graphs of indicators that were highly important to the respective units are shown in Figures 6–3, 6–4, and 6–5. Figure 6–3 is from the Comm/Nav unit which did maintenance on aircraft electronic equipment. The figure is a plot of one of their most important indicators, percent of bounces. Bounces are pieces of equipment which were repaired by the unit but did not function when they were actually installed. Thus, it is a measure of the quality of repair. The figure shows a major decrease in the percentage of bounces, averaging 5.9 percent during baseline and

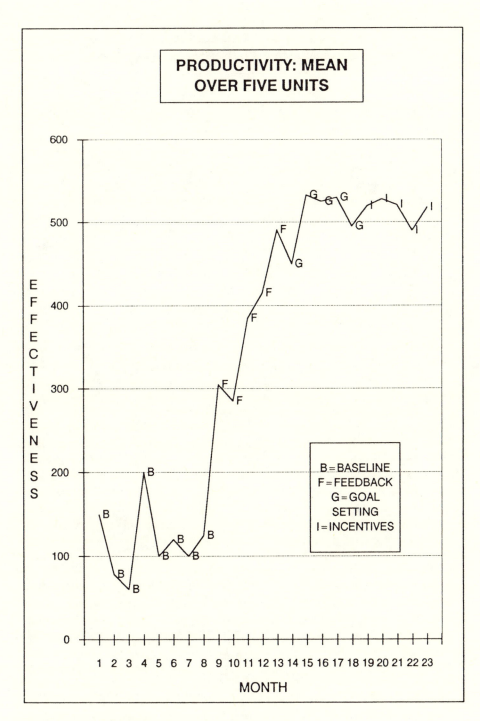

Figure 6–2 Productivity over All Five Units

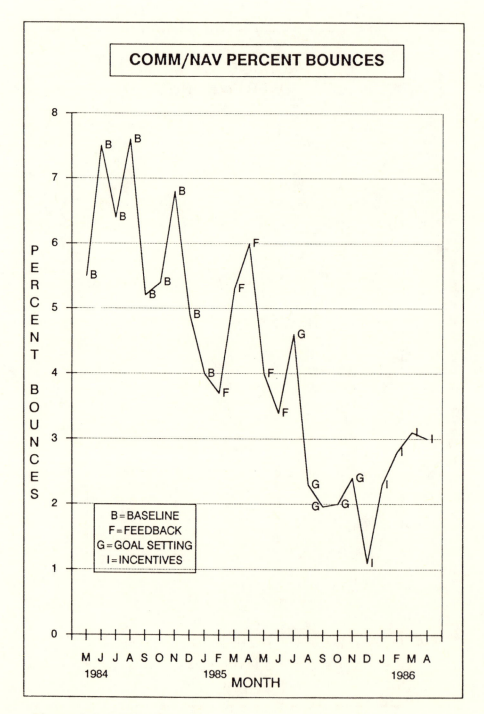

Figure 6–3 Percent Bounces

38

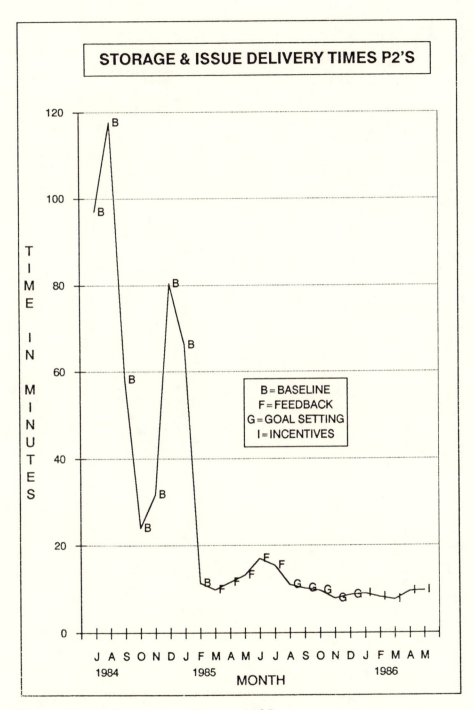

Figure 6-4 Delivery Time: Storage and Issue

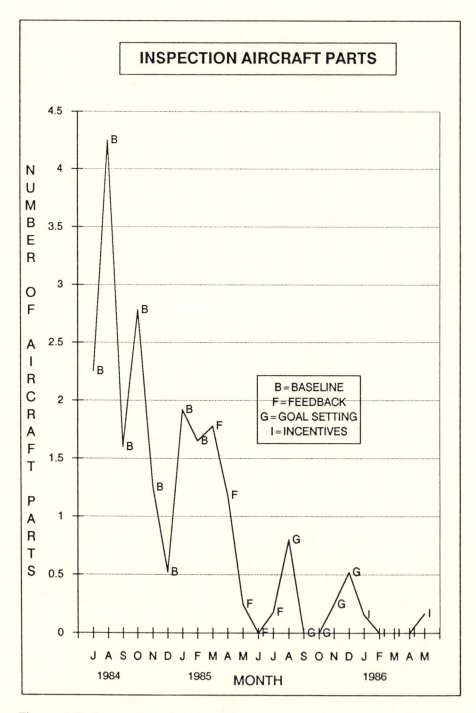

Figure 6–5 Inspection of Aircraft Parts

going down to 2.5 percent by the end of the project. Figure 6–4 is from the Storage and Issue unit. It stored material in the warehouse and retrieved it when ordered. The indicator shown in the figure is a delivery time indicator, the speed with which they filled the highest priority orders (P2's). This figure also shows a major improvement. During baseline, average delivery time was sixty minutes; after the start of the program it averaged about ten minutes. Figure 6–5 is from the Inspection unit. This indicator was the number of aircraft parts that had not been inspected by the end of the day. The fewer the number of parts, the more effective the unit. The results again show major improvement, going from 2.2 parts during baseline to an average of about 0.3 parts with ProMES.

Data were also collected on overtime. While the Comm/Nav unit did not have overtime, the four units in MS&D were doing considerable overtime at the start of the project. Overtime was tracked throughout the period and hours of overtime are presented in Figure 6–6. The figure shows a large decrease in amount of overtime under ProMES. Number of hours of overtime decreased from an average of 1348 hours during baseline to 892 during feedback, 404 during goal setting, and 416 during incentives. Thus, by the end of the treatments, overtime was less than one-third of what it had been during baseline.

Questions of Interpretation

Before one can confidently attribute these results as effects due to ProMES, several additional issues must be considered. The first is the possible presence of a Hawthorne effect, where productivity could have improved simply because the units had the special treatment of being selected for the project. While such an effect is possible, the project was designed to avoid such an effect. Specifically, the initial contact with the units during system development was quite intensive, and if a Hawthorne effect was going to occur, it should have occurred then. Since this contact started well before baseline, any productivity increase should have already occurred and would not contaminate the results. Thus, a Hawthorne effect can be effectively ruled out.

Another point in the interpretation of the results is that there could have been changes occurring in the organizations containing the five target units which caused general increases in productivity for all units. To explore this possibility, data were collected on several comparison/control groups that were similar to the target groups in the type of work they did and were part of the same larger organizations. These control units were not part of the ProMES program.

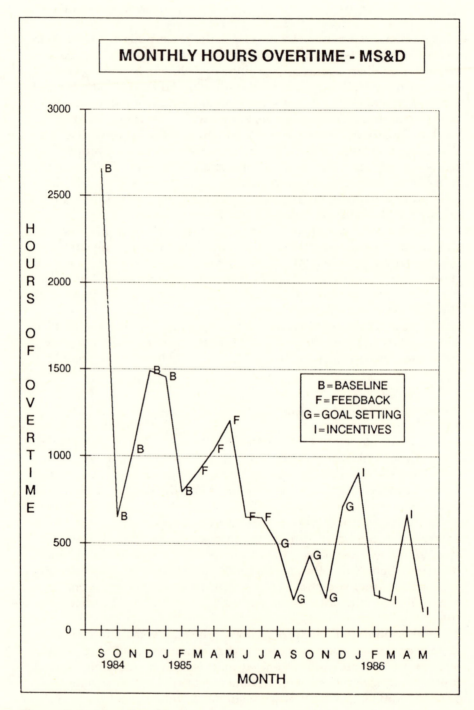

Figure 6-6 Overtime Hours

A number of measures of unit functioning were collected from these control units during the same period of time that the ProMES data were being collected from the five target organizations. These data are presented in Figure 6-7. The figure shows the average of the measures taken on the seven units serving as controls for the Comm/Nav unit and the average of the measures for the three units serving as controls for the MS&D unit. The figure is analogous to the figures presenting the productivity data (Figures 6-3, 6-4, and 6-5) in that the same time period is used, and the baseline, feedback, goal-setting, and incentive periods are indicated. There were, of course, no feedback, goal-setting, or incentive conditions done with these control groups. The symbols B, F, G, and I on Figure 6-7 are inserted only to show how the data for the controls correspond to the data for the groups under ProMES.

The figure shows that for Comm/Nav the control groups showed an increase in productivity towards the end of the period. However, this increase was not nearly as large as the increase for the unit under ProMES. In addition, these increases were primarily brought about by two of the ten comparison measures showing fairly large increases and do not reflect a general trend across the measures. The control group data for MS&D show no differences in productivity over the time period.

Taken together, the control group data indicate that the effects on productivity that occurred in the target units cannot be explained due to wider organizational changes in productivity.

ATTITUDE RESULTS

Data were also collected on work attitudes. A questionnaire was administered to unit personnel and first line supervisors in each of the units during baseline and again during feedback. It measured job satisfaction, morale, turnover intentions, clarity of objectives, role clarity, and evaluation clarity. Job satisfaction was measured by seven items adapted from the Minnesota Satisfaction Questionnaire (Weiss, Dawis, England, & Loftquist, 1967). The items for the morale scale were adapted from instruments developed by Seashore, Lawler, Mirvis, and Cammann (1983). Items for turnover intentions, clarity of objectives, and evaluation clarity were developed for this project. Items for individual role clarity were adapted from the Rizzo, House, and Lirtzman (1970) instrument.

Attitude results are shown in Table 6-1. The table shows that the measures of job satisfaction, morale, and evaluation clarity became significantly more positive under the system. Clarity of objectives became more positive, but the change was not quite statistically sig-

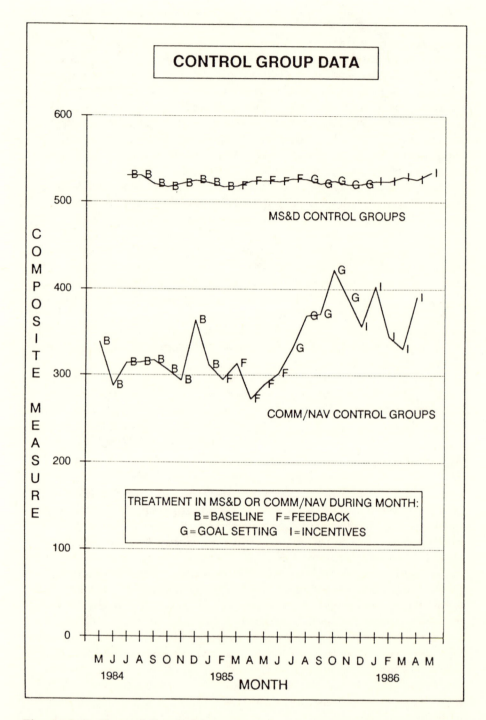

Figure 6–7 Control Group Measures

Table 6–1
Summary of Attitude Results

SCALE	RESULTS
JOB SATISFACTION	UP
MORALE	UP
TURNOVER INTENTIONS	NO CHANGE
CLARITY OF OBJECTIVES	UP*
INDIVIDUAL ROLE CLARITY	NO CHANGE
EVALUATION CLARITY	UP

* Clarity of Objectives improved, but the improvement was not quite statistically significant (p < .08).

nificant (p=.08). Turnover intentions, and individual role clarity showed no significant changes. In summary, the overall results of the attitude data indicate that job attitudes under ProMES either improved or stayed the same.

Other attitude data were collected on the subjective reactions to the system. After several months experience with feedback from ProMES, the unit personnel and supervisors of all five units were given a questionnaire to evaluate different aspects of the system. Answers to the questionnaire items were on a five-point scale with the options being Strongly Disagree, Disagree, Neutral, Agree, and Strongly Agree. The results are presented in Table 6–2. It shows each question and the percentage of people who Agreed or Strongly Agreed and the percentage who Disagreed or Strongly Disagreed. As the table indicates, reactions to the system were extremely positive.

Table 6–2
Subjective Reactions to the System

ITEM	PERCENT AGREE OR STRONGLY AGREE	PERCENT DISAGREE OR STRONGLY DISAGREE
1. The feedback system tells me how good a job I am doing.	64%	4%
2. The feedback system tells me how good a job the section is doing.	87%	1%
3. The feedback system helps me see the section's priorities.	77%	6%
4. The feedback system helps the section be more productive.	61%	4%
5. A system like this would help other Air Force bases be more productive.	62%	4%
6. The feedback system is clear and understandable.	58%	7%
7. It was worth the effort to develop the feedback system.	64%	10%
8. It was worth the effort to keep the feedback system in operation.	62%	10%
9. The information about section performance that goes into the feedback system is accurate.	52%	13%
10. The feedback system gives a good measure of productivity.	64%	13%
11. Overall, I like the feedback system.	62%	9%
12. I would prefer not to have this feedback system at the next organization I work in.	13%	54%
13. The feedback system is a better way of measuring productivity than what the section used to have.	75%	0%

CONCLUSIONS

This was an important research project because it formally evaluated the application of ProMES using an experimental design that allowed for clear conclusions to be drawn. These conclusions are summarized below.

1. The first issue was whether the ProMES could be effectively developed in an actual organization. Based on the results reported here and in Pritchard et al. (1988, 1989) it is clear that *the system can be successfully developed.* Personnel did develop the products, indicators, and contingencies. Unit personnel were cooperative in developing the system and, by the end of development, enthusiastic. The process of collecting the indicator data and putting the data through the system to provide feedback proved feasible. The system allowed for aggregation across units so that an integrated system could be developed across the four sections making up a larger organizational unit (MS&D). The application of this aggregation to much larger and more complex organizational units seems feasible. The system also allowed for the direct comparison of the productivity of different units to each other using the percent of maximum index and it helped both members of the unit and management identify the priorities for increasing productivity by the priorities listing feature.

Other support comes from the fact that the unit personnel were actually able to agree on the system. When the system was reviewed and approved by senior managers, what changes were made appeared to be totally accepted by all. Furthermore, the system operated for fifteen months without being changed, and when changes were made it was only to remove some indicators no longer needed. This supports the position that the system reflected policy well.

The system was seen as effective by unit personnel. They told us they were supportive; management and personnel within each unit wanted the system continued and asked that it be developed in other units. In addition, the questionnaire data indicate that subjective reactions were positive.

2. The second conclusion is that *using ProMES substantially increased productivity.* Feedback had a very strong effect on productivity. An average gain in productivity of 50 percent occurred across the five units during feedback. This increase occurred with a decrease in personnel time, at least in MS&D. These data indicate major increases in productivity; the effects were extremely large. In addition, the effects were consistent across organizational units. That is, each of the units showed a consistent pattern of increase for feedback and even greater increases for goal setting and incentives.

The development of the system and its positive effects worked well on units that were quite different from one another. The units differed greatly in the nature of the work, with Comm/Nav doing repair of sophisticated equipment and MS&D operating a large warehouse. The technologies were quite different between the two units, as well as between the four sections of MS&D. There were also great differences in the type of organizational structure and the work flow. The units varied considerably in size and the personnel varied considerably in academic as well as in technical education. They also differed in initial level of performance with MS&D acknowledged to be somewhat marginal in performance and Comm/Nav being perceived as fairly high. Yet with all these differences, the system was developed and worked extremely well in each unit. This adds considerable support to the generalizability of the approach.

3. *Attitudes either improved or stayed the same under ProMES*. This conclusion is supported from the attitude questionnaires. A concern at the start of the project was that personnel would feel that the system was intrusive and monitored their work too closely and that this might lead to a negative reaction. In fact, the opposite occurred. Personnel liked the system and felt it helped with the work.

4. *Other interventions can be added to ProMES*. It is clear that the interventions of goal setting and incentives can be successfully added to ProMES. Goals can be set and incentives can be awarded on the basis of the overall effectiveness measure. This makes these interventions much easier since it solves the problems of using goals and incentives with multiple measures.

ProMES IN OTHER SETTINGS

Aside from this formal evaluation of ProMES, the system has successfully been applied in a number of other settings. These include an assembly line manufacturing batteries, an assembly line manufacturing consumer products, a chemical-processing facility, life insurance agents and their managers, team-based manufacturing of printed circuit boards, sales and repair of office machinery, photocopier maintenance mechanics, an in-house corporate library research unit, team-based manufacturing of cardboard boxes, and a bar in a restaurant.

7

Why ProMES Works

It is clear that ProMES has some positive design characteristics and that its application in organizations has been successful. It is also worthwhile to explore *why* the system is effective. This chapter focuses on factors that seem to make it successful.

A number of different factors can be identified that contribute to the success of ProMES. While there is some overlap, these factors can be broken down into those related to (1) the structure of the system, (2) its motivational features, and (3) its informational features.

STRUCTURAL FEATURES

One structural factor that helps make the system effective is that ProMES *allows for integrating multiple, conflicting goals*. Most organizations and the units in them have goals that are seen as conflicting. The organization needs to be profitable yet protect the environment. It needs high production but also high quality. Dealing with these conflicting goals is frequently a problem. ProMES offers a way to rethink these apparently conflicting goals and to integrate them.

Specifically, ProMES uses the logic that these goals should not be thought of as being in conflict, but rather that they are all important for the success of the organization. All need to be met to some degree. The real issue is applying organizational resources to meet these goals in proportion to their importance. For example, while it may seem that quantity and quality are in conflict because doing more of one frequently means doing less of the other, *both* are important. The question that needs to be answered is how much organizational effort needs to be applied to each so that the final combination of efforts is maximally effective for the organization. In other words, what is the relative priority of the different objectives? Thus, at a logical level, ProMES offers a different way of thinking about conflicting goals by including all the apparently conflicting goals as products, thus defining all as important.

However, ProMES goes much further. It offers a concrete, numeric way of determining relative priorities through the contingencies. When the contingencies are developed, they are statements of the priority of the different objectives. They indicate what the priorities are in precise numerical terms since they show exactly what contribution is made when each is increased. This allows personnel to clearly see how much effort should be devoted to each activity. This ability to integrate apparently conflicting goals is one of the features of ProMES that make it an attractive system.

Another helpful structural factor is having the personnel who are going to be using the system be heavily *involved in its development*. Unit personnel frequently think that programs imposed from above are not going to be effective. They feel that such programs are not designed with an appreciation for their unique needs and environment and that the people designing them do not have a full understanding of the work of the unit. It is more effective to have heavy involvement from the unit personnel so that the final system will fit their work, and unit personnel will not feel that it is another project imposed on them from above. This also helps with the acceptance of the program and reduces the likelihood that unit personnel will ignore or sabotage it.

The strategy of developing the system from the *bottom of the organization up* is an important structural factor in its success in addition to the actual participation of unit personnel. The members of the unit and lower levels of supervision usually know the most about the functioning of the unit, the really critical issues in the day-to-day operations, and what are good measures. In addition, these are the people that will actually make the system work. It is important to have their involvement and knowledge from the start. By working out the details of the system with them first, the system becomes theirs and they are assured that it will measure what should be measured.

When the lower level personnel bring the developing system up the organizational hierarchy for approval, there are several additional benefits. Unit personnel develop a sense of ownership in the system because they must defend it to management. Management gets its chance to review the system and make any modifications that they see as necessary. Thus, management is included as a critical part of system development. Finally, the process of working out differences of opinion between management and unit personnel is a worthwhile process in itself because it increases communication between levels of the organization. We have had personnel from some units say that this was the first time they had ever sat down with higher management and had a real two-way dialog.

The approach to gaining *higher level management approval* of the system seems to help its success. The technique of getting approval on products and indicators before starting contingency development seems very valuable. It not only helps clarify policy early in the process and saves later revisions, but also helps prepare everyone for the eventual implementation. This approach of getting approval during development gives all levels of the organization a chance to learn about the system as it is being developed so that they know how to use it when it is finished.

Another reason for the success of the system is the use of a *single index* of productivity. Such a single index has the advantage of summarizing the effectiveness of a complex unit into one easily communicable number. Such a single index helps motivation because it tells the personnel in an easily understandable way how well they are doing, and whether they are improving or declining in productivity. Management, supervision, and members of the unit have reported that without this summary measure, they would not have been able to derive an overall sense of how the unit was doing.

The *perceived validity* of the system is also a factor in its acceptance as well as in the system's positive effects. Perceived validity means that the system is seen as being complete; it includes all the important aspects of the unit's work. A second meaning of validity is accuracy. The process by which products, indicators, and contingencies are developed promotes the type of repeated review that maximizes accuracy.

MOTIVATIONAL FEATURES

There are also a number of motivational features of the system that help its success. One such feature is that the system is *accepted* by unit personnel. This is a very serious issue for any intervention (Hurst, 1980; Tuttle & Sink, 1984). If the members of the unit do not accept a program, its effects will be limited and the possibility of its being sabotaged is present. Acceptance of this system is high because unit personnel are heavily involved in its implementation. They identify the products and indicators, they develop the contingencies, and they defend their work to management. Hence, they have a sense of ownership of it.

The use of the system also dramatically increases the *amount and quality of the feedback* unit personnel receive. Prior to the system many units have had some objective feedback on part of their activities.

However, the available data were not complete, were known to be influenced by factors beyond the control of unit personnel, and it was not clear what level of output was expected of the units. The formal feedback system from ProMES is effective because it provides more frequent, accurate, and specific feedback (Annett, 1969; Ilgen, Fisher, & Taylor, 1979; Ivancevich, Donnelly, & Lyon, 1970; Pritchard, Montagno, & Moore, 1978), as well as more positive feedback (Feather, 1968; Ilgen & Hamstra, 1972). In addition, the feedback that personnel receive contains evaluative information about how good or bad the unit is doing, not just descriptive information on how much was done (Dockstader, Nebeker, & Shumate, 1977; Hammond & Summers, 1972).

The positive feedback seems particularly important. Personnel from numerous units have indicated that the feedback from the system was unusual in that it represented one of the few times they were told they were doing a good job. They indicated that in the past they heard from management only when there were problems. The positive feedback also appeared to help them increase their sense of competence at doing the work, which should also help improve motivation.

Another motivational feature of the system is that personnel could *see the results of their efforts*. Most jobs are structured so that doing a better job does not show up in any measurable way. The frequent feedback provided by the system seems to improve the connection between the actions of the unit and their level of productivity. For example, when changes have been made to improve an indicator, the following month there is great interest in that indicator. There seems to be considerable satisfaction when the indicator does improve. This allows personnel to tell when their efforts have resulted in increased productivity.

Another plausible reason for the effectiveness of the system is that it makes units *accountable* for their productivity. The regular measurement of productivity and the public nature of the data provide a concrete performance history that is hard for the unit to ignore. The fact that the data exist generates a source of motivation for unit personnel. They want to look good and they know that they will have to answer for it if they do poorly. This accountability also appears to make personnel more objective about problem areas. There is much less of a tendency to make excuses and more of a desire to try to find positive solutions.

The system also improves *role clarification*. The process of developing, refining, and getting approval for the products, indicators, and contingencies helps personnel understand their roles more clearly (e.g., Rizzo, House, & Lirtzman, 1970). Unit personnel discuss what their objectives should be, disagreements surface and are resolved.

Expected levels of output are discussed and consensus achieved. Finally, these decisions are reviewed by higher management, debated, and a formally approved system results. When this process is finished, the units have a much clearer picture of what their objectives are, what they should be focusing on to achieve these objectives, what is expected of them in each area, and what is good and bad productivity in each area. This role clarification process should have positive motivational effects in and of itself.

The use of the system also *helps goal setting*, which should increase motivation (e.g., Latham & Yukl, 1975; Locke, Shaw, Saari, & Latham, 1981; Tubbs, 1986). Obviously, a system such as ProMES makes it easier to have a formal goal-setting program by having a single index of productivity upon which to set goals. However, just having the feedback makes informal and/or personal goal setting much easier to do and this should have positive effects on motivation.

INFORMATIONAL FEATURES

There are also several informational features of ProMES that contribute to its success. The system provides a considerable amount of *information about the work* to unit personnel that helps guide them. It indicates: (1) What activities they should be doing, and therefore what is important and what is not so important; (2) what is expected of them in each area; (3) what is good and bad productivity in each area; (4) how well they are doing in each area; and (5) how well they are doing overall.

The system also provides *information for developing productivity enhancing strategies*. It allows for the early identification and diagnosis of problems. The feedback reports show personnel when productivity is starting to slip in a given area. This allows the unit to deal with problems before they become serious. The system also allows personnel to know when the problems are fixed and it encourages them to persist until the problems are resolved. This appears to greatly reduce the tendency to ignore problems until they become serious. Finally, the system develops a formal, quantitative statement of priorities for increasing productivity that is useful in guiding action to improve productivity.

Another informational factor is that the system allows personnel to *focus on the same objectives*. In some units, personnel report that before the implementation of the system, different supervisors and different levels of management had different things on which they focused effort. Furthermore, what was high priority changed frequently. This led to a situation where there was a great deal of "firefighting." The process of developing the productivity measurement system and getting all levels of the organization to agree on it reduced this problem substantially. In essence, all levels of supervision and management agreed on what was important and what was not so important. When the process was finished, the amount of firefighting decreased greatly.

Finally, the system allows for *direct comparison across units* in terms of percent of maximum productivity. This can be done with units performing very different functions. One effect of this direct comparison is that personnel can assess how well the units are doing relative to each other and make decisions about resource allocation across units. A second effect of the direct comparison is that it allows for competition across units based on each unit's percent of maximum productivity. In places where such comparisons have been made, this competition was clearly present between units, was essentially friendly in nature, and seemed to have a positive effect on productivity.

PART II

Developing ProMES in an Organization

The second major section of this book is a concrete description of how to develop ProMES in an organization. Chapters 8 and 9 discuss conditions needed for implementing ProMES and preliminary issues that must be resolved prior to starting system development. The next three chapters, 10 through 12, cover the specific steps in developing the system. The last two chapters describe the process of combining the measurement systems of different units (Chapter 13) and issues of implementation (Chapter 14).

The material for this section of the book comes primarily from the author's experience in working with ProMES and other measurement and feedback systems in organizations. Other sources include published material about productivity systems in general. These sources include Belcher (1982); Kendrick (1984); Mali (1978); Muckler, (1982); Peeples (1978); Pritchard (1990); Pritchard, Jones, Roth, Stuebing, and Ekeberg (1986, 1987, 1988, 1989), Pritchard, Roth, Jones, Galgay, and Watson (1988); Pritchard, Stuebing, Jones, Roth, and Ekeberg (1987a&b); Riggs and Felix (1983); Tuttle (1981); Tuttle and Weaver (1986 a&b).

8

Conditions Needed for Implementation

Clearly, there are many advantages to measuring organizational productivity with a system like ProMES. We now turn to a discussion of how to do such measurement. Before the measurement process is even started, some conditions are necessary for a successful implementation. These conditions apply to ProMES or to any other productivity measurement system. Some of these are a fairly simple matter of getting the necessary information, while others are more complex, such as organizational attitudes needed for successful implementation of a productivity measurement and improvement system.

CONDITIONS PRIOR TO IMPLEMENTATION

Needed Background Knowledge

The first step in preparing for the implementation is to be completely familiar with the background and logic of ProMES and have an overall understanding of how the system works. This background can be obtained from a careful reading of Part I of this book. This should be done before serious consideration is given to implementation.

Important Organizational Attitudes

There are a number of organizational attitudes that should be present to maximize the success of a productivity improvement program such as ProMES. The first is that *productivity improvement is important*. If the organization is financially successful, is doing well against competitors, and believes it is providing its service effectively, there may be little motivation to try to improve productivity. While such complacency can frequently lead to problems in the future, the issue here is that such an attitude makes the institution of a productivity improvement system difficult.

Another important attitude is that *productivity improvement is not easy*. It takes work and constant vigilance. It is not easy in the sense that good productivity is a fragile thing, it is a careful balance of elements that can easily be disrupted. Productivity improvement is thus something that must be carefully attended to at all times. Productivity improvement takes work and constant vigilance in that we all like routines and once a set of procedures is learned, there is considerable resistance to changing. It takes commitment and dedication to break out of the old patterns and to systematically develop a productivity measurement system and use it to make changes.

The attitude that *productivity improvement must be considered as a long-range organizational change effort* is also important. A common failing of productivity improvement programs is that they are seen as projects with a fixed time period. The attitude is that the organization will try a certain technique and if it seems to work, it will somehow continue to operate on its own. Successful productivity improvement programs are long-term efforts that are permanent parts of the organization's operations. This also means that management has reasonable expectations about the time it takes to develop systems and get improvements in productivity. No productivity improvement program will provide an overnight answer to problems that may have been years in the making. Improvements take time and care.

The point is that these organizational attitudes are very important to successful productivity improvement efforts. If they are clearly present, productivity improvement programs are easier to institute and continue. If these attitudes are not adequately present, obtaining the needed management support over a long period of time becomes more difficult and the program is more likely to be short-lived, even if approval is obtained to start it. It is sometimes difficult to judge to what extent these attitudes are present, but attempting to make such a judgement will help in project planning.

Needed Organizational Beliefs

In addition to global attitudes there are also a number of more specific beliefs that need to be present for successful productivity improvement programs. The first is whether management believes that organizational performance depends heavily on the efforts of its human resources. Most managements realize that the success of the organization is heavily dependent on the proper functioning of organizational personnel. However, there are exceptions. For example, in organizations where there is high automation or which are heavily capital- rather than labor-intensive, managements may feel that the organization's human resources are not very important or are much less important than other factors. Such beliefs will lead to very low enthusiasm for expending organizational resources for efforts that are geared to these human resources.

Another important issue is whether all interested constituencies would view tackling productivity as a positive thing. These constituencies would of course include management and employees, but might also include unions, government regulating agencies, customers, etc. It is important that the attitudes of all important constituencies be considered. One classic mistake is that productivity improvement programs are started without any consultation with the union and serious problems start to develop during development or implementation. Such problems can be so serious that they lead to termination of a good program to avoid union problems. Working with the union(s) and other interested constituencies prior to starting a productivity improvement program is very important.

The issue of trust is also a key factor. Trust is especially important between management and workers. A productivity measurement system such as ProMES requires that workers, supervisors, and management work together in an atmosphere of mutual trust and respect. If employees do not have at least a minimum level of trust in their management, it will be difficult to properly institute a system like ProMES. This is because employees will be unwilling to help develop a system that makes them accountable to a management that they believe will use the information against their best interests. Even if a system is imposed on such a group, they will find a way to sabotage it or diminish its usefulness in some way. The trust issue also goes the other way: Does management trust the employees? ProMES is a bottom-up strategy in that measures are worked out by lower level employees and then presented to management for approval. To be comfortable with this approach, management must have at least some level of trust and respect for the employees.

The stability of the organization's management is also a factor to consider. If management is highly unstable such that key management personnel are expected to change during system development or change frequently after system implementation, this makes an effective system more difficult to develop and maintain. One solution is to wait for an expected change before instituting system development. A second approach is to make sure of support at the highest levels possible so that management changes at lower levels will be less of a problem.

Organizations differ considerably in their attitudes and sophistication about measurement. Some are very measurement oriented and the introduction of an involved productivity measurement system would seem a natural extension of measurement already done. To other organizations, the idea of measuring what is done will be very foreign. It is important to assess where the organization is on this issue and whether some education on the importance of measurement is needed before launching a productivity measurement and improvement program.

A final issue is that some organizations take the attitude that "If we didn't invent it, it's no good." This is especially true of organizations which are highly technologically sophisticated. Such an attitude would make instituting a program such as ProMES more difficult.

While it is not necessary that a formal assessment be made of whether these attitudes and beliefs are present in the organization through such procedures as questionnaires or other formal techniques, it is advisable to make an informal assessment of where the organization is on these issues. If the organization is fairly positive on all of them, sound productivity improvement programs will probably be welcomed. If the organization is more towards the negative end on these issues, preparatory work to improve these attitudes and beliefs would be worthwhile.

The Importance of Management Commitment

It is critical that management commits to the productivity improvement program. Management must see such a program as important, must commit resources to it, must be interested in the results of the effort, and must protect the program when it is challenged. Without this support, the program will most likely fail no matter how successful it is in improving productivity. It is particularly important that the most senior manager in the functional area where the productivity project will be done be committed to the project. For example, if it is in a production unit, the vice president of manufacturing should be committed.

Not only must this commitment be present, but it must be perceived to be present. This means that the support be very visible to everyone in the organization. This can be formal public announcements of support from top management, personal visits to the implementation site(s), and requests for information about the program.

To get this commitment, the attitudes and beliefs discussed above about productivity improvement being valuable, human resources being important, etc., must first be present. Even if they are already present, reminding management of their importance and applicability to a successful productivity improvement effort is worthwhile. In addition, management should be given a realistic picture of (1) the potential benefits of the system; (2) the costs of development and implementation of the system; (3) a methodology for how these benefits will be assessed; (4) a realistic timetable for obtaining these benefits; and (5) the importance of visible, long-range support from them. To insure continued management commitment, it is important that management be kept informed of the progress of the program and be given tangible evidence of its success.

MAJOR IMPLEMENTATION PRINCIPLES

The last section on general information has to do with major principles that must be understood in using a system like ProMES. These are important general guidelines that should influence all phases of the design and implementation.

The first principle is: *What you measure is what you get.* This means that what the organization chooses to measure, and particularly what is both measured and fed back to personnel, will cause a change in what is measured. For example, if there is a problem with excessive long distance phone bills in a unit, simply measuring the dollars spent by each individual each month and giving this information back to the individuals will decrease phone costs even if nothing else is done with the data that is fed back.

This is a very powerful principle and is at the heart of why feedback is so successful at changing things. What it says is that if you can develop measures of important organizational functions and give this information back to the unit responsible, things should improve. However, this is a two-edged sword. If what you measure is not carefully thought out, problems can develop. One of the biggest problems is that what is measured and fed back is what is most easily measured. For example, in a manufacturing process it may be easy to count the number of units an operating team produces from a machine. This measure could then be divided by the time the operators worked at the machine. The resulting measure would be a measure of units per hour of team effort. It would be easy to get and feed back. The message is that the operating team should make this number look good. That is, have a high output per hour of team effort.

On the surface, this sounds like a perfectly good measure and improvements in the measure would probably result if the data were fed back to the team. However, it may have some unintended negative consequences. For example, if the machine starts turning out units of poor or unacceptable quality, the best thing would be to stop the machine and make the needed adjustments so that good quality units are being produced. However, to do this, the operating team must stop the machine and thus their output per hour goes down. Because of the nature of the measurement, there would be pressure on the team to continue making poor quality units because if they stop the machine, they look bad.

Another potentially negative effect of using such a measure is in doing preventative maintenance. If preventative maintenance is needed which slows or stops the machine, there will be a tendency to omit such maintenance because it "hurts their numbers." In this example, the measurement system is essentially telling the team to do something different than what is optimal for the organization. Because of the power of such measurement, this issue can be a serious problem.

It is thus vitally important that the measures be carefully thought out and thorough consideration given to their unintended negative consequences. The measures need to be adjusted so that if they are improved by the unit, this is in the best interests of the organization.

The power of feedback also implies another issue about measurement: completeness. A good system must measure all the important functions of the unit. If the system measures only some of the important activities of the unit, this creates the potentially very serious problem of improving activities that are measured while not improving activities that are not measured. In our example above, if only quantity is measured it may improve, but quality may in fact get worse. This can be extremely counterproductive. If the measurement system includes *all* the important activities of the unit, this problem will not be present.

The next major principle is that *measures used for decision making are different from those used for motivation.* Typically, many different measures are collected by an organization. In fact, there are usually more available than can be used. The temptation when designing a productivity measurement system is to use measures that are already available. Sometimes this is a good strategy but frequently it is not. Measures used to make management decisions are frequently not appropriate for a motivational productivity measurement system. Such measures frequently have to do with the functioning of large parts of the organization or are measures which were developed for monitoring how well a human-machine combination is functioning.

If you want to motivate, you must measure somewhat differently. The issue is that the things measured and fed back must be those things that are under the control of the personnel for which the measurement is designed. Giving feedback on measures over which the unit has little or no control will increase frustration, not motivation. If the measurement is based on large sections of the organization, the resulting information may be very valuable for making important policy decisions but have very little utility to lower level personnel. Their contribution to such broad measures is so small that they effectively have no control over them.

Other measures that may be available but not under the control of unit personnel are measures developed by specialists in the organization to monitor some specific aspect of the organization's operation. For example, the industrial engineering unit will probably have many measures of the functioning of a manufacturing process. However, these measures are designed to evaluate how well a technological process is operating. Such measures are developed for a different purpose than motivating personnel and thus may not be appropriate. If the measures describe how a technical process is operating, they will frequently be a combination of human input and the functioning of a machine. If the resulting measure is one that unit personnel have little or no control over, it will not be a good measure for a motivational productivity measurement system.

A third principle is that *acceptance of the measurement system by those being measured is essential to its success*. If the personnel in the unit where the measurement system is being used do not accept the system, they will resist it. If it is forced on them, they will find ways of decreasing its effectiveness. The most important factor in getting acceptance of a measurement system is for the unit personnel to have a major role in developing the system. People do not like to have things that affect their lives imposed on them from above. There is an almost automatic resistance when this occurs. In addition, these personnel know a great deal about the work they do, much more than supervision and management in many areas of the work. For them to be ignored in the development of the measurement of their work implies that they have nothing to contribute. This is resented.

Another thing that contributes to acceptance is a complete understanding of the system. If the unit develops the system, they will understand it thoroughly, thus helping promote acceptance.

A final factor aiding acceptance is the perceived validity and accuracy of the system. The better the system, the more likely it will be accepted. Systems imposed without the expert knowledge of the unit members will tend to be less accurate. In addition, the more effectively the system includes design features that make it a good system, the better. For example, the more the system includes all aspects of the work, provides for different activities being differentially important, and uses measures that have no negative unintended consequences, the greater the perceived validity.

A final general principle is that when implementing a productivity measurement system, *people do not like surprises*. It is essential to keep everyone informed during development of the system and after implementation. All interested parties should be kept informed. This includes all levels of management and supervision in the chain of command, unit members, and, when appropriate, other constituencies such as unions, government regulators, customers, etc. The best way to avoid resistance to the effort is to keep everyone informed about what is happening and answer questions as they come up. Failing to do this will result in a much greater effort needed later to overcome the ever-present problems and concerns that will develop.

9

Developing the System: Preliminary Steps

In this chapter, we shall start with a discussion of some decisions that must be made before starting system development. Then some general factors that will guide system development will be presented.

PRELIMINARY DECISIONS

The basic process of ProMES is to work with a design team to develop a productivity measurement system for units of the organization. The measurement that results from this system is then fed back to the members of the unit (incumbents) and their supervisors and management. The primary process used to develop the system is group discussion where measurement issues are discussed until consensus is reached. The results of these discussions are then brought to higher management for discussion and final approval. Within this general structure, a series of decisions must be made about how to proceed.

The Design Team

The first decision is the structure and function of the design team. The role of the design team is to be responsible for designing and implementing the system. They go through the steps to develop the system, they have the discussions to generate the measures, they keep everyone informed of progress, and they implement the system when it is finished. The design team is composed of three types of people: facilitators, supervisors, and unit members.

The person or persons who serve the role of facilitator in the design team are important to the success of the effort. The facilitators are responsible for (1) making sure the development process proceeds correctly and in a timely manner; (2) serving as moderators and discussion leaders in meetings where the system is developed; (3) seeing that all the essential people are included in the process; and (4) making sure the design personnel get the information they need. The facilitators are objective, independent helpers of the process, not representatives of management, supervision, incumbents, or anyone else. They are to help the organization develop a sound productivity measurement system in the units with which they work.

The selection of a facilitator or facilitators is very important. A person outside the organization who is familiar with ProMES and is skilled in group processes (conducting meetings, listening, achieving consensus, etc.) would be ideal. However, it is frequently not feasible to obtain such a person, and someone from inside the organization must be selected. Such a person need not be an expert at the work itself since it is the expertise of the supervisors and incumbents who will be used to design the system. However, it is important that the facilitator have a complete knowledge of ProMES and have good skills at working with groups. The facilitator should also be someone who is respected by the other members of the design team. Ideally, two facilitators should be used so that they can help each other and review the progress of the design team together. This is especially true when the facilitators have not had much experience with ProMES. By having two facilitators, they can give each other feedback about how they are handling the process.

The supervisor of the unit for which the system is being developed must also be part of the design team and attend all the meetings. His/her role is to (1) provide information to the group on pertinent matters, such as what different measures mean, how the unit interacts with other units, etc.; (2) offer guidance to the team so that they do not overlook important issues or policies; and (3) serve a translation function between the incumbents and the facilitators. This translation function is important because the incumbents will have a very different frame of reference about the nature of the work and the measurement effort than will the facilitator, and having someone to help the two types of people communicate is desirable.

Deciding how many levels of supervision to include in the design team is also a decision that must be made. On the one hand, it would be desirable to have several levels of supervision always present so that all the issues that need to be addressed can be dealt with on the spot. However, having too many levels of supervision and having supervisors who are fairly high in the organizational hierarchy can inhibit frank discussion. In addition, these higher level supervisors may have firm ideas about what the system should look like and tend to put too much pressure on the design team to make the system match this preconceived idea.

As in many issues about an intervention such as ProMES, it becomes a matter of judgment in which the factors identified here need to be weighed against each other and a decision made about the best way to proceed. The first line supervisor of the unit must be included, and other supervisors could be added as the situation indicates, but care must be taken that supervisors do not dominate the discussions.

The design team should also include some (typically 3 to 5) incumbents. If the unit is small, the entire unit could be included in the design team. As the unit size increases, this becomes progressively more impractical. If a selection must be made, the best choice is for the supervisors and facilitators to select key opinion leaders or individuals in key jobs in the unit. It would also be reasonable for personnel in the unit to select some or all of the incumbents who become members of the design team.

If only some of the unit's incumbents are selected for the design team, an issue to consider is whether to have the same incumbents stay on the design team throughout the entire process or to rotate people. Rotating people has the advantage of exposing more incumbents to the process and thus increasing knowledge and acceptance of the system. However, it has the disadvantage of losing the rapport and continuity of the process that starts to develop. On balance, it is better to pick a group of incumbents and stick with them as the core design team. If the involvement of more people in the unit is desired, one alternative is to have a small core of incumbents that are permanently on the design team and one or two unit members each meeting that participate on a rotating basis as observers so that more unit members can see the process. In any event, steps should be taken to keep the rest of the incumbents informed about the design team's activities and progress.

The total size of the design team should be between five and eight members. Since at least one facilitator, one supervisor and some incumbents are needed, five is probably a reasonable minimum. With more than eight members the process starts to slow down because of the size of the group.

The Unit to Be Used

A series of decisions must be made about the organizational units for which the system will be developed. The size of the units is one such issue. In theory, ProMES can be used for individuals so that measurement is done for each individual and each individual gets unique feedback about his/her work. At the other extreme, the system could measure the work of a large unit, such as an entire division which encompasses many smaller units. If the system is developed for such a larger unit, information fed back will concern how the larger unit is functioning.

There are two issues to consider when deciding unit size. First, the design team should consider the nature of the work and the nature of the organization. If all individuals in a unit are doing essentially the same job, individual level measurement may be appropriate, since one set of measures could be developed that covers all the individuals in the unit. However, if different individuals in the unit are doing different work and the work of some individuals is dependent on what others do, one should measure at the level of the unit since individual efforts cannot easily be separated from group performance. There are a few situations where everyone is doing the same work and they are independent of each other. However, in most jobs this is not the case. Unit members are doing different things and are interdependent.

Second, the design team must consider the tradeoff between the power of feedback and practicality. Feedback tends to be more powerful the closer it is to the individual; the more the feedback gives performance information about how individuals are doing their work, the greater will be its positive effects on performance. This means that feedback about the performance of individuals or small units (5 to 30 people) within an organization will be more powerful than feedback about the performance of much larger parts of the organization. This is because feedback about large organizational units has little meaning for the work of individuals in those units. Although feedback indicating that the organization is doing well can give individuals a sense of pride, a given individual cannot take much credit for it. Also, the person does not know if his/her individual contribution was good or not. It is lost in the generality of the overall measure.

In contrast, if the measure is for the work of a small group, individuals are much more likely to feel a sense of accomplishment when the unit does well. In addition, such factors as feeling accountable, seeing better how to focus efforts, correcting mistakes, and diagnosing reasons for problems all operate more strongly when feedback is closer to the individual.

This concern for the power of the feedback system must be balanced with the practical need to make a system efficient to develop and maintain. It would take a great deal of effort to develop a feedback system for every individual in an organization if each one was doing different work. In fact, it is often not possible to separate each person's work from the work of the group. In addition, it would take too much effort to collect the measures and give individual feedback.

Taken together, these factors suggest that, in general, feedback should be given to the smallest unit possible that does not separate groups that must work interdependently. This often balances the need for feedback to be close to the individuals with the need for having a manageable system. The design team should balance these concerns when they determine the size of the unit for which feedback will be developed. Most often, this comes down to a unit which works together daily and ranges in size from three to fifty people. Another way to think about such groups is that they are typically the smallest groups on the organization chart.

Needed Organizational Resources

Another factor to consider is what commitments of organizational resources are needed to design and implement ProMES. The main thing needed to develop the system is the time of the personnel involved, the facilitators, the supervisors, and the incumbents. The design team must have a series of meetings to design the system. Typically these meetings should be from one and a half to two hours long and be held once every two weeks, although variations from this schedule are quite possible if required by the situation. It is difficult to estimate the number of meetings required because this depends on the experience of the facilitators, the complexity of the unit's work, how well the design team works together, the availability of existing measures, etc. However, a rough estimate with a facilitator with some experience would be one meeting to review the program, two to identify products, five to eight to develop and refine indicators, one to get management approval, three to four to develop contingencies, one for final management approval, and two to design the feedback report. In addition, the design team would be doing tasks between meetings, such as preparing written summaries of what the group does and gathering information about measures. However, this work would most typically fall to the facilitators and the supervisors.

A number of other things are needed during this development phase. These would include a place to meet which is reasonably comfortable and quiet, access to data on existing organizational measures, and resources to analyze such data.

Once the development phase is completed, implementing the system would require the collection of the indicator data and the preparation and distribution of the feedback reports and charts. Finally, every time the feedback report is distributed, a meeting must be held between unit personnel and supervision to discuss the report.

THE DEVELOPMENT PROCESS: GENERAL CONSIDERATIONS

The basic process used in developing ProMES is discussion by the design team. This discussion continues until consensus is reached. That is, the design team discusses the issue at hand until there is general agreement on the solution. For example, when products are discussed, the design team continues to discuss the list of products until there is general agreement on what the list should be and how the products should be worded. It is not essential to get complete unanimity on every issue, but unanimity should be obtained on the major issues and a very strong majority/consensus on all the rest.

The Importance of Participation

This face-to-face discussion is one of the key features of ProMES that makes it successful. Different individuals in the unit will have different ideas on what the objectives of the unit are, what should be used as measures, how well the unit is expected to do on each measure, etc. It is this open discussion of different ideas and perspectives that results in a quality system. The different perspectives and ideas usually all have some validity, they are typically a result of looking at the work from different perspectives. Exposing all the members of the design team to these different views broadens the perspective of all the members and makes for a better system. Thus, group techniques that decrease face-to-face discussion should be avoided. For example, techniques where ideas are passed from person to person but no actual face-to-face meeting takes place will not be as effective at capitalizing on these different perspectives as will an actual face-to-face group.

The nature of the participation of the members of the design team is thus very important. The facilitators should make sure that all members of the design team have the opportunity for full participation. If some members dominate while others do not participate, the facilitators should take the necessary steps to make sure the more quiet members of the team are heard. If a supervisor is directing the group towards his/her point of view, the facilitator should discuss this with the supervisor in private and stress the importance of full participation of all group members and the negative effects of a dominant team member, especially if that dominant person is also the supervisor.

Participation Versus Control

One of the most difficult things for the facilitators is the balance between participation and control. We have discussed the importance of the group having a major influence on the nature of the system and their feeling a sense of ownership of it. This means that they should speak freely, indicate when they disagree, and have final say in the nature of the developing system. Thus, the role of the facilitators is to guide this process and support full participation so that all opinions are heard, no single person dominates, etc. However, the facilitators will be the most knowledgeable about the system and how the decisions made earlier in the process will affect what has to be done later. Because of this knowledge, the facilitators can save a great deal of the design team's time by pointing out when they are going in a direction that will create later problems or when they are not really doing what the process requires at a given point in time. This dual role is somewhat conflictual in that the facilitators must push for participation yet also do some controlling.

Finding the balance between these two roles can only be done through experience and by monitoring the group process as it occurs. If the design team is spending too much time on tasks that are not really important to system development or are making decisions that will clearly cause later problems, the facilitators should speak up and in a supportive manner help the group get back on track. On the other hand, if the group is giving verbal or nonverbal indications that they feel that the facilitators are being too controlling, the facilitators should reduce their directing efforts.

The Importance of Time

Time is also an important issue in the process. The process cannot be rushed. To do a thorough analysis of products and indicators, and to develop contingencies are steps that are very difficult and take time to do properly. Different ideas must be expressed and the design team personnel must have the time to think over the ideas they develop. It also takes time for the design team to discuss these ideas with personnel outside the team, such as other supervisors and especially with other incumbents in the unit.

Rough guidelines were given above on the time it will take to develop the system. However, a productivity measurement system can be developed faster. Some approaches to productivity measurement would develop products and indicators in two or three meetings and proceed to put these measures into a feedback report. We would very strongly argue against such an abbreviated approach. It is true that a system can be developed in that time, but not a *good* system. Doing it in that way glosses over disagreements in points of view, typically results in using measures that are the easiest to come up with but not the best, and will almost always result in problems when implemented. This will lower acceptance and potentially result in a generally negative experience for all concerned.

It is also important to allow time between meetings. Ideally there should be about two weeks between meetings, with a minimum of one week. This will allow the personnel to think about what was discussed in the meeting and talk it over amongst themselves and others. Frequently this will lead to very useful revisions of the work done in the last meeting. Simply letting time pass is also an excellent tool for dealing with disagreements. If disagreements in the meetings occur that are not immediately resolvable, postponing discussion of that point until the following meeting will frequently lead to the problem being resolved between the meetings or at least in it being easier to resolve in the next meeting.

Interaction in the Design Team

How the design team members interact with each other is an important consideration. Expect disagreement in the meetings. It is important to realize that in these meetings, disagreement is a good thing. Personnel will have different points of view and the fact that such different perspectives are being expressed is an indication that the process is going well. It shows that people are willing to express their ideas and opinions. This can only help the quality of the resulting system. However, the facilitators should make sure that the disagreement is constructive. That is, it should not be personal in nature and should focus on issues pertinent to the work. Doing this is usually not a problem if the facilitators are sensitive to constructive disagreement.

It is important that a sense of rapport develop between the members of the design team. This is most often an issue for the facilitators. They are strangers to the supervisors and incumbents and their role is not exactly clear. Consequently, it is desirable that the facilitators spend some informal time with the design team by sharing lunch, spending some time working side by side with them to get a first-hand picture of the unit's activities, etc. The facilitators should also have as much knowledge as possible about the unit. A guided tour of the unit's work area is essential. It is also desirable for the facilitators to read any available written material about the functioning of the unit.

Another issue to consider is that the facilitators and supervisors must be totally honest with the incumbents about what is happening. Issues ranging from the purpose of the project to how the data will be used must be answered with total accuracy. Leaving personnel with inaccurate impressions about sensitive issues can only cause more harm when dealt with later.

Preparing the Unit

A final issue before turning to the actual process is the question of how to prepare the unit for the project. The unit for which the system is being developed should know as much as possible about the project. The entire project should be explained to all unit personnel. This explanation must include the objectives, the steps that will be taken to develop the system, how it will be implemented, and what will be done with the feedback data. This can be done by a meeting with all the unit personnel where these issues are discussed by the supervisor. The facilitators should also be present and their role described. In addition, management support for the project should be clearly evident. This is best accomplished by having as high a management person as possible attend this meeting, or at least introduce the project and indicate management's complete support of the effort.

The concerns of the unit personnel should be dealt with at this time. These concerns will include whether the data from the system will be used for evaluations of personnel, whether jobs will be lost if productivity increases, whether standards will increase if productivity increases, and how the system fits into the existing reward system. This last issue is of particular concern and includes issues about whether employees will receive increased compensation or other rewards if they increase their productivity. The answers to these questions should be determined before starting the project and honest answers to these and any other questions given to the unit personnel.

Another common concern that should be discussed with the group is why they were picked to participate in the project. The biggest concern is typically that they were picked by management because their productivity was poor. The reasons for their selection should be stated. A related issue is why other units were not selected. Other units who are not part of system development can feel left out and this can create some resentment. These other units should be told the plans for them. It could be that they will get the system later, or that some units are starting the system as a pilot to assess whether it should be used more broadly. In such cases, they should be told that if it works out well, they will be included later.

10

Steps in Developing Products and Indicators

With the preliminary decisions made about how ProMES will be implemented, we now turn to a discussion of the specific steps to construct the system. Developing ProMES for a unit consists of four basic steps: (1) developing products; (2) identifying indicators; (3) constructing contingencies; and (4) designing the feedback report. If multiple units are to be combined (aggregated) into one measurement system, another step is required to accomplish this. Once the system is developed, it is implemented by collecting the necessary information each measurement period (e.g., by week or month), preparing the feedback reports, and having unit meetings to discuss and evaluate these reports.

IDENTIFYING PRODUCTS

Products are the major things that the unit does to make its contribution to the organization. Products can also be thought of as the objectives of the unit. Another way to think about products is that a given unit is a part of the organization. It uses resources such as personnel, equipment, space, and materials to produce some product or service. The unit transforms these resources into some sort of end result such as refrigerators, circuit boards, deliveries, sales contracts, transactions on customers' accounts, aid to clients, etc. The products of the unit are the list of these major results and their characteristics, such as amount, quality, timeliness, etc. The following are examples of products that might be found in different kinds of units. Examples of products and indicators for several actual units are shown in Appendix A.

Meeting production demand as efficiently as possible (manufacturing unit).

Making items (whatever the unit makes) of high quality (manufacturing unit).

Meeting repair demand as quickly as possible (maintenance unit).

Delivering material as quickly as possible (delivery unit).

Operating safely (many different kinds of units).

Keeping up with appropriate paper work (many different kinds of units).

Meeting training needs (many different kinds of units).

Keeping customers satisfied (many different kinds of units).

The Product Identification Process

To identify products, the facilitators ask the design team to list the things that the unit contributes to the objectives of the organization. A good way to start is to ask: "What does this unit do for the overall organization?" The design team then discusses this and many ideas come out. The discussion will probably be fairly lively once the group gets going, but other questions to stimulate discussion would be: "What is this unit paid to do?" and "What is the basic contribution of your unit to the overall organization?"

The ideas of the group should be written down, not only for all to see while they are working, but also so that a permanent record can be made of the list that results at the end of the meeting. Using flip charts is one good way to do this. One facilitator writes the group's ideas down on the charts while the other facilitator takes notes. Using a blackboard will also work well if there is enough blackboard space available so that it will not be necessary to erase any of the ideas. A written copy of the proposed products should later be produced, typically by the facilitators, and left with the group or delivered to them as soon as possible. By doing this, the supervisors and incumbents have a written record to study and discuss prior to the next meeting.

The group should continue having meetings to discuss the list of products until they are satisfied that it is complete and accurate. At the end of this process, a unit will typically have between three and six products.

Since only three to six products should ultimately result, the phrasing of the products must be fairly general, such as "Maintaining high quality." However, the group will typically start the discussion with much more specific things. For example, instead of the product of meeting production demand as efficiently as possible, they might get

very specific about different kinds of production demands for different items on different machines at different times. In other words,
they will tend to think about the specifics that they must deal with
every day rather than the more general products that the unit
generates.

This is not a bad thing, since it helps get the group working together
on something that is fairly easy for them. It also helps insure that
important products will not be omitted. However, the facilitators
should guide them from this very specific listing to consolidate the
things that they do into the more general products. One good strategy
is for the facilitator to let them deal with the specifics during the first
meeting and make sure everything of importance that the unit does is
put on the list. At the end of this meeting or at the start of the second
meeting the list would be consolidated into products by summarizing
the specific functions into more general objectives. This is one instance
of the balance the facilitators must achieve between taking control on
the one hand and having the group develop the system on the other.
One strategy is to present this reformulation of the products as a
rephrasing of what they had come up with rather than as something
new.

This may still result in too many products, but that is really not a
problem at this stage of the process. Later, when indicators are finalized, the list of products can be consolidated. The basic idea is to make
sure the list is complete, then consolidate/summarize the product list
to three to six products by the end of the process.

During the process of product development, the group will sometimes start to discuss measures of the products. One situation when
this occurs is where they confuse a product with a measure of a
product (an indicator). If this continues for much time, the facilitators
should remind the group of the difference between products and
indicators and move the group back to considering products. Another
situation where a premature discussion of indicators occurs is when
there is a discussion of whether a given product is in fact measurable.
For example, someone may say that it is not possible to measure the
quality of something that the unit does. In this case it is better for the
facilitators to suggest that the first step is a complete list of products,
and that assessment of how the products will be measured will come
later.

Criteria for Good Products

There are several criteria for the products. A single product should
be *clearly stated* and should be something that *if the unit did exactly what*

the product says, the organization would benefit. This sounds like a fairly obvious point, but it is not. Frequently, products are stated in the early stages of development that need to be revised when carefully thought through. For example, in one maintenance unit a product was first defined as "Make repairs as quickly as possible." The idea was that if each repair was done as quickly as possible, this would help the unit meet its objectives. However, it was later realized that it was not doing each repair quickly that was important, but meeting the repair demand that existed. In other words, the critical factor was that no matter whether the amount of material to be repaired was large or small, the unit had to meet that demand quickly. Thus, the product was later revised to "Meeting repair demand." This resulted in very different measures than would have been used for making repairs quickly.

Equally important is that the set of products be *complete.* It is crucial that no meaningful part of the unit's work be omitted from the product list. If the list is not complete, the resulting measurement system will not be complete. This will encourage neglect of the organizational objectives that are not part of the measurement system. What is measured is attended to, and what is not measured may be neglected. If important things are not measured and thus not attended to as much, the effectiveness of the organization will suffer.

In order to insure completeness, the group should discuss the product list until they are satisfied that it is complete, and some time should pass so that they can think about anything left out. The strategy of discussing products and finalizing them at a second or third meeting will accomplish this. In addition, as indicators are developed, the facilitators and other design team members should be sensitive to additional products that come up that were not originally listed. Finally, when the products and indicators are submitted to management for approval, there is a final check on the completeness of the list.

DEVELOPING INDICATORS

Once the design team is satisfied that the product list is complete and worded in a way that most accurately captures the objectives of the unit, the next step is to develop indicators of the products. An indicator is a concrete measure of how well the unit is generating the product.

The Process of Identifying Indicators

After reminding the group of the purpose of the indicators, the facilitators should start with questions such as "How would you

measure how well the unit was doing on each of the products?";
"What sort of concrete measure could be used to indicate how the unit
was doing on each product?"; and "What would you point to for
showing your boss that the unit was actually achieving the objectives
listed in the products?" Questions such as these can get the process
started, but once the group gets the idea, little prompting should be
necessary.

The group starts with the first product and goes through the list
generating ideas for measures. As with the development of the
products, flip charts or some similar mechanism should be used so
that the ideas can be seen during the meeting and a written record can
be made.

The group keeps working on the list of indicators until they are
satisfied that it is complete and accurate. This will take a number of
meetings. The best approach seems to be to start with the first product
and work on it until no more progress seems to be occurring, then
move to the next product. Once all the products have been covered
once, then repeat the process. That way the group does not get stuck
on one product, more progress will be felt by the group, and it will
give the group time to think about where they are having problems
with measures. This additional time usually results in many good
ideas for solutions to measurement dilemmas.

When the process is completed, the number of indicators will
typically range from five to fifteen. Each product will have at least
one indicator and may have as many as five or six. It is important to
keep the number of indicators to a manageable number, probably a
maximum of fifteen, and typically no more than twelve. Any more
than this and the system will begin to become too complex. In our
experience, the average number of indicators has been between eight
and ten. Examples of indicators for several actual units are shown in
Appendix A.

Typically, the unit will have some measures that already exist and
are in use. Expect to use some existing measures, to modify others,
and to create yet others. It is important that any existing measures
be carefully scrutinized. Do not assume that just because a measure
is in use, that it is a good one. Do not make this assumption even if
the incumbents and supervisors agree it is a good measure. All too
often, measures are developed in other parts of the organization
such as in industrial engineering or in personnel for a specific
purpose that is different than increasing productivity through
motivation. Thus, it is essential that each measure be evaluated by
determining (1) exactly what is being measured and (2) whether
that is what should be measured for the productivity measurement
system.

Criteria for Good Indicators

There are a number of criteria of a good indicator. First, the indicators as a set must *cover all the products* and *cover each product completely*. The idea is the same as that mentioned under products. If something important is left out, that aspect of the work will tend to get less attention and this can be very detrimental. Getting such completeness is frequently a difficult thing to do, but the quality of the resulting system is heavily dependent on how well it is accomplished. This is best done by continuing to work on the indicator list until it is complete.

The indicators must also be *valid*. This means that what is measured is an accurate index of product accomplishment. This is not as easy as it sounds. One example comes from a maintenance unit. One measure originally suggested was the number of units repaired, divided by the number of personnel hours expended during that period. This is a typical labor efficiency measure and sounded good at first. However, the unit's objective (product) was to meet repair demand. Thus, if the demand was low, there would be personnel with less work to do. Even if the work to be done was done very quickly, the hours of personnel time in the unit would stay the same and the unit's productivity numbers would go down since a smaller amount of work was done with the same amount of personnel hours. This would not be a valid measure of their contribution since they had no control over the amount of work to be done. This measure was discarded and an index of the percentage of material brought in that was actually repaired was used since this more accurately captured the product.

Coming up with the best indicator is a difficult and subtle business which takes creativity on the part of the design team. One example of this complexity comes from a manufacturing unit which ran large sheets of cardboard through a complex machine which then cut cardboard boxes out of the sheets and imprinted the boxes with the client's name, logo, etc. The machine would pull in one sheet of cardboard, then a large drum would revolve and cut out and imprint the boxes. To get a measure of quantity, one indicator suggested was the number of boxes produced. This sounds like a good measure of quantity. However, a varying number of boxes could be cut from one sheet of cardboard. If small boxes were being made, there were several boxes made with each sheet, if large boxes were being made there would be only one made from each sheet. Thus, the number of boxes cut was in part beyond the unit's control. It depended partially on the number of boxes that were cut out of one sheet. The next idea was number of square yards of cardboard processed. This would take care of the problem of the number of boxes per sheet varying by the size of the box. However, the size of the sheets also varied, so this measure had the same problem as the number of boxes measure. It was partially out of the control of the group. Finally, the number of revolutions of the cutting and inking drum was chosen as the measure. Thus, it is not always clear what the measure should be; the issue must be carefully thought out.

A test of the validity of an indicator can be made by answering two questions. First, "If the unit was very high on the measure, would this be good for the organization?" This can highlight some potential problems of an indicator. For example, an indicator of quality for a manufacturing unit might be the score on an index of quality resulting from an inspection of a sample of the unit's output. The higher the score, the higher the quality. However, it may well be that maximizing quality is not really the best strategy but instead meeting quality requirements is important. The idea is that exceeding minimum quality requirements would take time and slow down production resulting in a decrease in quantity and be unnecessary for the needs of the customer. Thus, the measure should assess how well the output stays within a quality range. This is a very different type of measure than just quality level.

A second and related question to ask is "What are the long-term implications of the unit making such an index look good?" Consider the maintenance example used in the previous paragraph where a measure of number of repairs divided by personnel hours was considered. One way for the unit to look good on such a measure over time is to decrease the number of personnel hours by, for example, not replacing personnel who leave. Doing this will decrease the number of personnel hours and increase the unit's score on the index. However, by reducing personnel, even though the unit can still repair a given piece of equipment just as fast as before, it cannot meet repair demand when there is a lot of equipment to be fixed. This is exactly the opposite of their objective, which is to be able to meet repair demand, no matter how much that demand is. Consequently, such an indicator has negative long-term consequences.

Another critical criterion for an indicator is that it be *controllable by the unit*. The resulting indicators must be measures which are under the control of the unit. If the unit is being measured and evaluated on elements which are beyond their control, it is very frustrating to personnel and will decrease the effectiveness of the system. In fact, it is this controllability of indicators that most clearly distinguishes ProMES from the measurement systems used by the typical industrial engineering approach and a management information system approach to measurement. In these two approaches, whether the personnel in a given unit have direct control over the measures is not important. This is one of the main reasons why measures developed for such purposes are frequently not usable in ProMES.

Measures that the unit does not have control over are typically of two types. The first type is a measure that is influenced by factors that are beyond the unit's control. For example, in one organization an indicator for a manufacturing unit was the average amount of time it took the unit to complete orders. However, the time it took to complete orders was heavily influenced by the quality of the raw materials they had to work with. Since they had no control over the quality of these raw materials, time to complete the orders was a poor measure.

A second type of measure to be avoided is one which combines the unit's activities with those of one or more other units. For example, a suggested measure in a maintenance unit was the turnaround time for a malfunctioning part to be removed from where it was being used, repaired, and reinstalled. This was a bad measure since included in the total time was the time that the mechanics from another unit took to remove and reinstall the part. The repair shop had no control over this. A better measure would be the time from when the repair shop received the item to when it was delivered back.

Another criterion of a good indicator is that it be *cost effective to collect*. Some measures are fairly easy to collect, others are quite time consuming. A judgment must be made about the tradeoff between completeness and cost-effectiveness. If a measure is very costly to collect and is only of minor importance, it could be dropped. If the measure is important but costly, techniques should be explored to decrease the cost. Examples of such techniques would be taking only samples of work for measurement, developing simpler coding systems, etc.

Finally, indicators must be *understandable and meaningful to personnel in the unit*. This means that the indicators must make sense to unit personnel. Highly complex measures which are poorly understood are weak motivators. Indicators should also be expressed in terms which have the most meaning to unit personnel. For example, in one unit a measure was needed for how the unit's production was above or below production requirements. The best measure seemed to be the percent of production requirement met by the unit. However, some unit personnel had difficulty fully understanding percentages but understood absolute numbers much better. Consequently, the number of units above or below production requirements was used as the final indicator. Another example which is more common is where a measure is calculated by a complex procedure that unit personnel do not understand.

Once the group gets some experience at developing indicators (after one meeting, for example), it is a good idea for the facilitators to mention these criteria and have the group use them to evaluate each indicator. This will help train the group in developing indicators. As the process of developing and refining indicators continues, it is the role of the facilitators to help point out where a specific indicator has problems if the group does not detect these problems.

Types of Indicators

Developing good indicators is the hardest part of doing ProMES. It is difficult to measure some things and it is difficult to carefully think through indicators to make sure they are really good measures. One thing that may help to generate ideas about indicators is to list some different types of indicators that would apply to different measurement situations. This will help give some feel to the types of indicators that could be included in ProMES.

One common type of indicator for a manufacturing unit is output: the amount of work done. These indicators are usually fairly obvious, although they must be phrased very carefully as some of the examples above indicate. Efficiency is another type of indicator. Here output is divided by the resources (inputs) it took to produce the output. Output divided by labor hours or labor costs is a common example of an efficiency indicator. Other examples would be output divided by cost of materials used by the unit. Such indicators are used when efficiency of the operation is important and the unit has some control over both the input and the output in the measure.

Another general type of indicator is readiness. Readiness means that the unit must be ready to deal with something. Maintenance units frequently have indicators of this type. Typically the workload varies greatly and the effectiveness of the unit is determined by how well they meet the demand whether it is light or heavy. Percent of the demand met during a period of time (week, month, etc.) is a common way of measuring this.

Meeting objectives is another class of indicators. Such indicators are commonly seen in production situations where a unit must complete a specified number of units to keep the overall production process on schedule. Here the issue is not really output itself but whether the unit meets the production schedule. Consequently, rather than "number of units completed," such measures are typically expressed relative to the production quota. Percent of quota attainment is one common method of doing this. Here, 100 percent means that they met the production quota, above 100 percent exceeds the quota and below 100 percent means the unit did not meet the quota.

Having enough of something on hand is another class of indicator. It is used when the group actually has control of whether there is "enough" on hand. A good example is training, where enough trained personnel must be available to conduct various functions and the training is done by the unit as on-the-job training. An indicator could be developed by determining how many of each type of person must be available and then expressing the number actually available as a percentage of those needed. Another example of this type of indicator is having adequate supplies when it is the unit's responsibility to order the supplies.

A particularly difficult type of indicator is getting measures for the prevention of something that rarely occurs. Examples would be preventing accidents or a security unit preventing property damage. The problem is that the actual events (accidents, break-ins, etc.) occur so rarely that most of the time there would be nothing to measure, thus the indicator would be zero. In such a situation, the best solution is to measure the actions that could lead up to or help cause the rare event. In accidents, for example, unsafe acts would be measured such as not wearing safety equipment, working on a machine without turning it off, or leaving tools or scrap around the work area.

Customer satisfaction is another type of indicator that is important in some situations. One way this is commonly measured is by counting the number of customer complaints. However, such a measure usually has problems. Complaints frequently occur a long time after the work is done, so their use as feedback to guide behavior is weakened. In addition, sometimes no complaint is registered but the customer is dissatisfied. For example, customers may not complain because they are forced to use the inferior product or service to meet their own work schedules. Another alternative to getting a customer satisfaction measure is to take samples of customers and directly contact them to assess their satisfaction with the product. Another possibility is to measure repeat business. For example, a hair salon or medical clinic could measure the percentage of clients who returned for services. A completely different approach is to survey customers for the reasons for possible dissatisfaction and then measure these factors directly. For example, if factors such as late deliveries, improper documentation, and not meeting quality specifications were the primary customer problems, these could be measured directly.

A common type of indicator is one where there are interdependencies between the unit developing the system and another unit. Thus, a measure is not a pure measure of either unit's work. This is a complex topic and a discussion of it will be saved for a later section.

Getting Management Approval

Once the list of indicators has been completed to the satisfaction of the group, the next step is to obtain formal approval of the list of products and indicators from management. This is an important step in the process and one whereby the accuracy and completeness of the system is once again checked. The approval step is done when products and indicators are finished and again when the contingencies are complete. By doing this approval step, management has the opportunity to suggest revisions to the system. This approval is important not only for acceptance of the system by management but also so that all agree that the system will indeed represent organizational policy for the unit.

It should be made clear from the start that this approval process is going to occur. That is, at the beginning of the development of the system, all participants are told that incumbents and supervisors will develop the products and indicators, and then they will be presented to higher management for approval. That way they will know from the start that whatever they come up with for the unit's measurement system will be studied by management and a final system agreed to.

This approval needs to be obtained using the entire chain of command from the unit up to and including the most senior manager who has routine management responsibility for the unit. Put another way, it should go up to the person who has complete authority for setting the policy for the unit. How far up the management hierarchy to go in getting approval depends on the particular organization. On the one hand, the higher up the hierarchy one gets support for the system, the more powerful the resulting system will be. On the other hand, the higher up, the more complex the management approval group will be and the more difficult it will be to satisfy all levels of management. The decision is a matter of judgment that should also take into consideration the management style of the particular managers involved and the precedents already set in the organization.

The management personnel should be reminded of the goals of the project and what the process has been so far. They should be given written versions of the proposed products and indicators and given time to study these documents before a meeting is scheduled for the formal review. They should also be told that their formal approval of the products and indicators will be sought at the end of the meeting. Typically this can be done in one meeting of an hour or less for one unit. If the systems of multiple units are being presented, it will take longer. In this meeting the products and indicators are presented, discussed in detail, and, after any required revisions, approved by management.

It is important that the supervisors and incumbents in the unit present the system as theirs. While it is acceptable for the facilitators to explain how ProMES works and make a presentation of the resulting products and indicators, all questions from management should be addressed to and answered by the supervisors and incumbents. The idea is that the system belongs to the unit, not the facilitators. Unit personnel should answer questions and be prepared to defend the choices made.

In the approval meetings, management typically asks for clarification of numerous points and wants to hear the unit's defense of their system. While the majority of the products and indicators will probably be left as originally developed by the unit, there will likely be some changes made as a result of the approval meeting. The process can be quite positive. The resulting discussion can clarify the position of higher management to the unit personnel and the position of the unit personnel is made clearer to higher management. In most cases, the resulting changes will represent compromises that should satisfy both groups.

The facilitators' role in the approval meeting is very important. The mind-set going into the approval meeting should be one of mutual problem solving, not a negotiation session. The facilitators should make this clear to the design team and to the managers as well. During the meeting, the facilitators should make sure that the supervisors and incumbents are the ones answering management's questions so that all see the system as being something belonging to the unit. The facilitators should also keep the discussion on a constructive level, suggest compromise positions when there is disagreement, and generally keep the meeting on track.

11

Steps in Developing the Contingencies

Once products and indicators have been finalized and approved, the next step is to develop the contingencies. The idea in contingency development is to take each of the indicators and generate a function that shows how much the different amounts of the indicator contribute to the overall effectiveness (productivity) of the unit. The idea is that by relating each of the indicators to overall effectiveness, they are put on the same measuring scale. In that way, the different things the unit does can be combined into a single measure. As was indicated in Chapter 3, having a single index is very useful and it is a critical feature of a good productivity measurement system.

Contingencies are graphs that show the different levels of the indicator on the horizontal axis and the contribution of that level of the indicator on the vertical axis. Examples of contingencies were shown in Figures 4–2 and 4–3, in Chapter 4. Other examples of actual contingencies developed in different units are shown in Appendix B.

As was also discussed in Part I, the contingencies do several other important things, such as show the relative importance of the different unit activities, show what level of output is expected on each, show what is a good and what is a poor level of output on each indicator, reflect non-linearities, enable the system to identify priorities for improving productivity, and allow for direct comparison of the productivity of units doing different things. Thus, the contingencies do many things and are very important to the system.

DEVELOPING CONTINGENCIES

When first studied, developing the contingencies seems like a very difficult task, especially since it is critical that they be very accurate.

However, developing contingencies is typically fairly easy and takes surprisingly little time, typically three or four meetings with experienced facilitators. Part of the reason that the task is easier than it sounds is that contingency development is broken down into small steps, each of which is quite feasible for the design team to do, and following these steps results in the complete set of contingencies.

An Extended Example

To present the steps involved in developing the contingencies, we shall use an extended example. The example is based on one of the units for which ProMES has been developed. For this example, we shall use a maintenance organization that diagnoses and repairs aircraft electronic communications equipment. The organization's primary responsibility is to repair the items that are brought in as quickly and as accurately as possible. If a repaired item does not function properly when installed in the aircraft, it is returned to them to re-do the repair. The unit is periodically inspected by a *quality control* function, which determines whether maintenance personnel are accurately following the procedures for repair that are detailed in the repair manuals. The maintenance unit also has responsibility for conducting on-the-job training, and a technician can repair a piece of equipment only if he/she has passed the training certification required for that piece of equipment. Thus, it is important that a sufficient number of people be qualified through training so that all the items can be repaired in a timely manner.

Assume that after the development of products and indicators the final set looked like this:

Product 1. Doing high quality repair.
  Indicator A: Return rate: percentage of items repaired that were returned as malfunctioning immediately after installation.
  Indicator B: Percentage of quality control inspections passed.

Product 2. Meeting the demand for repairing equipment.
  Indicator: Number of units repaired divided by total number of units brought in for repair.

Product 3. Meeting training needs.
  Indicator: Number of people qualified to work on each type of item to be repaired, divided by number of people needed to be qualified.

In actual fact, there were more products and indicators in this unit. However, since our intent here is to explain the logic of the system, we shall use only these three so that the example remains simple enough for clear presentation.

Identifying Maximums, Minimums, and the Zero Point

The first step in developing the contingencies is to identify the maximum value of each indicator. The design team is asked what is the maximum feasible value that the unit could do on each of the indicators under ideal conditions. In other words, if everything went perfectly, everyone worked as hard as they could, and all equipment worked well, how high could the indicator go with existing personnel, facilities, etc.

There will be considerable discussion and initial disagreement on these maximums, so the facilitators should not be surprised at this. Getting accurate values for the maximums is a very important part of the system, so this discussion must not be rushed. The design team discusses the question and comes to consensus on the maximum for each indicator. Thus, if there were ten indicators, there would be ten maximums.

In our example, assume that for the four indicators the maximums came out as follows:

Indicator	Maximum Possible Value
1. Percent return rate	2%
2. Percent quality inspections passed	100%
3. Percent repair demand met	100%
4. Percent qualified/needed	130%

The next step is to get the minimum possible values each indicator could take on. This is the lowest possible value the unit could show on each indicator. It is a much more difficult judgment for the design team to make because it depends on how "lowest" is defined. The best approach is to ask the design team to identify the point on the indicator where major negative consequences would start to happen if the indicator got that bad. For example, this would be the point at which large numbers of unit personnel would be replaced. This is still a very difficult judgment for the design team to make, but in contrast with the maximums, the value selected for the minimum is not very critical for the system, so an approximate value is sufficient. There are two reasons why the maximum values are more important than the minimums. The first is that the unit will probably never be near the minimum and the second is that while the maximum is used in later calculations, the minimum is not. Consequently, the design team should not spend much time debating the minimums.

Assume in our example the minimums were as follows:

Indicator	Minimum Possible Value
1. Percent return rate	20%
2. Percent quality inspections passed	80%
3. Percent repair demand met	50%
4. Percent qualified/needed	70%

After the values for the maximums and minimums have been agreed to, the next step is to determine the zero point for each indicator. The zero point is defined as the expected level of the indicator. It is the level that is neither good nor bad, neither positive nor negative. It is the point where the unit would not get complimented nor would they get criticized for being at that level of the indicator. Discussion should be continued until there is a clear consensus since the zero point is also quite important to the system.

Assume the zero points came out as follows:

Indicator	Zero Point
1. Percent return rate	10%
2. Percent quality inspections passed	100%
3. Percent repair demand met	80%
4. Percent qualified/needed	100%

Establishing Effectiveness Values

The next step is for the design team to determine the effectiveness values of the maximums and minimums. To do this, the facilitators ask the design team first to rank the maximums in terms of the contribution of each to the overall effectiveness of the unit. In other words, they should rank the indicator maximums in terms of overall importance to the unit's work. A good way for the facilitators to get at this is to ask, "If each of the indicators were at their zero points and only one of the indicators could be at the maximum, which indicator should be chosen to get the highest unit effectiveness?" The group discusses this until consensus is reached.

The maximum that the unit personnel believe to be the most important is given a rank of 1. The question is then repeated for the second most important thing the unit could do and this indicator is given a rank of 2. The process continues until all the indicators are ranked.

Next, the maximum with the highest importance rank is given an effectiveness value of +100, and the group is asked to rate the other maximums relative to this. The idea is that the most important thing the group could excel at is given the value of +100 and the rest of the maximums are to be compared to this one to determine how important each is relative to the standard of the most important one. To do this, the group is told to rate the other maximums as percentages of the +100 maximum. For example, if the maximum of a given indicator was only half as important to the effectiveness of the unit as the most important maximum, they would give it a value of +50.

In our example, suppose the indicator maximum which was most important was meeting 100 percent of repair demand. It would get the +100 value. Quality as reflected by the indicator value of a 2 percent return rate was somewhat less important. Thus, it received a value of +80. Training was next most important, but much lower than the other two and judged only 10 percent as important as meeting 100 percent repair demand. Finally, passing all the quality inspections was given a value of zero because passing all the inspections was the expected level, or the zero point. The zero point is at 100 percent because these inspections are not inspections of the final work but rather, inspections of the process the technician goes through in doing the repair. It is an index of how well the person is following the manual in doing the repairs. It is expected that all repairs will be done in accordance with the manual. Thus, 100 percent is the zero point.

The resulting effectiveness scores for the maximums would then look like this.

Maximum	Effectiveness Score
1. 2% return rate	+80
2. 100% quality inspections passed	0
3. 100% repair demand met	+100
4. 130% qualified/needed	+10

An analogous process is then done for the minimum values of each indicator. Each minimum is first ranked as to which would be the worst for the unit if all indicators were at the zero points and one was at its minimum. Next what would be second worst must be determined, and so on.

The only difference in doing the minimums is that the most negative minimum is not automatically given a value of -100. To give the most important negative a value of -100 would be to assume that it is equally as bad as the most important positive (+100) is good. This is not a safe assumption to make. The idea is that the amount of positive contribution made by the best positive thing for the unit is not necessarily equal to the amount of negative contribution made by the worst negative thing.

Deciding on the effectiveness value for the most important negative is done by comparing it to the most important positive. The idea is to compare how bad the worst negative is to how good the best positive is. The most negative minimum might be seen as only 80 percent as bad as the best positive indicator value is good. In that case, the most negative minimum would get a value of 80. If it was seen as substantially worse than the best positive was good, it might get a value of 120. It will be difficult for the group to make these judgments of relative negativity, but the facilitators should not be too concerned. As with the case of determining the minimum indicator values, complete accuracy here is not very important and only a rough idea of the maximum negative value is necessary.

The other minimums are then rated relative to the most negative minimum in a fashion analogous to how the maximums were done. At this point the zero point has been determined for each indicator as has the effectiveness value for the maximums and minimums. The resulting values in our example might look like this.

Indicator	Zero Point	Min.	Max.
1. Percent return rate	10%	-80	+80
2. Percent quality inspections passed	100%	-40	0
3. Percent repair demand met	80%	-85	+100
4. Percent qualified/needed	100%	-60	+10

This process of ranking and then rating is one of the steps done to insure the accuracy of the resulting contingency set. The idea is that when the contingencies are finished all the values of an indicator that could reasonably occur are converted to their overall effectiveness equivalents. The design team agrees where each point on a given contingency goes so that it is accurate relative to the other points for the indicator values. However, it is also important that the contingencies be accurate relative to each other. For example, if one indicator is more important than another, this should be indicated by a steeper slope. The process of rating and ranking insures that the extremes are accurate relative to each other, so that when the remainder of the contingency is completed, all the contingencies will be accurate relative to each other.

Once the zero points are identified and the effectiveness values of the maximums and minimums established, the outlines of the contin-

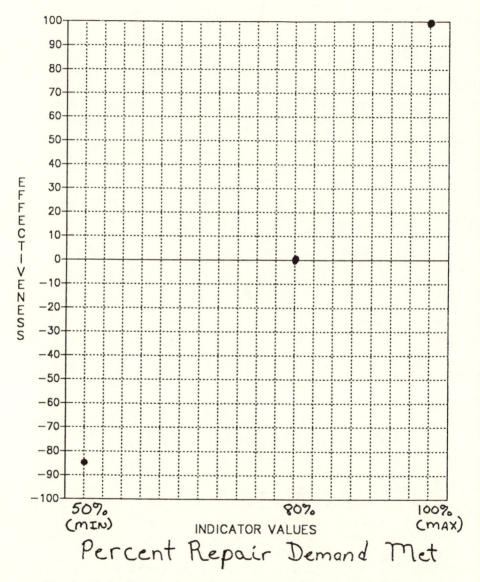

Figure 11-1 Contingency Template with Maximum and Minimum

gencies can be drawn, as shown in Figure 11–1. As the figure indicates, the horizontal axis for each contingency goes from its minimum to its maximum. The vertical axis goes from a high of +100 to a low of -100. (If the most negative indicator is less than -100, it will go to whatever that value is.) A horizontal line is drawn at the effectiveness value of 0. Plotted on each contingency is the effectiveness value of its maximum, the effectiveness value of its minimum, and where the zero point falls.

Contingencies with this information drawn in are prepared for the design team. Next, the remainder of the points in each contingency are filled in by the group. The best strategy for this is an overhead projector, where transparencies have been prepared showing a draft of the contingency as it has been developed so far. The maximums, minimums, and effectiveness values can be hand drawn on the template, as shown in Figure 11–1. A copy of the template is presented in Appendix C for copying and use by the facilitators in actually developing the system.

As with the steps on contingency development already discussed, the group's discussion of the effectiveness values of the different levels of the indicators will probably be very lively. This should be expected and reflects differing opinions on the nature of the work. The process of developing the contingencies brings out these different opinions and allows for open discussion and eventual consensus. This is an important aspect of ProMES.

Another thing to expect is that the contingencies will probably not be linear. That is, they will not be a straight line graph from minimum through the zero point to the maximum. This non-linearity is to be expected. As can be seen from the example contingencies shown in Appendix B, non-linearity is typical. (Note that the actual contingencies in the first example in Appendix B are similar but not identical to those used in the example in this chapter. Those used in this chapter were based on the Comm/Nav unit described in Appendices A, B, and C, but are hypothetical. The information shown in the Appendices is the actual system developed for that unit.)

During this process the facilitator should keep the discussion on track, help resolve disagreements, and point out issues that seem relevant but that the group is not apparently considering. Again, the facilitators must balance the need to give the group control over the system with the need to add inputs that only the facilitators can give. Another function of the facilitators during this step is that he/she can be at the projector to indicate where on the graph the group is indicating the point should be for a given level of the indicator. In this way the group can see graphically what they are suggesting.

Sample Contingencies

An example of the complete set of contingencies for the hypothetical example is presented in Figure 11–2. The *contingency for return* rate is steep, indicating that it is an important aspect of the work. In addition, the contingency shows that going above the neutral point results in increasing positive values, but that they are not linear. In the example, once a return rate of 6 percent is reached, lower return rates do not represent as great an increase in effectiveness. Likewise, at the low end, once the return rate reaches 14 percent, the unit is doing very badly, and any rate below that is proportionally not as bad. The second contingency is for the percent of Quality Control inspections passed. Note that the expected level is that 100 percent of these inspections be passed. Recall that these inspections are not inspections of the final work but inspections of how well the person is following the manual in doing the repairs. It is expected that all repairs will be done in accordance with the manual. Thus, this contingency shows that the expected level is doing all repairs (100%) in accordance with the manual. Anything less is below expectations, and results in negative effectiveness. In this particular case (since it is not possible to pass more than 100 percent of inspections), there are no positive values. Together, these two contingencies cover Product 1, Quality of Repair.

The second product, meeting demand for repairing items, has only one indicator; and hence, only one contingency. This is the contingency with the steepest slope, indicating that it is the most important thing the unit does. The contingency is steep at the low and high end, and fairly flat in the middle section.

The third product, meeting training needs, also has only one indicator: number of people qualified (through training) to repair equipment, divided by the number needed, expressed as a percentage. For this indicator, it is possible to go above 100 percent qualified since, although the organization needs only fifteen people to be qualified to repair a given piece of equipment, it could actually have more than fifteen. However, the contingency becomes flat after 110 percent, indicating that having more than 110 percent is no more effective than having 110 percent. The idea is that once there is a small excess over the maximum number needed, having additional trained personnel is not important.

As indicated earlier in the discussion of contingency development, the process sounds very complex and involved. However, in practice it is fairly simple and straightforward and takes much less time than one would expect. In addition, members of the design team seem to enjoy this part of the process very much. They report that it is a way of capturing the way the work should really be done.

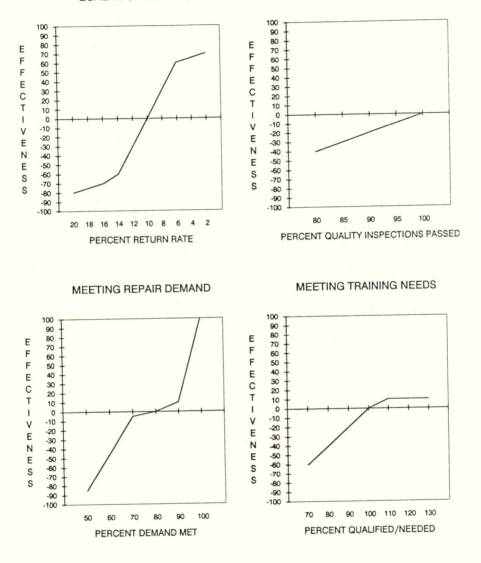

Figure 11–2 Contingency Set: COMM/NAV

Management Approval

Once consensus is reached and the contingencies are finalized, management approval is once again sought. The process is analogous to that for getting approval for products and indicators. The purpose of the meeting is indicated to management and they are given the completed contingencies along with the list of products and indicators for their study prior to the meeting. The same group of managers is typically used as was present for the approval of products and indicators. At the meeting, the project is summarized, the products and indicators are briefly reviewed, and the contingencies are presented. It is a good idea to break down the contingencies into maximums, minimums, zero points, effectiveness values of maximums and minimums, and the shape of the function. In other words, get approval in the same step-by-step process as was done by the design team to develop the contingencies. This makes the task easier for the managers and they get a clearer picture of what they are agreeing to.

As with products and indicators, there will be disagreement, discussion, and compromise. In fact, there will probably be more discussion about contingencies than there was for products and indicators. The resulting system will probably be somewhat different after this process, but if the discussion is handled well by the facilitators, both the group and the managers should see the validity of the other's point of view and feel that the final system is a sound one. At the end of the meeting, formal approval of the system should be sought from management. Typically, the entire approval process can be done in one meeting of an hour to hour and a half.

12

Developing the Feedback Report and Feedback Meetings

Once contingencies have been approved by management, the next step is to design the feedback report. This is the formal report that the unit and its management get that describes the productivity of the unit and is the basis for discussions (during the feedback meetings) about improving productivity. In this chapter, we shall first present several issues that must be decided in designing the feedback report and then discuss what it should include and how the feedback meeting should be conducted.

DESIGN OF THE FEEDBACK REPORTS

There are several issues involved in developing the feedback reports. One is how frequently feedback should be given. This is really an issue that will come up in designing indicators, but can also be discussed here. To decide this question, two issues should be considered by the design team. The first is the timing of the job cycle. That is, how long does it take to do a unit of work? For some work, such as a simple assembly job, the job cycle could be as short as a minute or two. For more complex tasks the time to do a unit of work could be weeks or even months.

Thus, the job cycle is one factor in determining the timing of feedback. Feedback should not be more frequent than the job cycle, since information on complete units of work will not be available to be fed back, nor should the delay be so long that many cycles of the job have occurred, thus making the feedback too late to make changes. For example, if it typically takes a week to do a repair job and find out how well the repaired part functioned, feedback once a month would be appropriate. Once a week would be too frequent since only one unit of work would have been completed. Feedback every other month would be too long to wait to see what happened to productivity. If the job cycle is one hour to one day in length, weekly feedback would be appropriate.

The frequency of feedback is also dependent upon the feasibility of preparing feedback reports. If, for example, critical data needed to generate a feedback report cannot be obtained more frequently than once a month, the program will necessarily be limited to monthly feedback. There may also be situations where logistical difficulties do not allow feedback reports to be generated as frequently as the job cycle would indicate. In this case, there must be a trade-off between the decreased effectiveness of the less frequent feedback and the difficulty of preparing reports more frequently. In most applications, feedback will be given either once a week or once a month.

The timing of the feedback is also important. The feedback report should be distributed as soon as possible after the completion of the reporting period. For example, if the reporting period is a week and it ends on a Friday, the report should be distributed on the following Monday or Tuesday. The sooner after the performance period the report is distributed, the more powerful it will be in improving productivity.

Another aspect of feedback delivery is the manner of presentation of the feedback. The best approach is to prepare written feedback reports. In this way, involved personnel have a document to refer to and study.

Who gets the feedback report is also an important issue to decide. Certainly, all levels of management who have been involved in developing or approving the feedback system should get copies of the report, and they should have been trained in how to read and interpret the data. In addition, it should be made available to all incumbents. Frequently, it is logistically difficult and/or costly to give each incumbent a copy of the report. In such cases, it is acceptable to post the report in a common area where all can see it.

Whether feedback information should be public or private is another question to be answered. If feedback pertains to individuals, it should be given privately. That is, only the individual and his/her supervisor(s) should be given the report. If feedback pertains to a group, it should be made public. It should be posted in the work area. This creates an even greater desire in the unit to perform well; and, if they are doing well, it becomes something they take pride in showing to visitors.

CONTENT OF THE FEEDBACK REPORT

What to include in the feedback report is also important for the design team to resolve. The basic information would be the indicator and effectiveness data for the period. This includes the list of products and indicators and the level of each indicator for the period, along with its associated effectiveness value. Total effectiveness for each product would also be shown along with overall effectiveness. Table 12–1 shows the basic information for our hypothetical example.

Historical Data

In addition to this basic information it is also worthwhile to include historical data in the feedback report. One good technique is to include data from the previous period (e.g., the last month) along with data from the current period, and show the amount of change between the two sets of data. This allows personnel to readily see improvements or decrements in productivity.

Table 12–1
Completed Hypothetical System
Electronic Maintenance Unit

PRODUCTIVITY: MAINTENANCE UNIT

DATE: March, 19XX

	INDICATOR DATA: MARCH	EFFECTIVENESS SCORE
I. Quality of Repair		
A. Return Rate	6%	+60
B. Percent Quality Control Inspections Passed	95%	-10
Total Effectiveness: Quality of Repair = +50		
II. Meeting Repair Demand		
A. Percent Demand Met	90%	+10
III. Meeting Training Needs		
A. Percent Qualified/Need	80%	-40
OVERALL EFFECTIVENESS = +20		

Other important historical data is information on productivity over a considerably longer time period. A good approach is to show productivity since the start of the program, in graphic form, posted in some public place. For example, the overall productivity of the unit could be plotted by time periods (e.g., by month, if the reporting period is months). This allows one to easily see trends in the productivity of the unit. It also becomes a source of pride for units that are improving.

Priorities

ProMES also offers a way to develop a clear set of priorities for improving productivity. Recall from Table 12–1 that for a given time period (e.g., a month), the system presents the actual output on each indicator for that period, and the associated effectiveness levels for those amounts. It is a simple matter to look at the contingency for each indicator and calculate the effectiveness gain that would occur if the unit went up one increment on each of the indicators during the next period. If, as is indicated in Table 12–2, the unit had a Return Rate of 6 percent in March, for them to improve one interval to a 4 percent Return Rate the following month would mean an increase in effectiveness from +60 to +65, for a gain in effectiveness of +5 units. A gain of this type could be calculated for each indicator. Once it was calculated, one could rank order the changes from highest to lowest. Such a listing for our example would look like that in Table 12–2.

This information communicates exactly what should be changed to maximize productivity. In the example it says that the best thing the

Table 12–2
Priorities for Increasing Productivity
Electronic Maintenance Unit

PRIORITIES FOR: APRIL, 19XX

CHANGE	GAIN IN EFFECTIVENESS
Percent Demand Met from 90% to 100%	+90
Percent Qualified (Training) from 80% to 90%	+20
Percent Quality Control Inspections Passed from 95% to 100%	+10
Return Rate from 6% to 4%	+5

unit can do is to increase their meeting of repair demand. That is where they should focus their efforts if they want to best increase their productivity. Once this is done, or if increasing on this factor is not possible, the next best thing they could do is to improve training so that more people are qualified. Improving return rate and improving quality control inspections are the least important in increasing productivity, with improving on quality control inspections being slightly more important than improving return rate.

Thus, the system can generate a set of priorities that unit personnel can use to guide efforts to increase productivity. This can be calculated for each indicator and be part of the feedback report. While it is necessary for unit personnel to combine the priorities data with information on factors such as cost and difficulty of making each change, the priorities information should aid in decisions about resource allocation, and where to focus in identifying barriers to productivity.

Comparing Units

One useful feature of ProMES is that it allows one to directly compare the productivity of very different units. This feature can be incorporated into the feedback report and used to compare different units in the same section of the organization or different units in different sections. It might be tempting to think that this could be done simply by comparing the overall effectiveness score of two different units. If unit A had an overall effectiveness score of +210 and unit B had an overall effectiveness score of +150, unit A did better than unit B. However, this approach is not valid. The overall effectiveness score is in part determined by the number of indicators and the values of their maximums. For example, if unit A had 15 indicators and unit B had only 6 indicators, it would probably be easier for unit A to get high overall effectiveness scores. Thus, a simple comparison of overall effectiveness scores is not appropriate.

In order to compare units, a different approach is necessary. The correct approach is to compare the overall effectiveness score of a unit to its maximum possible effectiveness. In order to make this comparison, one first determines the maximum possible overall effectiveness for each unit. This is done by determining the effectiveness score for the maximum possible value of each indicator, and summing these effectiveness values. In our example, this maximum comes from an examination of the effectiveness scores for the four maximums. These values are +80, 0, +100, and +10, for a total of 190.

This sum of maximums represents the effectiveness value that would occur if the unit was doing as well as it was possible to do on every aspect of their work; in other words, it is their maximum possible effectiveness. Recall that these maximums were developed by consensus among the supervisors of the units, and discussed and approved by management. Thus, they should represent realistic maximums, and the effectiveness scores represent the value of the maximum contribution each of the units could make to the organization.

Once the maximum possible effectiveness is calculated, the actual monthly overall effectiveness score for each section is expressed as a percentage of maximum possible effectiveness. In our example, the maximum possible effectiveness for the unit is 190. If their actual productivity for a given month was +80, their percent of maximum would be 80/190 or 42 percent. This value is calculated each month and included as part of the feedback report.

This index is a measure of how well the unit is doing relative to how they could be doing. Therefore, it is a measure that is comparable across units. If one unit is doing 42 percent of its maximum and another is doing 65 percent, the second unit is doing better than the first. Thus, different units can be compared to each other.

Another benefit of the percent of maximum measure is that when there are multiple units in the same part of the organization on ProMES, giving each unit the data on their percent of maximum as well as the percent of maximum for the other units in their section can promote a healthy competition between units.

In making the decisions about the design of the feedback report, the design team should consider the issues discussed above and decide how the feedback report can best fit their needs. In addition, they should discuss the design of the report with other personnel in the unit and with the various supervisors and managers that will be using the report.

Sample Feedback Reports

Appendix D shows two examples of actual feedback reports. The first example comes from the unit which was the basis for our hypothetical example. The appendix shows examples of the basic report as well as the change from the previous month to the current month and gives priority information. For these units, percent of maximum was put on another report, so it is not shown in the sample reports.

GENERATING THE FEEDBACK REPORT

After final decisions are made on the design of the feedback reports, the process of actually generating the reports is started. This means that the indicator data would be gathered for the period (e.g., a month) and used with the contingencies to calculate effectiveness scores and other information in the feedback report. This report would then be distributed to unit personnel, supervision, and management. Appropriate graphics such as overall monthly effectiveness would also be posted.

It is also valuable to plot the contingencies and post them in the working area. They should also be explained to unit personnel. In this way, the personnel can see how the effectiveness scores were calculated. In addition, they can see the relative importance of each indicator, what the expected level is on each, the non-linearities, and what constitutes a good and poor level of output on each indicator.

FEEDBACK MEETINGS

After feedback reports are ready, there should be a meeting with supervisors and all incumbents, or at least a large representative group of incumbents, to review the feedback reports. Such a feedback meeting is held after each feedback report is available. Thus, if feedback reports are done monthly, there would be one such meeting each month. This is a very important part of ProMES. Higher level managers who were involved in the approval of the system may want to attend this meeting as well. This will turn out to be a major planning meeting.

The meetings should be conducted by the supervisor, but the facilitators should be present at least for the first few meetings and occasionally thereafter. During the meeting, the feedback report should be reviewed and areas where productivity increased or decreased should be explored. The group should then focus on the reasons for improvement or decrement in each area.

The meeting should be conducted as a factfinding exercise, not a search for excuses or a method of attaching blame. The purpose of the meeting is to identify the barriers and facilitators to productivity. In this way, needed changes can be identified and implementation strategies discussed. This meeting can also be used as a planning session, focusing on events that could affect productivity for the next month. If handled properly, these meetings are very powerful, and quite important to the successful operation of the system. They can be very motivating for the participants and lead to invaluable improvements in operations.

13

Aggregation Across Units

One of the unique features of ProMES is its ability to aggregate across organizational units. It is quite valuable to have a productivity measurement system for a given unit, or several units. It would be even more valuable if one could aggregate the measurement system from the several different units into one measure that indicates the total productivity across all the units. For example, if a branch of the organization were composed of several separate sections, it would be valuable to have a measure for each section, and be able to combine those section measures into a single measure for the entire branch.

While a discussion of the aggregation process fits logically at this point in the development of the system, this topic is a more advanced feature of ProMES and would not be used if the system is being used for only one unit. However, if the system is being used for multiple units in the same part of the organization, it is quite pertinent.

In many productivity measurement systems this aggregation is not possible, since the measurements vary from unit to unit. Thus, it is not possible to combine them into one measure reflecting productivity of the different units. An advantage of ProMES is that it is possible to do such across-unit aggregation. Each unit is measured on a common metric: overall effectiveness. Since each of the sections is measured on this common metric, it becomes possible to simply add the overall effectiveness of each of the sections to get a measure of the overall effectiveness of the branch, as long as one more step is done in the process of system development.

If one were to simply add the overall effectiveness scores of the different sections to determine the productivity of the branch, one would be essentially assuming that each section contributes equally to the effectiveness of the branch. Although this may indeed be the case, it is not safe to assume it. It could easily be that the work of one unit is more critical than that of the others. Thus, this one unit's effectiveness would contribute more to overall effectiveness than that of the others. Another likely possibility is that a section with forty people is going to make more of a contribution to the organization than a section with five people.

THE AGGREGATION PROCESS

Dealing with this problem is actually a fairly straightforward matter which can be done with one meeting and some simple calculations. When the system is developed for a single section and all levels of supervision and management have agreed on the values, we assume that the contingencies are accurate for that unit. Specifically, we assume that the values for each contingency are accurate relative to the other values for that contingency, and that all the contingencies for the given section are accurate relative to the other contingencies for that section. After the contingency set for each unit has been developed, all that remains to be done is to rescale the contingency sets for relative accuracy *across* sections.

An Example of Rescaling

To explain this rescaling across sections, let us use an example from a maintenance function like that used in the previous two chapters. Suppose we have a division composed of branches, where each branch is in turn composed of sections, like that shown in Figure 13–1. The division is the Maintenance Division and is responsible for main-

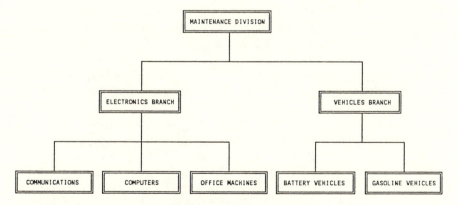

Figure 13–1 Structure of Sample Organization

tenance of all organizational equipment. One branch is the Electronics Branch, doing maintenance of electronic equipment. Assume that this branch has three sections. One section is the electronic communication maintenance section we have been using as the example; we will call this unit Communications. The branch also has two other sections, one doing maintenance on Computers and one maintaining Office Machines.

To do the rescaling, a process is used that is analogous to the development of contingencies for a single unit. We start with the fact that the most important indicator for each section will have an effectiveness value of +100. This is true because in the development of the contingencies, the most important indicator is always defined to have an effectiveness value of +100. Thus, by definition, each of the sections will have at least one indicator value of +100. In doing the actual rescaling, we take the indicator with the +100 effectiveness score for each section. With the three sections in this branch, there would be three such indicators, one for each section. Assume that all three sections had an indicator for meeting repair demand and that the indicator value with the +100 effectiveness score was meeting 100 percent of repair demand.

The list of maximums would then look like this.

Section	Maximum
1. Communications	100% repair demand met
2. Computers	100% repair demand met
3. Office Machines	100% repair demand met

These three +100 indicators from the three sections would then be shown to a group of the managers, supervisors, and representative incumbents from the branch and the three sections. After explaining the task, the group would be asked to rescale the three levels. To do this, they first rank the three levels in terms of overall contribution to the branch. That is, they are asked which of the three outcomes they would most value for the overall effectiveness of the branch. Put another way, they are asked to indicate which of the three outcomes would make the greatest *contribution* to the effectiveness of the Electronics Branch. They discuss this and come to a consensus. It could be that they believe that since all three types of equipment are crucial for organizational functioning, they are all equally important. In this case they will say they are equal. In contrast, they may feel that the three are not equally important. This could come about for a variety of reasons. For example, one section might repair more items and have a correspondingly larger number of personnel. Thus, that section makes a larger contribution to the overall functioning of the branch than the other sections. Differential importance could also occur because there is a sufficient backlog of repaired equipment (office machines, computers, etc.) in supply for two of the sections, but not for the third. Thus, repair of the non-backlogged equipment is more crucial for meeting organizational needs than repair of components for which there is already a sufficient backlog.

Assume that in the discussions, unit supervisors and managers decide that meeting 100 percent repair demand in Communications is the most important thing for the branch, meeting 100 percent repair demand in Office Machines is next, and meeting 100 percent repair demand in Computers is next.

Once this ranking is completed, the indicator ranked highest in effectiveness is given a value of +100, and managers are then are asked to rate the remaining indicators relative to this one. In doing this, they are told to think in terms of percentages; that is, they should ask themselves whether the second most important thing is 95 percent as important as the most important, 90 percent, etc. Assume that the second most important maximum is given a value of 90, and the third a value of 75. This means that the group is saying that meeting 100 percent repair demand in Office Machines is almost as important as meeting 100 percent repair demand in Communications, but not quite as important. In fact, they are saying that it is 10 percent less important. Meeting 100 percent repair demand in Computers is somewhat less important, and in fact is only three-quarters as important as meeting demand in Communications.

The Rescaling Step

Once the relative ratings of the top indicators for the sections are agreed upon, the next step is to rescale the individual contingencies for each of the sections. This is done by reducing the effectiveness score of each level of each indicator in a given section by the percentage its own maximum indicator was reduced in the rescaling. For example, in Office Machines the original +100 maximum was reduced to +90 in the rescaling process. This represents a decrease of 10 percent. In essence, it is saying that to be comparable with the other sections in the branch, the effectiveness of this level of the indicator must be reduced by 10 percent, since it is not quite as important to the branch as the maximum of the Communications section. Since the effectiveness value of the maximum was reduced by 10 percent, to retain accuracy it is necessary that the effectiveness levels of each of the indicators for that section also be reduced by 10 percent. This means that if the original positive values of one of the indicators for that section were +10, +20, +40, and +75, the values after the rescaling process would be +9, +18, +36, and +67.5. This process of reduction by 10 percent is done for the points between the zero point and the maximum for each contingency in that section. Thus, the positive effectiveness scores for each level of each indicator in that section are reduced by 10 percent.

A similar process is then done for the Computers section. Here the maximum was reduced by 25 percent, from +100 to +75. Thus, each positive effectiveness score for each level of each contingency in that section must be reduced by 25 percent.

The effectiveness values for the Communications section do not change. Since the original maximum of +100 was unchanged in the process of rescaling across sections, the effectiveness values for the contingencies in Communications are not recalculated.

An analogous rescaling process is done for the negative effectiveness values of the indicators. The three indicator levels with the most negative effectiveness scores are listed for each of the branch's three sections. These three levels are then ranked as to which constitutes the poorest level of effectiveness. Once the ranking is done, the other minimums are rated relative to the minimum with the most negative effectiveness score. For example, if the largest negative effectiveness was –120, the other negatives would be compared to that. If the next most negative indicator was only half as bad, it would get a value of –60. Finally, just as with the positive values, the negative values of each level of the indicators are each adjusted by the percentage that the original minimum indicator level was reduced. Thus, if the original maximum negative was –80 and the value was –70 after ranking and rating, this would mean a reduction of 12.5 percent since the effectiveness value was reduced 10 points and 10/80 = .125. Each value of the indicators from the maximum negative to the zero point would then be reduced by 12.5 percent. An original value of –40 becomes –35.

This rescaling process has the effect of adjusting the effectiveness scores of the different sections in the branch for any differences in importance of the different sections. It also changes the contingencies. If any rescaling is done, this is essentially changing the effectiveness values associated with levels of the indicators. Thus, new contingencies result. Once it is finished, the overall effectiveness values from the different sections are calculated just as before. The only difference is that the contingencies have been changed to the revised versions. These revised contingencies are used for the calculations of effectiveness and are the basis for the feedback reports.

The overall effectiveness scores from each of the sections can now simply be summed to produce overall effectiveness of the entire branch. For example, if the monthly overall effectiveness based on the revised contingencies for Communications was +250, for Internal Navigation was +150, and for Office Machines was +200, the total branch effectiveness would be +600. This value can be interpreted just like overall effectiveness for a single section. If it is 0, the branch overall is meeting expectations. If it is above 0, the branch is exceeding expectations and the higher it is above 0, the greater they are exceeding expectations.

Percent of maximum for the branch can also be calculated. It is the actual total overall effectiveness across all three sections divided by the maximum possible overall effectiveness for the branch. Actual total overall effectiveness is the sum of the effectiveness scores based on the rescaled contingencies for a given time period, such as a month. Maximum possible overall effectiveness is the sum of the maximums from the rescaled contingencies for the entire branch.

EXTENDING THE AGGREGATION

This approach to aggregation can be extended to increasingly larger units of the organization, so that a single index of the productivity of the entire organization can be developed. For example, one could aggregate branches into a division index. Assume that in the Maintenance Division we have been discussing there is not only an Electronics Branch like that described above, but there is also a second branch called Vehicles. As is shown in Figure 13–1, this branch has two sections, Battery Vehicles and Gasoline Vehicles. Battery Vehicles repairs and rebuilds battery powered carts, forklifts, etc., while Gasoline Vehicles works on cars, trucks, grading equipment, etc.

To aggregate this second branch up to the level of the division, the first steps are to develop the products, indicators, and contingencies for the two sections in the Vehicles Branch. Once this is done and the system for each section is approved up the chain of command, the next step is to aggregate the two sections into the measure for the Vehicles Branch, and to aggregate the two branches into a measure for the Maintenance Division.

To achieve these two levels of aggregation (section to branch, and branch to division) is fairly straightforward. In essence, we do the same thing that was done for the Electronics Branch. Instead of rescaling the three maximums from the three sections in Electronics, we rescale the five maximums from the five sections in the Maintenance Division at the same time. Put another way, if one wants to aggregate up to the level of the Division, the aggregation to the branch and to the division is done at the same time, and by the same process.

One important point should be made about this rescaling process. The description of the rescaling makes it sound rather complicated, but its implementation is really quite simple. It only requires that the appropriate supervisors and managers be brought together to rank and rate the maximums for the sections to be aggregated. While this can be a difficult set of judgments for them to make, it takes only a short time, typically one meeting. This is especially true since at this point in the process these personnel have been involved in the development of the system for some time and should be quite familiar with the issues. Once the judgments are made, it is a simple matter to recalculate the effectiveness scores. Once this is done, the rescaling is finished.

An Example of Extended Aggregation

Specifically, we would take the maximum indicator value from the five sections and list them, just as we did when aggregating the three sections of Electronics to the branch index. This would result in a list of the five levels of the indicators that received the +100 effectiveness value. For the three sections in Electronics, this would be meeting 100 percent of repair demand in the three sections of Communications, Computers, and Office Machines. Added to these three would be the indicator levels in the two sections in the Vehicles Branch that had received the +100 effectiveness scores. Assume that for the Battery Vehicles section the indicator level with the maximum effectiveness value (+100) was having 6 or more vehicles repaired, inspected, and ready for use. Assume that for the Gasoline Vehicle section, the indicator level with the +100 effectiveness score was having 0 percent vehicles that had been repaired by the section returned as malfunctioning.

These five maximum indicator values would be ranked and rated just as in the example of using only the three maximums from the Electronics Branch. Assume that the rankings and ratings came out as follows.

Section	Maximum	Ranking	Rating
Communications	100% repair demand met	1	100
Battery Vehicles	6 or more vehicles ready	2	98
Gasoline Engines	0% vehicles returned	3	95
Office Machines	100% repair demand met	4	90
Computers	100% repair demand met	5	75

In other words, the indicators from the Vehicles Branch were seen by the group as slightly less important to the functioning of the division than the most important maximum from the Electronics Branch, but more important than the other maximums from the Electronics Branch. Once these values have been determined, the next step is to recalculate the positive effectiveness values of the indicators, as was done in the previous example. Positive effectiveness scores for the Communications section contingencies would remain unchanged since the original maximum, with its value of +100, is still +100 after rescaling. The positive effectiveness values of the contingencies in the other four sections change. Each positive value in Battery Vehicles is reduced 2 percent, by 5 percent in Gasoline Vehicles, by 10 percent in Office Machines, and by 25 percent in Computers.

As before, an analogous process is done with the indicator values which have negative effectiveness scores. The five negatives are ranked and rated by the group. Then the negative effectiveness scores are rescaled by the percentage that the maximum for that section is reduced.

Once the rescaling of the contingencies is completed, overall effectiveness for each section can be calculated as usual, using the revised contingencies that have resulted from the rescaling. Branch overall effectiveness is simply the sum of the section overall effectiveness scores, and division overall effectiveness is simply the sum of the two branch overall effectiveness scores. By going through this process of rescaling, the sections in each branch and the branches in the division are made comparable to each other. This simple summing of overall effectiveness scores preserves the relative importance of the different sections and branches.

This same logic of rescaling to make the different units comparable with each other can be continued to larger and larger units. In theory, it is possible to use this approach to develop a single index of productivity for a large organization.

One potential problem that could come up in this rescaling process is that the shape of the original contingency could change. Recall that rescaling is done on the positive effectiveness values, then repeated for the negative effectiveness values. In other words, the rescaled effectiveness values for the best possible levels of the indicators are determined, then the process is repeated for rescaling the effectiveness values for the worst possible levels of the indicators.

This two-step process could have the effect of changing the shape of the contingency that was originally developed by the unit and its supervision. For example, suppose a given section developed a contingency that was linear. That is, the contingency was a straight line from the worst level of the indicator (e.g., with a –75 effectiveness value) to the best level of the indicator (with a +75 effectiveness value). After rescaling, the maximum could stay at +75, while the minimum was rescaled to –50. This would mean that the rescaled contingency was no longer linear in shape. It would be steeper from the zero point to +75 than it would be from the zero point to –50.

This in and of itself is not a problem. The new non-linear contingency would be the most accurate reflection of the contribution of amounts of that indicator to overall organizational effectiveness, and the new contingency would be used in calculating effectiveness values for unit feedback reports. The only potential problem is that the unit personnel had developed a contingency that has now been changed by the aggregation process. This could lead to a lack of acceptance of the new contingency by unit personnel. Thus, it is important to explain to unit personnel from the start what the aggregation process will do and how it could change the contingencies. In addition, if contingencies are changed, the reasons for these changes should be explained to unit personnel by the unit supervisors who were present at the meetings that did the rescaling.

As was mentioned above, while this description of the process of rescaling and aggregation sounds complex, actually doing it is quite simple. One meeting and an hour of so of recalculation of the effectiveness scores are all that is required. The revised contingencies then become the basis for generating feedback reports.

Aggregation Versus Percent of Maximum

We have introduced two different measures from the system that have to do with looking at different units at the same time: aggregation and percent of maximum effectiveness. It is important that the difference between the two be clearly understood.

Percent of maximum is a measure of the overall effectiveness of a unit compared to the maximum possible overall effectiveness the unit *could* achieve. By calculating percent of maximum for different units, a direct comparison of the units can be done. If one unit is at 58 percent of their maximum and another is at 73 percent, the second unit is doing better. This information is useful to see how well one unit is doing compared to another and it is meaningful no matter how many indicators the two units have or what their contingencies look like.

Aggregation and the accompanying rescaling is a way of combining the effectiveness scores of units in the same part of the organization into one overall measure reflecting the productivity of the larger organization. It is interpreted just like the overall effectiveness scores for individual units in that a score of 0 means that the larger organization is just meeting expectations, positive scores mean the larger unit is above expectations and the higher the score, the more above expectations they are.

Thus, percent of maximum is a way of *comparing* units, while aggregation is a way of *combining* units. Aggregation would be started with units in the same part of the organizational hierarchy, percent of maximum could be used for the units in the same part of the organization, but also would be used for comparing units in very different parts of the organization. Aggregation results in an overall effectiveness score for the combined organizational unit that is interpreted the same way as overall effectiveness for an individual unit; percent of maximum is a measure different from overall effectiveness and must be interpreted differently. Aggregation is used to track the productivity of the larger unit over time; percent of maximum is used to compare different units at the same time.

14

Issues in Implementing the System

After the system has been developed, the next step is to implement it. This chapter discusses how this implementation process is done. It covers what to expect during the process of ProMES development and implementation and offers suggestions to aid implementation.

WHAT TO EXPECT DURING THE PROCESS

There are a number of issues that come up during the process of development and implementation of which the facilitators and other members of the design team should be aware.

Relative Difficulty of Each Step

The steps in developing ProMES vary considerably in difficulty. Developing products is moderately easy. The only real problem is getting the group to focus on objectives that are general enough to be considered products rather than more specific functions of the unit. Having the facilitators help by summarizing the more specific functions into draft versions of products for the group to respond to helps in this step. The other difficulty with products is the exact wording. It takes some time to get this exactly right. Typically, the facilitators keep raising issues that the group should consider. This can become a bit frustrating to the group since they do not appreciate at this point in the process the importance of the exact wording. If the frustration gets too high, the best bet is to go on to indicators. It will become clear during the process of developing indicators if the products need to be revised and the group will begin to see the importance of precise specifications of products by this time.

The most difficult step is the development of indicators. It requires great care and a considerable amount of creativity. One difficulty is that the group will not realize the precision and careful thought that must go into each indicator. The continual reassessment, rethinking, and refinement of the indicators may become frustrating. The group members may feel little progress is being made and that this step will never end. To deal with this, the facilitators should point out that the work the unit does is complex. If there were a simple way to measure it, it would have been done long ago. In addition, it should be stressed that if measures have problems, they will need to be fixed at some time because the flaws will show up when the system becomes operational. The facilitators should point out that it is far easier to fix problems now than after the system is operational. Another valuable strategy is for the facilitators to acknowledge the group's frustration and point out to the group that it is normal and typical for this phase of the process.

Development of the contingencies is fairly easy. It is also frequently the most enjoyable step in the process. It takes little time and the design team can start to see how the whole system will fit together. Developing the contingencies is essentially formalizing the policy of the unit. As members of the design team start to see this, they frequently realize how important it is to be able to specify policy and that contingencies are a tool for making this policy explicit.

The other steps in the process are fairly easy. While the anticipation of getting management approval can be an anxious time, this process usually goes fairly smoothly. It helps if management has been kept well informed about the progress of the project and if both the design team and the management group have an expectation that different points of view are possible and should be listened to. Designing the feedback reports is a fairly simple matter. The only real issue is to try to make the reports as usable and meaningful as possible to the users and to get inputs on the design of the report while it is under development. Getting input from all eventual users is important so that it can be maximally useful to everyone. In addition, getting inputs is a good way of promoting acceptance of the report and doing preliminary training in using and interpreting the report. If rescaling of the contingencies is done to aggregate different units, this process is also quite easy. The only real difficulty is that formally stating that one unit is less important than another is a sensitive issue. No one wants to be told that their unit is less important to the organization than another unit. Thus, this issue must be handled with sensitivity and the reasons for such a decision carefully explained.

Predictable Patterns of Understanding

Another thing to expect is a predictable pattern of understanding of the unit's work by the facilitators. When the facilitators first get a tour of the unit and its work is explained, there is typically a sense that the facilitators have a good understanding of what the unit does. Thus, they confidently go on with the meetings to design the system. As these meetings progress, especially during indicator development, it becomes clear that the work is much more complex than was first realized. As these details, conditions, exceptions, and so on, come out, the work of the unit seems more and more complex. It is at this point that the facilitators can start to become somewhat discouraged. The feeling is "If I cannot understand what the unit really does, how can we ever develop a good productivity measurement system for this unit?" The facilitators should realize that this is a natural and typical phase of developing the system. As system development continues and the facilitators keep trying to understand the work, it will eventually become clear. When this last stage of the learning process occurs for the facilitators, they do indeed have a solid grasp of the unit's work.

There is also an analogous, predictable pattern of understanding of the system by the unit personnel. At first they will probably be somewhat skeptical about outsiders (the facilitators) doing something in their unit. When the system is explained, they will probably be somewhat more positive, but still skeptical. Even if this explanation is very complete, they will probably have only a very general and incomplete understanding of the system. They will understand the idea of developing measures, but will probably not have a clear idea of how the contingencies work or how the system will fit together. It is not really important at this point that they have a full understanding, so if this is the case, the facilitators should not worry about it. The facilitators can explain the logic of the later steps when it is time to work on them. As the work progresses, the general pattern will be for the group to become increasingly more positive, with the occasional frustrations that were noted above at certain points in the process. At some point, typically around the time of contingency development, group members will see how the whole process fits together. At this time, real enthusiasm for the system is typical.

Other Things to Expect

Another thing to expect is that during the process of developing the system, the steps start to become somewhat indistinct. Writing about the steps of developing products, identifying indicators, or determining contingencies makes it sound like each is a discrete step and one is finished before the next is started. In fact, the process is not this distinct. During product identification, group members will be discussing indicators. During indicator identification, the group may realize that a product is not really stated correctly and go back and revise it. During contingency development it may become clear that an indicator is not appropriate and should be constructed differently. After the system is operational, it may become necessary to change an indicator, a contingency, or some aspect of the feedback report because of problems that were not anticipated.

Expect problems to come up about how the unit is functioning. As the process of developing the system proceeds, the design team will probably see problems in how the unit is doing its work. This could lead to conflicts within the unit or between the unit and other units. This is perfectly normal and is actually a good sign. It shows that the unit is examining how they do their work. Dealing with these problems will help the unit work more effectively.

Following the implementation of ProMES it should be expected that some revisions will be necessary. In designing the system, it is impossible to anticipate every possible problem. An indicator may be defined in a such a way that it is not as meaningful as originally thought, a contingency may need to be revised, etc. These changes should be made as needed.

It is also important in implementation to remember to introduce new personnel to the system. When a new manager or supervisor joins the part of the organization where ProMES is operating, they need to know about it in detail before they will be willing to support it. Remember that there may be some resistance by a new manager or supervisor to support a system that they had no part in developing. Thus, care must be taken to educate them about the system. This means explaining the system carefully, including its background, the process that was undertaken to develop it, and the results that have occurred since its implementation. Having the support of higher level management can be especially important at this time and such support should be communicated to the new supervisor or manager. It is also important that new incumbents to the unit have the system explained to them, although acceptance of the system is not as difficult a problem with a new incumbent as with new managers and supervisors.

Another concern is that if productivity does go up and stays up, there will be a tendency to take this high productivity for granted. The high level can become the norm and the only time the unit gets any reaction to their work is when their productivity goes down. The managers and supervisors of the unit must guard against this tendency. This creates a situation where the only thing that can happen to the unit as a result of the system is something bad. This can easily result in resentment. A unit that is consistently high in productivity should be regularly recognized for this effort. The high productivity must not be taken for granted.

A related point is that once productivity is very high and is maintained at a high level, there may be a temptation to discontinue the system. The logic would be that because productivity has been so high for so long, it is not really worth the effort to gather the indicator data, put the feedback reports together, and hold the feedback meetings. If a decision is made to discontinue the system in such a circumstance, the result will probably be a gradual decrease in productivity. Without the system to help maintain the high productivity, the unit will not have the information, not be given the motivation, and not get the recognition for high productivity. Thus, discontinuing the system can have very negative consequences. Adopting a system such as ProMES should be seen as a long-term commitment. If it is helpful to the unit's productivity, it should be maintained permanently.

SUGGESTIONS FOR IMPLEMENTATION

In considering a productivity improvement strategy such as ProMES, one needs to make decisions about how to go about the process of implementation. There are several issues that should be considered.

One recommendation is if one wants to begin using ProMES, start with only a few units. This allows for a trial of the system in the particular organization and lessons learned in this pilot program will make implementation in other parts of the organization easier. In addition, such a pilot gives inexperienced facilitators a chance to work with the system before implementing it on a broader scale.

Units should be selected where there is a good chance of success. In other words, do not choose the most difficult situation for the first trial of the system. This means selecting a unit where the management is enthusiastic about trying the system, there is reasonable trust of supervision and management, the unit is fairly stable and at least willing to try such a system, and there is a reasonable expectation that the work of the unit can be measured. Such an approach of starting where there is a good chance of success makes it more likely that the overall program will be successful. It allows for learning about ProMES and how it will operate in that specific organization. In addition, such a start means that there will be people in the organization who will be able to support the program from their own experience when expansion of the system is being considered. In addition, if inexperienced facilitators are used, they should have some experience with a more favorable situation before attempting a more difficult one.

Periodic Review

When ProMES is implemented there should be a formal plan for periodic review of the system. All organizations change. The objectives, methods, and priorities for the units will not always be the same. Thus, the system will need periodic review and alteration. This should be done at least once a year and also after any major change in the unit's tasks, equipment, or personnel.

If the review is the annual, regularly occurring review, the design team should go through each step of the process. Products should be reviewed, then indicators, contingencies, and the feedback report. This can usually be done rather quickly if done by the original design team. Two or three meetings will frequently be sufficient. If the review is in response to a specific change in the unit's work, such as the addition of a new task, the review can focus on that change only.

The addition of a new task is a common change. This may require the addition of a new product, but typically will only require one or more new indicators. Once these are identified, the contingencies are developed. This is done by first determining the maximum and minimum of the new indicator(s), and getting the zero point(s). Next, the list of maximums from the existing indicators is prepared and a determination of where the new maximum(s) fall in that list is made by the design team. For example, suppose a new indicator fell between the maximums that were originally second and third in importance, and the effectiveness values of these original maximums were +80 and +65. In this case, the maximum for the new indicator would be somewhere within this range, the exact value to be determined by the design team. An analogous process would be done for the minimum of the new indicator(s). The other points on the new contingency would be developed as before.

Once this was done, the new system could be used by simply adding the new effectiveness values to the calculation of overall effectiveness. Note that the calculation of percent of maximum would also be changed since the new indicators mean the maximum possible effectiveness has increased.

Another common type of revision is the deletion of an indicator for a task that is no longer done or one for which it is no longer worth the effort to collect the indicator data. That indicator is simply removed from the feedback report and the maximum possible effectiveness recalculated.

Changing a specific contingency would also be a common type of revision which is sometimes needed after a major change in equipment, procedures, or number of personnel. Anything that would move the maximum or the zero point of the contingency should result in a reassessment. For example, if a new piece of equipment was installed that was much faster than the old one, output would be expected to be higher. In such a situation, the contingency should be changed.

One case where it is not appropriate to change the zero point of the contingency is where the unit's productivity is very high and has continued to be high for a long period of time. One could argue that the unit is now expected to be at this level, so the zero point should be adjusted upwards. However, this is not the case. Raising the zero point in such a situation has the effect of lowering the overall effectiveness score of the unit. This can be very demotivating. It is related to the point discussed before about changing the standards. The feedback report should show that the unit is making a very high level of contribution to the organization and any revision that appears to reduce the extent of this contribution should be avoided.

The only situation where the contingency should be changed as a result of high productivity is where it becomes clear that the original maximum level of the indicator was too low. That is, the unit's productivity is so high that it is exceeding the original maximum. In that case, it is appropriate to increase the maximum for that contingency. However, the effectiveness level for the new maximum must also be raised. For example, suppose that serving fifty clients a month was the old maximum and it had a maximum effectiveness of +85. The unit is now regularly servicing sixty clients. The new, higher maximum should get an effectiveness value of greater than +85. It would not be appropriate to retain the original maximum effectiveness because that would be the equivalent of lowering the effectiveness score for the same output. In other words, serving fifty clients before the change resulted in a +85 effectiveness score. If doing sixty clients still resulted in +85, serving fifty clients would have to result in an effectiveness score of less than +85.

Existing Organizational Problems

Another question that comes up has to do with existing problems in the unit where ProMES is to be developed. Where problems in the unit already exist, it is not clear whether to first work on fixing the unit's problems and then start ProMES or just proceed with ProMES.

The resolution of this issue depends on the nature of the problems. If they are of a type that will seriously detract from the unit's ability to develop ProMES, they should probably be worked on first. Issues such as lack of trust between incumbents and management, strong unions who are against productivity improvement programs, or a supervisory structure for the unit that is soon to be changed are of this type. If the objectives for the unit are not clear, priorities are not communicated, or the group is not performing well, ProMES should help and should be instituted. Unit problems of other types should be assessed on an individual basis. The general idea is that if the problem is serious and will disrupt the institution of ProMES, it should be worked on prior to starting.

It is also common that the unit is not functioning well, but the nature of the problems is not clear. In such a case, if there are no clear impediments to starting, the process of doing ProMES can frequently uncover the problems and help in their solution.

Other Interventions

A final issue to consider is the use of other productivity enhancing interventions such as goal-setting and incentive systems, in addition to ProMES. Specifically, in what order should they be done, and what combinations should be used? The order of implementation should be first to develop ProMES. ProMES is the measurement and feedback system, and good measurement and feedback are the foundation of all other productivity enhancement systems. The feedback should be allowed to operate for at least a few months. This allows time for the inevitable changes and revisions in the system to be made. The feedback system should be allowed to operate until the unit's productivity has leveled off. At this time, a decision can be made about the desirability of adding other interventions. If the unit is near its maximum with only feedback, adding programs such as formal goal setting and incentives would probably not be of value. In addition, having a stable productivity base from feedback alone provides good productivity data from which more realistic goals can be set, and productivity levels for awarding incentives can be more accurately established. Finally, having ProMES in place makes implementation of other interventions much easier. Programs featuring goals, incentives, forms of recognition, or gainsharing can be based on the overall effectiveness measure from ProMES.

If the decision is made to add other systems after productivity has leveled off from ProMES alone, the best bet is to first add the simplest program before adding the more complex. For example, formal goal setting is a simpler intervention than incentives or gainsharing and should be used first. After that, other interventions could be added to feedback and goal setting.

Additional information on goal setting and incentives can be found in Chapters 18, 19, and 20. These chapters present a comparison of feedback, goal setting and incentives and offer concrete suggestions for designing goal-setting, and incentive systems.

PART III

Questions and Answers About ProMES

The third part of the book covers many details of ProMES that have not been covered so far. A series of questions are posed and answers given. Chapter 15 covers questions of a broad, general nature. Chapter 16 deals with questions about the measurement system. Chapter 17 discusses questions about the feedback reports and feedback meetings.

15

Questions and Answers About ProMES: General Questions

In this chapter, various questions will be raised and answered about the use of ProMES. These questions are divided up into the categories of (1) alternate features and applications; (2) general implementation questions; and (3) further information.

ALTERNATE FEATURES AND APPLICATIONS

Can productivity measurement be used for individual performance appraisal?

It is possible to use a system like ProMES for individual performance appraisal, but only under certain circumstances. Individual performance appraisal is an attempt to measure how well the individual fulfills his/her role. It is usually an index of the outputs of the individual (e.g., dollars of sales) or more commonly an evaluation of how the individual's behavior compares to organizational expectations such as is done in written performance appraisals. Such measures are used to evaluate the contribution of a single individual to the functioning of the organization, typically for the purpose of making decisions about how that individual should be treated in areas such as raises, promotions, or training.

In contrast, productivity measurement more explicitly acknowledges that the functioning of a unit requires interdependence between individuals to achieve the unit's objectives. Because of this interdependence, the productivity of the unit is not the simple sum of the performances of the individuals involved. Productivity also includes factors such as how well personnel cooperate with each other, how well the personnel are coordinated and managed, and how well priorities are set so that organizational objectives are reached. Consequently, productivity should be thought of as a measure of the unit's contribution and performance appraisal is a measure of the individual's contribution.

This means that while it is theoretically possible to use a system like ProMES to develop performance appraisals, it is frequently not practical. The interdependencies that exist between individuals in a unit would make it difficult to develop a system for each person. Interdependencies must be carefully considered when developing the system for a unit, and considerable time is used to develop measures that correctly deal with this interdependence. It would in most cases be too time consuming to do a similar process for each individual. In addition, since the different individuals in a unit typically do different things, it would be necessary to develop separate products, indicators, and contingencies for each individual. It would also be necessary to collect the indicator data for each individual. These steps would be very time consuming.

However, there are two situations where it would be quite appropriate to use ProMES for performance appraisal. When all individuals are doing exactly the same work and the productivity measurement system is based on individuals, ProMES can and should be used as a measure of individual performance. For example, in one unit of repair technicians, all the repair personnel had essentially the same job and worked independently. In such a situation, ProMES works quite well as a performance appraisal instrument.

The other situation is that the productivity of the unit can be a very important element in the performance appraisal of the supervisor of the unit. The primary job of the supervisor is to manage the human and material resources under his/her control to maximize the accomplishment of the organization's objectives. How well the units under the supervisor or manager score on ProMES is a good index of how well this supervisory function is being done. Thus, if each of the units is using ProMES, overall effectiveness scores are an answer for the common organizational problem of how to get good measures of supervisory and managerial performance. The overall effectiveness score of the unit under the supervisor's control would be used as his or her performance appraisal score. For a manager, the combined overall effectiveness score of all the units under his/her control would be the measure. Other things would typically be measured in addition to ProMES (keeping upper management informed, developing subordinates, etc.), but the productivity of their units as measured by ProMES would be the major factor in supervisory and managerial evaluation.

There is also a way for the basic ProMES methodology to be used in the development of rating instruments for performance appraisal.

This is different from using ProMES for individual productivity measurement where products and indicators are developed for individuals based heavily on objective measures, contingencies are formed, etc. Here we are discussing using the *logic* of ProMES to improve the ratings of performance frequently done in performance appraisal. One of the problems in performance appraisal has been the lack of an overall index of performance. This overall rating is very important because it is needed for decisions about such matters as raises, promotions, and terminations. Typically, ratings of performance are made on performance dimensions such as technical knowledge and planning ability, then an overall evaluation is made as a separate general rating, or as a summation of the ratings of the individual dimensions.

The logic of ProMES could be used to develop the appraisal system. Once the dimensions of performance such as technical competence and planning skills were identified, they would be analogous to indicators. The rating anchors for a scale would be analogous to the different values on indicators. The rating anchors would represent how well the person was doing on that dimension (indicator). These rating anchors would then be used to develop contingencies. Once this was done, the overall rating would then be obtained by summing the effectiveness scores for each dimension in a fashion similar to how overall effectiveness is calculated in ProMES.

This approach to performance appraisal has several advantages. An overall measure of performance would be generated which would not only weight the dimensions of performance according to their importance, but would also preserve non-linearities. This could be an improvement over traditional methods. Another advantage is that by keeping the ratings more molecular, the rater would not have to make the more general judgment about overall performance. The overall judgment would be generated by ProMES, which reflects agreement between managers and incumbents about organizational policy. This could decrease rater errors. A third advantage is that the very process of developing the system could help in role clarification as it does when used as a productivity measurement system. Finally, such a system should also be useful for performance feedback. The system itself communicates what is important, what is less important, and what level of performance is expected in each area. The ratings from the system would indicate what the person did well and not so well. It would give an overall index of performance. The priorities that come out of the system for increasing performance would be a good source of information for the ratee, a basis for performance counseling by the supervisor, and a logical starting place for a goal-setting program.

Can ProMES be used at higher levels in the organization?

The system can be used in several ways at higher organizational levels. The most straightforward application is to develop the system in the usual way, but applied to higher level personnel. ProMES can be developed for professional and technical units such as engineers, accountants, or geologists by going through the normal process of developing products, indicators, contingencies, and feedback reports.

As discussed earlier in this chapter, the system can also be used as a measure of the performance of managers. The performance of the manager is determined in large part by the productivity of the units under his/her supervision.

Another application for higher levels in the organization is to use ProMES as the foundation of a management information system. Managers are typically given large amounts of data on many aspects of the functioning of the organization under them. Interpreting this information is a difficult task. There is too much of it, it is difficult to distinguish what is important from what is not, and it is difficult to see trends.

ProMES offers a solution to this problem. The idea is to go through the development of the system, but measure the functioning of the broader organization. For example, the functioning of a group of retail stores in a geographic region might be the focus of the management information system. The steps in doing ProMES for such a large part of the organization are quite similar to doing it for a small unit. The major difference is that the measures will not usually be controllable by any specific units in the organization. These measures of the functioning of a large part of the organization will be the product of many different units as well as the actions of forces outside the organization such as competitors, regulating agencies, the market place, etc. In the retail stores example, the resulting measures will be a function of the activities of each individual store, the economy, the time of year, the actions of competing stores in the same areas, etc.

To use ProMES as such a management information system, the products (objectives) for that part of the organization would first be formally identified. A process would be used that is analogous to that used to develop products for a single unit, but the products would be much broader in scope. Next, the indicators would be developed. To do this, each existing measure would be evaluated in terms of its applicability to the products. If it is a good indicator of that product, it would be retained for that product. In order to get good coverage of all the products, some measures would probably be dropped, others modified, and some new ones added. Contingencies would then be developed for each measure. An analogous report to the feedback report would then be developed.

How would ProMES be different in a service organization?

The majority of the examples used in this book have been of organizations producing a product rather than a service. However, ProMES is quite appropriate to service organizations as well. The logic and process of developing ProMES for service organizations is exactly the same as for other types of organizations. There are some special issues for such organizations, though.

One feature especially relevant for service organizations is that there is frequently another organization which funds the service organization or has regulatory power over it. The controlling organization(s) must be satisfied for the service organization to continue its existence. This situation is especially true for public service organizations. This creates a somewhat unique situation, where the service organization provides a basic service but can spend substantial time in activities for the controlling organization that are not part of its direct service. For example, the primary function of a community mental health agency is to provide mental health services to the public. However, a great deal of personnel time may be spent in writing proposals for funds, dealing with questions from government agencies, and compiling numerous reports justifying its existence in one way or another.

This kind of reporting, proposing, and justifying activity is very important to the organization in that the work must be done in order for the organization to continue to survive and prosper. The problem is that this type of work is frequently not predictable. This results in situations where the unit must quickly change priorities. An example of this is where it is common to have unexpected reports for a regulating agency that need to be written immediately. It is also hard to formalize these multiple, unpredictable, and sometimes even conflicting demands for information into a measurement system.

While including such tasks into the system is difficult, a productivity measurement system which ignores the reality of this kind of work will have severe problems. If it measures only the quantity and quality of the service provided, the system implies that the unit must only focus on service. However, everyone knows that responding to the parent organization must also be done.

One solution to this problem is to have one of the products of such an organization be something like "Appropriately respond to needs of the parent organization," or "Maintain the viability of the organization." In this way, this function will be formally acknowledged. Then measures should be developed that are as valid as possible. For some predictable tasks, indicators could be used such as percentage of reports completed on time, and percentage of reports returned as inadequate. For less predictable tasks, an indicator could be developed such that if a report, proposal, etc., were designated by the supervisor as high priority, a measurement would be made of whether it was completed by the deadline. The indicator could be the number of such high priority items not completed.

Another problem in service organizations is the evaluation of the quality of the service. This is often a very important aspect of the work, but difficult to measure. While measures such as numbers of client complaints, percent of repeat customers, or even regular customer surveys can be used, they may well be incomplete measures of quality or be inappropriate for that unit. In such situations, quality may need to be assessed with subjective judgments, such as subjective evaluations made by the supervisor.

Using subjective judgments is sometimes viewed as a problem for a productivity measurement system. The concern is typically that personnel will not accept subjective judgments as well as they will accept objective data. While this is usually true, it is usually better to use subjective judgments rather than have a system that incompletely measures something important to the unit's work.

The problem with subjective data is not the subjectivity itself, but rather its susceptibility to distortion. For example, a unit would normally have little problem accepting the results of a short survey completed by a random sample of customers, assuming the questions were seen as appropriate. While this is subjective data, there is no reason to believe that it will be distorted. However, if it is a judgment made by a supervisor, such judgments can be seen as easily distorted.

The resolution of the issue is to minimize the possibility of distortion when subjective judgments are unavoidable. For example, suppose the work of the unit is to deal with customer complaints on the phone and the only way to get a good measure of quality is for the supervisor occasionally to monitor the calls and make a quality rating. To minimize possible distortion in the ratings, the supervisor might do the ratings with a representative incumbent and with the stipulation that both must agree on the rating.

There are several techniques to help insure acceptance of such ratings. One method is to have a formally discussed and agreed upon set of criteria for what constitutes being courteous and what behaviors result in what ratings. Another technique is to report the ratings back to the unit only as group measures, not individual measures. With group level measures, the supervisor would have little reason to distort the ratings of specific individuals. This can best be done by doing the ratings without the supervisor knowing which individual is being rated, if this is feasible, or by only reporting to the group the totals or averages for the group.

Another way to increase acceptance would be to do the ratings on a regular basis using a formal system where the process is known. For example, the supervisor might spend one hour each day at some randomly determined time doing the evaluations, and the average of the scores for the week would constitute the measure. Finally, such judgments should go into the system just like any other indicator. They should be discussed, agreed to by the design team, and approved by management. Contingencies should be developed and they should be part of the feedback reports and feedback meetings.

Must data from a productivity measurement system be reconcilable with profitability data?

Some approaches to productivity measurement take the position that to be maximally useful, the data coming out of a productivity measurement system must be reconcilable with profitability data. The idea is that if productivity data can be *mathematically* tied to profitability, upper management will give it more attention and productivity improvement programs will be more successful.

Having productivity data that are mathematically reconcilable with profitability data is definitely worthwhile. However, the way productivity must be measured to make it reconcilable imposes severe limitations on the productivity measurement system. Specifically, the measurement is limited to the efficiency approach of outputs divided by inputs. Effectiveness measures where output is compared to goals or expectations is not possible because of the mathematical formulas used to calculate profitability. Being unable to use effectiveness means that many desirable features of productivity measurement are lost when reconcilability is required. For example, the efficiency measures required by reconcilability result in measures which do not help clarify roles, do not identify priorities, cannot typically be used with all types of units, and do not easily allow for direct comparison of units doing different things. Finally, reconcilability also requires that all inputs and all outputs be transformed into their dollar value. This is very difficult to do for many units.

While overall effectiveness is clearly a factor in profitability, ProMES does not produce productivity data that are directly and mathematically reconcilable with profitability. Whether to use ProMES or a system which is exclusively reconcilable with profitability depends on the purpose for measuring productivity. The purpose of a system like ProMES is motivational. It improves productivity through the actions of the personnel in the organization. A system that is reconcilable with profitability is more a management information system type of productivity measure. It is designed for top management to make broad decisions. It is not designed to help lower level personnel do their work better. If such a management information type of system is desired, an excellent source of information is Kendrick (1984).

In what kind of situation will ProMES not work?

While ProMES will work in many situations, it has its limits. The single biggest problem is where there is a rapidly changing environment. If the objectives of the unit are frequently changing in unpredictable ways, this creates problems for a measurement system such as ProMES. For example, if products, indicators or contingencies change weekly or monthly, it would not be worth the effort to continue revising the system to meet the changing situation. Another example would be where the unit's work is so changeable that it is impossible to get enough historical experience to make any judgments as to what is high or low output. A final example of low stability is where work groups form for only short periods and then disband to form other groups doing totally different work. It will not be worth the effort to develop ProMES in such a situation. Fortunately, most units have more stability than this, but where such instability is present, ProMES is not recommended.

Another situation where ProMES is not recommended is when the facilitating conditions discussed in Chapter 8 are not present to any extent. For example, if there is little trust between incumbents and management, a strong union is present which is strongly opposed to productivity measurement, and a bottom-up strategy will have doubtful acceptance, ProMES is not recommended. It is better to deal with these problems first, then consider a technique such as ProMES.

GENERAL IMPLEMENTATION QUESTIONS

Is it worth doing ProMES in a unit that already has measures and feeds these back to the unit?

Situations can come up where what appear to be sound measures are already taken and fed back to the unit on a regularly occurring basis. The question that comes up in such a situation is whether doing ProMES is worth the trouble when much of what ProMES does is already being done.

To make such a decision, the first issue is whether the measurement system already in place is well designed for motivating the unit to high productivity. An assessment must be made of whether the measures are good ones, validly reflect what the unit should be doing, are under the control of the unit, are complete, etc. In other words, do they meet the criteria outlined earlier for good measures?

The best source of information for such an assessment is typically personnel in the unit. However, they may be reluctant to criticize a system installed by their management, especially when the exact role of the person asking them about it is not clear. It is frequently important to establish good rapport with them to get a clear picture of their views.

If the assessment is that the measurement system is not adequate, the process of doing ProMES can be used to revise, replace, or supplement it. However, this must be done with some delicacy if the existing program is highly regarded by some people in the organization.

Even if the assessment is that the existing system does use good measures, it still may be advisable to use some aspects of ProMES to supplement it. Taking the measures and going through the process of developing contingencies for them can add features to the existing system. Specifically, a single index of productivity can be obtained, personnel in the unit can see how well they are doing relative to expectations, priorities can be developed, the productivity of the unit can be aggregated with other units, and productivity can be compared with other units. If adding these features to the existing measurement and feedback system is seen as worthwhile, using ProMES contingencies can be valuable even to a high quality existing system.

Should the meetings to develop the system be done on company time?

The personnel should be paid for their time in the meetings to develop ProMES. While the personnel should directly or indirectly benefit from attempts to improve productivity, it is the organization who is sponsoring the effort. Thus, the organization should be prepared to invest in it. This also shows the organization's commitment to the project. If the organization is reluctant to do the development work on company time or to pay personnel for their time in some other way, it is doubtful that sufficient commitment exists for a successful productivity improvement program.

Is there a problem with the facilitators becoming consultants?

One of the problems that comes up in the development of the system is that there will be a temptation for the facilitators to become organizational consultants. That is, they could take on the role of directly aiding in solving organizational problems. This issue comes up most often when there is a problem that surfaces in the system development meetings and it is clear that if the facilitators were to discuss it with management or with other supervisors, a solution could be worked out. Such situations are not uncommon, and it is frequently the case that the facilitators are in a unique position to help solve the problem. Thus, there is some pressure for the facilitators to meet with personnel external to the design team in an attempt to solve it.

However tempting it may be for the facilitators to take on this role, it is usually a mistake. The facilitators should not become a problem solver for the unit, they should only help in the process of developing the system. The problem is that if the facilitators start the process of meeting with personnel outside the design team to help solve problems, this can quickly become a very complex task which takes up a great deal of time. In addition, once it is started, it is difficult for the facilitators to extract themselves from the process. Finally, if the facilitators take on the role of consultant, they can be seen as being advocates for one position or another. This can lead personnel inside or outside the unit to see the facilitators as less than fully objective when they do work on the system.

The dilemma is that in some situations the facilitators *should* meet with personnel outside the design team to get information, keep them informed, or solve problems that are directly related to the development of the system. Thus, it becomes a matter of judgment about when the facilitators should take on the role of representative of the design team to external personnel. The only guideline is to do this when it is directly needed to develop the system. When it is not directly related to developing the system, it should be avoided.

FURTHER INFORMATION

Where can I get more information on organizational productivity?

A list of suggested readings on productivity has been compiled in Appendix E. The list is divided into (1) further background on the conceptualization and measurement of productivity; (2) further background on ProMES; and (3) readings on other approaches to productivity measurement.

Where can I get more information about other interventions to improve productivity?

Chapters 18, 19, and 20 offer references to other interventions and give an extended discussion of how to do goal-setting and incentive programs.

16

Questions and Answers About ProMES: Questions About Measurement

This chapter continues the discussion of questions and answers about the system. The focus of this chapter is on questions about developing the measurement system. The chapter is divided into (1) general measurement questions, (2) issues of interdependence, (3) questions about indicators, and (4) questions about contingencies.

GENERAL MEASUREMENT QUESTIONS

How do you deal with the trade-off between the completeness of the system and the difficulty of getting the measures?

This trade-off is not an uncommon issue in developing measures. It comes about when there are important aspects of the work that are difficult or expensive to measure. Completeness of measuring the important tasks is critical or the resulting system can be dysfunctional. However, there is a limited amount of time and effort that can be devoted to collecting the measures.

Ultimately, the issue becomes a matter of judgment. How much will be lost if the measures are not collected must be compared to the cost and effort of actually collecting them. It should be assumed that unmeasured functions will not get as much attention from the unit as will the measured functions. If the unmeasured function is not done well, the question to be addressed is how much that will hurt the overall effectiveness of the unit. If the damage is substantial, it is worth spending considerable resources to gather the information.

Another strategy for dealing with the problem is to try to reduce the cost of the measures. There are several ways to do this. Sampling is one such technique. It is frequently possible to take a sample of the work and use it to make the measurement. For example, in one manufacturing unit quality was important, but it was too time consuming to make the fifteen different quality measures that had to be made on each piece the unit assembled. A 10 percent sample of the output could be taken, however, and the quality measures done on these. This would cut the cost of data collection substantially. Sampling is an effective technique if it is done in such a way as to be representative and the sample is large enough to give an accurate reflection of the total.

Developing simplified scoring systems is another cost saving technique. Consider the example above with fifteen different quality measures for a product. Rather than get a quantitative measure of each of the fifteen factors, a satisfactory/unsatisfactory evaluation could be made on each factor. This would take substantially less time.

One possibility is to combine sampling with simplified scoring. This is especially useful when there are many measures that must be considered and collecting them all would be too time consuming. Take our example of having fifteen measures of product quality. One could start by taking only a 10 percent sample of the output. Then use the satisfactory/unsatisfactory scoring system to reduce the time to take each measurement. To further reduce costs, one could make only the first five of the 15 quality measures for the first third of the sample of output, collect the second five measures for another third of the sample of output, and collect the last five measures for the final third of the sample.

Another cost-saving technique that works for some indicators is using a longer time interval for the measurement. For example, it may be important for an inspection unit to keep up with the inspections of a certain type of item. Rather than count the number inspected each day, the measure could be the number left to inspect at the end of the week. In this way, a count has to be taken only once a week rather than once a day.

Using subjective judgments was discussed earlier, in Chapter 15. It is sometimes possible to use subjective judgments in place of expensive direct measurement techniques. Sometimes it comes down to a choice of measuring an important function through subjective judgment or not measuring it at all. In such a case, using subjective judgment as the measure is usually better than omitting the function from the system.

Sometimes what cannot be measured directly can be measured by going back to its determinants and measuring them. If customer satisfaction cannot be measured directly, a survey could be conducted to identify the determinants of customer satisfaction. A carefully done telephone survey could identify that the factors critical to customer satisfaction were (1) quality of the product, (2) delivery on schedule,

(3) quantities correct, and (4) paperwork done properly. Each of these could then be measured directly and the assumption made that if they are done well, customer satisfaction will be high.

How do you deal with resistance to measurement?

There will frequently be some resistance by personnel to developing productivity measurement systems that affect them. This is in part due to the general resistance to change that occurs in any organization. People generally do not like to change established routines. However, other reasons for resistance are possible.

The task of the facilitators or design team is to identify the causes of the resistance. In some cases, it may be concern about the extra work involved to develop the system. Another possibility is concern about the additional paperwork that the program might generate when operational. Issues such as these are fairly easy to resolve. The potential benefits of the program can be explained and the unit personnel assured that the amount of administrative work to develop and run the system will be monitored carefully. In other words, it should be made clear that the system will be cost effective or it will be revised until it is.

It is more difficult to deal with the fact that most people simply do not want to be evaluated. Although personnel would like to have feedback about their work, ideally they would like for the feedback to be known only to them and to no one else. Only when the information is positive would they want anyone else to see it. This is a very natural feeling and a very common one. However, people are accountable for their work, and the information must be made available to others, even if it is negative.

People may therefore resist the development and implementation of the system simply because they do not want to be evaluated. Rarely, however, will they admit this is the reason they resist it. Instead, they bring up other reasons why the system should not be used. This creates a problem for the facilitators and/or the design team, because no matter what facts or assurances such individuals are given, they continue to resist the idea. One must be sensitive to this issue and attempt to recognize when the issues that are being raised about the system are legitimate concerns, and when they are really manifestations of the fear of being evaluated. One approach that may help is simply to acknowledge the fears by making it very clear that concerns about being measured are perfectly natural and are a typical consequence of a productivity measurement system. It should also be made clear that such concerns should not stop the development of a system that could improve the functioning of the unit.

There are some specific forms of resistance that are worth noting. One is the notion that: "You can't measure what this unit does!" Such

a perception is common. Because there has been no system of measurement in the past, personnel assume that none is possible. One way
to deal with this is to ask if they have any idea how well they are doing
their job or if they can tell when they are doing a better or worse job.
If they say yes to either of these questions, point out that they are
measuring how well they do the job. They are looking at things that
lead to concluding that the job is being done well or poorly. The
question is how to make that measurement system more public and
less subjective.

This argument will probably have some effect, but will not put their
fears to rest. One approach that has been successful is to get agreement
from unit personnel to try the system and see how it goes. Once they see
the process and have the typical successes at coming up with measures
when they all work together, their doubts will probably disappear.

Another reaction expressed about productivity measurement systems is: "We don't want a bunch of 'bean counters' around here!" In
some organizations, productivity measurement has received a bad
name, "bean counting," because the systems that have been used have
measured and fed back poor measures. They have used only indicators that are easy to collect and which do not really assess the
important functions of the unit. As a result, the measurement is seen
as trivial and a waste of effort. In such measurement systems, there
has been insufficient attention given to the objectives of the unit and
what are proper measures of the objectives. Such systems are typically
imposed from above and are perceived as being less than totally
relevant to the actual functioning of the group. This concern can be
dealt with by explaining to the personnel that ProMES is not this type
of system. When they have the experience of going through the
process, they should see that it is relevant to their work and the
concern should be minimized.

*How do you deal with the point that because of the contingencies, ProMES
is a subjective measurement system?*

ProMES is based on pooled judgments and thus incorporates subjectivity. Subjectivity is present in the listing of the products and
indicators, and especially in the ratings that are used in the contingencies. Traditionally, subjectivity implies lack of accuracy, un-
verifiability, and measures that are of poorer quality than those based
on "objective" data. Our position is that such subjectivity is not only
acceptable, it is both desirable and unavoidable in dealing with organizational productivity. This is because the determination of
whether a given level of output represents high or low productivity is
a matter of policy.

The elements of ProMES are statements of this policy. Products,
indicators, and contingencies indicate what activities are important to

the functioning of the unit (and therefore by omission what activities are not important), the relative importance of the different activities, the level of output that is expected on each (the zero point), and how other levels of output are evaluated. This is policy, and policy is by nature a matter of judgment and thus inherently subjective. ProMES offers a way of formally deriving and communicating policy. It represents a way of reducing ambiguity in policy by formally discussing it, quantifying it, and subjecting it to formal review and approval by the management of the organization. It can also be a way to develop an explicit policy where there was none before.

What is critical is that the policy of the decision makers is correctly reflected in the productivity measurement system. This means several things. It means that the listing of products and indicators must be complete, so that important activities are not omitted. It also means that the system accurately identifies what the unit should be doing. This means that the products, indicators, and contingencies used in the system must be consistent with policy and be correctly scaled on effectiveness.

These aspects of correctly identifying policy are dealt with in the development of the system by having a clear process of approval of the system at higher levels of the organization. The products and indicators are discussed at length by incumbents and supervisors. When consensus is reached, they are taken up the organizational hierarchy for modification and approval. Next, the process is repeated for the contingencies. Thus, all levels of the organization directly involved with the functioning of the unit have two separate opportunities to review and formally agree to the policy that will guide the unit. This developmental process should maximize the chances of a correct translation of policy into a productivity measurement system.

How do you deal with an overly directive supervisor during the process of system development?

It can happen that a supervisor on the design team is too controlling. He/she tries to make the system conform to what he/she thinks it should look like, rather than let everyone on the design team help design the system. If this becomes a regular occurrence, the facilitators should take action to solve the problem. A highly controlling supervisor, being more powerful than the incumbents, will reduce open discussion and participation. This will weaken the power of the resulting system.

The facilitators should meet with the supervisor in private to discuss the matter. The importance of open discussion and participation should be reviewed with the supervisor and the problem with his/her controlling the meetings pointed out. The facilitators should give specific examples where the supervisor was too controlling and make suggestions for how he/she could have behaved differently. Sometime after each of the next few meetings, the facilitators should meet with the supervisor and discuss where he/she improved and where more work is necessary.

Is it ever appropriate to meet with only a part of the design team?

Sometimes a situation arises where it is appropriate to meet with only part of the design team. This can occur when some members of the team do not have the necessary expertise to make reasonable judgments. Usually this is during the process of contingency development where some incumbents may simply have no knowledge about what is a reasonable maximum, what the shape of the contingencies should be, etc. In such a situation it is reasonable to meet with only those supervisors and incumbents who have reasonable expertise, as long as those who are to be excused are completely comfortable with not being present. However, it is essential that at least one or two incumbents be present to describe the process to the absent team members and the other members of the unit.

How do you deal with feelings of lack of progress in the design team?

There will be occasions when the group feels frustration at what seems to be lack of progress in developing the system. As was discussed earlier, this is most likely to occur during the long process of developing indicators. It can also occur if other members of the organization, such as unit members or managers, are putting pressure on the design team to complete the task.

The best procedure here is to have carefully explained to all concerned how long the development process was expected to take. Having done this, those involved can be reminded of this. Second, the group can be told that other units which have developed the system also took this long. That can sometimes help with the frustration. Also, it is useful to point out where the group is in the process and that they have made considerable progress already. Finally, it is important to strongly point out that it takes time to develop a truly good system. The time invested in the development phase pays strong dividends when the system is operational.

INTERDEPENDENCY ISSUES

How do you deal with interdependencies between units?

Interdependency between units is common and sometimes difficult to deal with in productivity measurement. Consider the following examples. One unit can only work on something when another unit is finished with it. In another example, the quality of the final product is partially dependent on the quality of the raw materials the unit has to work with. Another case would be where the speed of doing work is dependent on the speed of getting parts or materials when needed. As a final example, how efficiently the output is produced depends on how production scheduling has arranged the orders. These and many other examples of interdependency are common.

The problem is how to get a good measure when there is interdependency. With interdependency, the unit does not have complete control over the work. Consider the situation where the unit to be measured can only do the amount of work that is finished by the unit before them in the process. In this case, the unit is dependent on the other unit. By definition, the unit does not have complete control over its output. It can only do as many as the prior unit provides.

This lack of control of the measure thus violates one of our key criteria for a good measure: it must be controllable by the unit. This creates a dilemma. If controllability is necessary, and interdependency means lack of controllability, what should be done?

There are several ways to deal with the interdependency problem. One approach is to form the indicator such that the interdependence is removed. The basic idea is to make the measure relative to what the unit can control. For example, in one situation, a repair unit was dependent on a supply unit for spare parts. If the time it took to repair the item was the indicator, this would include waiting on supply for the parts. To reduce interdependency, the measure could be the amount of time it took for the repair to be done once the parts were delivered. Another example would be where output of a unit was dependent on the output of another unit. Rather than amount of output, the measure could be percent of items completed of those available. Thus, 100 percent means that the unit completed all the work they had available.

Separating measurement of the interdependent units is another approach. In one organization there were two units in a warehouse which dealt with orders for material. One unit took the order and removed the material from the shelf, the other unit delivered it. The measure available was the time from when the order was made to when it was delivered. However, this measure could be separated for the two units. The time from when the order was made to when the material was placed in the delivery area could be determined separately from the time it was placed in delivery to when it was delivered to the customer. Thus, each unit would have its own measure that was not dependent on the other.

In some cases, it is impossible to redefine the measure or separate it to remove interdependency. The way to deal with such a situation is to make all the interdependent units jointly responsible for the measure by including it in each of their measurement systems and feedback reports. In the warehouse example, one indicator was the number of orders for which the paperwork was lost. In this case it was impossible to determine which unit in the warehouse was responsible for losing the paperwork since one unit must pass it to the next. If it was lost, it could have been that the person filling the order misplaced it, or it could have been the delivery person. To solve this, the frequency of lost paperwork was made as an indicator in the measurement system for both units. When paperwork is lost, the productivity of both units suffers.

In assessing interdependency and the amount of control a unit has over an indicator, the facilitators should be aware that personnel frequently tend to underestimate the amount of control they have over the actions of other units. A maintenance unit may say they cannot control when they receive the spare parts for doing repairs, for example. However, if they take the trouble to interact more carefully with the supply function, they can speed up the process; thus, they have some control over how quickly they get the parts. The unit generally prefers to only be measured on indicators over which they have total control. If they do not have total control, they will sometimes say they have no control.

The issue is that it is not necessary for the unit to have total control over every indicator. If there are one or two indicators where the unit has only partial control, this is not a problem for the system. A judgment must be made if the unit has enough control over the indicator to justify measuring it.

In dealing with interdependencies, there is another problem to consider. Most of the techniques described here serve to make the measurement system for the unit independent of the other units. This is a major way to avoid problems of interdependency and control. However, in some cases this can have the effect of reducing needed cooperation between units. Consider again the warehouse example. Suppose the measure used for the unit filling the order is the average time it takes from receiving the order to placing the material in the delivery area. The measure for the delivery unit is the average amount of time it takes to deliver the material. However, the delivery unit can do its job much faster if personnel from the other unit put the material to be delivered to different locations in different containers at the delivery area. By doing that, the delivery unit does not have to sort the orders by intended location before delivery. In this case it takes the order-filling unit longer to do their work since they have to determine the location and find the correct container. They may be motivated to do this rather haphazardly since doing it carefully slows them down and makes their times look worse.

Thus, removing the interdependency can reduce needed cooperation between units. This issue must be kept in mind when dealing with interdependencies. If this is seen as a potential problem, the measures should be redefined so that cooperation is encouraged. This can be done by having measures for which both units are responsible and which are on both reports, or by redesigning the measures so that cooperation is not implicitly discouraged.

Is there a dilemma between having measures over which the unit has control and dealing with interdependence?

A dilemma can occur in such a situation. In order to maximize control, the measures should be constructed so that the unit has as complete control as possible over the measure. However, to deal with interdependence, it is sometimes desirable to help foster cooperation by having some measures where the functioning of two or more units is combined in the measure. Thus, by including interdependence in the measure, the control a given unit has over its measures is decreased.

This dilemma must be solved by judgment on the part of the design team. Both control and maintaining appropriate interdependence are important and the relative importance of the two factors must be weighed in each situation. Sometimes one is more important than the other, sometimes both are equally important. If the design team cannot decide on a compromise, one possible solution is that both are reflected, but in different measures. One measure reflects the functioning of only the single unit, another measure reflects the interdependent functioning with another unit(s). For example, a measure reflecting the functioning of the single unit could be number of items processed by that individual unit divided by the number received by that unit. A second measure would be number of items processed by the combined units divided by number received by the combined units. This measure would reflect the interdependent functioning of all the units and having all units responsible for it would help facilitate cooperation.

INDICATORS

What should the facilitators do if incumbents and supervisors cannot agree on a measure?

There may be times when after discussion, incumbents and supervisors in the design team simply cannot agree on how something should be measured. This can also happen when the design team presents the system to management.

This actually happens much less often than one might expect. If the design team is working well together, it usually becomes clear that both sides have valid points and compromises are easily reached. However, a situation can come up where this is not the case. In one case, there were two opinions about whether the amount of unscheduled maintenance in a manufacturing unit should be part of the measurement system. This unscheduled maintenance was typically due to breakdowns of the equipment. The supervisor felt it should be included in the system because how the unit used the equipment would determine the frequency of breakdowns. The incumbents felt they should not be held responsible for unscheduled maintenance since management did not allow them time to do all the scheduled maintenance called for in the equipment manuals. Thus, they believed that the breakdowns occurred from lack of proper maintenance.

If the incumbents and supervisors cannot agree, the first strategy is to try for compromise. The facilitators should encourage compromise and, if necessary, suggest possible options. The compromise agreed to in the example was that if the unit was allowed to do all the scheduled maintenance, it would be accountable for the amount of unscheduled maintenance.

Other strategies are also possible. If a compromise is not apparent, simply letting time pass frequently helps. Rather than let the level of conflict in the group get too severe, the facilitators should postpone discussion of that indicator with the request that the group think about it for the next meeting. Frequently, they will come up with a solution in the meantime. Finally, bringing in an outside authority of some type to resolve the disagreement might be possible, especially if the disagreement rests on an issue of fact or information. If all else fails, one resolution is to get the group to try it one way for a period of time with the understanding that it would be reevaluated later.

The most important thing in such a disagreement is for the facilitators to prevent each side from getting too firmly entrenched in their positions. If this happens, it is much more difficult for one side to change their minds and "give in" to the position of the other side. Compromise then becomes much more difficult.

Is the variability of an indicator an important factor to consider?

The variability of an indicator is the extent to which the value of that indicator changes over time. Variability becomes an issue in two situations: where it is very high or where it is very low. If it is very high, this means the things that determine the value of that indicator are changing a great deal from measurement period to measurement period. High variability can be a problem, because if the value of the indicator is changing dramatically, it may be hard to detect when it is really improving.

The question to ask here is why the measure is changing so much. If the reasons for the change are largely due to the actions of the unit, this is not a problem. For example, if the number of days of voluntary absence changes dramatically from week to week, this change is under the control of the unit members. If it is felt that a more stable measure is needed, the measurement period can be lengthened. Voluntary absences for the month will be more stable than absences for a week.

If the reason for the variability is not because of actions of the unit personnel, this indicator may not be a good one. It probably means that factors beyond the control of the unit are having a major impact on the measure. In this case the indicator should be reviewed. The real issue is control by the unit, not variability. To remedy the problem, the measure should be redefined so that it is determined as much as possible by the actions of the unit.

Variability also becomes an issue when there is little or no variability in an indicator. For example, in one manufacturing setting the unit was expected to work on high priority orders first. These were identified by the unit supervisor. The unit did these first, so there was hardly ever a case where the measure would show that the high priority orders were not done first.

The question is whether such a measure should be included in the system. There are some situations where such a low variability measure would be excluded. Usually this is when the indicator will always be a constant. For example, if the measure was percentage of low priority orders done before high priority orders, the value of the indicator will always be 0 percent. Thus, making the effort to collect the indicator data might seem a waste of time.

However, excluding low variability indicators must be done with caution. If the indicator is an important one and the unit is consistently doing well on it, dropping it would be risky. This could result in greater attention being paid to the new measures with a decrease in attention to the previous, well-done part of the work. Consequently, including such a low variability measure as part of the system will help insure continued high performance.

Another reason to keep a low variability measure is when the unit wants credit for doing something. They may feel that it takes considerable effort to keep the indicator where it is and would like that contribution to be formally recognized by the feedback system.

Is it a problem if indicators are not independent?

Sometimes the indicators under consideration for a unit will be dependent on each other, or correlated. This means that if one is improved, the other will tend to go up as well. For example, if attendance goes up, a measure of output will go up also. This is generally the case and is typically not a problem. The idea is that the factors making the indicators change are different from one another. For example, the factors making personnel come to work are different from those determining the amount of output. Thus, it is appropriate to measure both indicators so that personnel are motivated to do both things. The only time correlated indicators become a problem is when they are really measures of the same thing. In this case, only one should be used.

There is another aspect of indicators that is related to the dependency issue. You can think of the indicators for many units as chains of measures influencing a final measure. Sales units we have worked with are a good example of this. The ultimate indicator may be something like dollar volume of sales. However, sales depend on making sales presentations, making presentations depends on getting prospects, and getting prospects depends on activities such as telephone work and social activities.

These factors leading to sales volume are, by definition, not independent. The more presentations, the more sales; the more prospects, the more sales; and so on. It is quite appropriate to measure at multiple points along this causal chain in developing the system. In fact, it is highly desirable. The idea is that keeping up with telephone work and social activities will help with future sales. Ignoring it and only focusing on presentations will cause problems in the long run.

The only problem with having dependent indicators is that the function being measured potentially could be overweighted in the final measurement system. For example, suppose our sales unit in the above example also had responsibility for a significant amount of record keeping on customer accounts and this could be measured by a single indicator of number of non-current customer records. In addition, sales represented 60 percent of their work and keeping the records represented the other 40 percent. If the final measurement system had only one indicator for record keeping and five indicators for sales (e.g., volume, presentations, prospects, calls, social events), this could be a problem. The values of the five sales indicators could wind up with sales weighted more than it should be in overall effectiveness.

Normally, this problem is taken care of when contingencies are developed. The process of ranking and then rating the maximums of each indicator will usually insure that these dependent indicators are weighted properly. However, when there are several dependent indicators such as in our sales example, or there is concern about correct weighting of the different functions of the unit, it is a good idea to make one more check to make sure the different functions are correctly represented.

To do this, add up the maximum effectiveness values of the indicators for each product and compare them. For example, the maximum effectiveness value for the only indicator for record keeping in our sales example might be +70. If the sum of the maximum effectiveness values for the five indicators of sales was +300, this would be considerably different from the 60/40 split in the overall importance of the two functions. The maximum effectiveness values for the sales indicators should probably be lowered. It is not necessary to get the sums to show exactly the 60/40 split since the maximums are not that precise. However, they should be somewhere near that value if 60/40 really does represent a good measure of the relative importance of the two functions.

CONTINGENCIES

What if the design team comes up with linear contingencies?

Based on considerable experience with the system, it should be unusual to get a completely linear contingency and almost impossible for the majority of the contingencies to be linear. Thus, if the design team is developing linear contingencies, something is probably wrong in the process. It could be that they do not fully understand the contingencies and what they represent. One solution for this problem would be for the facilitators to review what contingencies are and show them some examples from other units such as those in Appendix B.

One common cause of this type of problem comes from the contingency templates as shown in Figure 11–1 in Chapter 11. Once the contingency templates are prepared with the minimums, maximums, and zero points drawn in, there may be a tendency for the group to simply draw a straight line from the zero point to the maximum and from the zero point to the minimum. If this occurs, it is helpful to ask if there are any points between the zero point and the maximum where a jump occurs. That is, a point where things change for some reason. In the vast majority of situations, there are such points where somewhere from the zero point to the maximum or minimum the effectiveness increases or decreases at a different rate. This will help the group identify inflection points that will have the effect of reducing the linearity.

Why do you use the term "effectiveness" on the vertical axis of a contingency?

Technically, measures of output relative to expectations or goals are called effectiveness measures (Pritchard, 1990). When a contingency is developed for something like units produced or return rate, the output of the unit is compared to expectations. The effectiveness score is how that level of output compares to expectations. A value above zero means it is above expectations, the higher it is above zero, the higher above expectation it is. The reverse is true for scores below zero. Thus, the scores coming out of the system are technically effectiveness measures. Even if the indicator is actually an efficiency measure such as units produced per personnel hour, the contingency is a way of showing how the unit's level of efficiency compares to expectation. In other words, the effectiveness of that level of efficiency.

However, it is certainly possible to use another term if the design team feels that "effectiveness" will be misunderstood. Possible substitutes are "productivity" and "overall contribution." Whatever best communicates that the index is the contribution the unit is making to the overall organization is perfectly appropriate.

What do you do if there are ties when contingencies are ranked?

It is not uncommon for the design team to be unable to decide which of two indicator maximums are more important. In this case it is perfectly appropriate to give them both the same rank. For example, suppose that the system for a dentist's office results in ten indicators. The most important four indicators deal with the quality of the work and the volume of patients. The design team has no trouble ranking the maximums for these four. The next two maximum indicator values are having 80 percent of the patients in a dentist's office return and having 0 percent accidental double bookings. However, the design team cannot decide whether return patients or double bookings are more important. In other words, they see them as equally important.

In such a case each should be given the same rank. In this example, each should be given a rank of 5. The next most important indicator would be given a rank of 6. When the determination of the effectiveness value for the maximums is done, the tied indicators should both be given the same maximum effectiveness value. Thus, if having 80 percent of the patients in a dentist's office return is given an effectiveness value of +45, having 0 percent accidental double bookings should also be given a +45.

Other situations are also possible. It is possible for two or more maximums to be tied for the most important maximum. In this case, each would be given a ranking of 1 and be given a maximum effectiveness value of +100. Another situation is to have several ties at different points on the list of maximums. This is not a problem. Simply follow the procedure for ties whenever they occur.

Is it important that the intervals on the contingencies be equal in size?

In the examples used in earlier chapters, the size of the intervals for the indicators have been equal. That is, if percent returns is the indicator, the horizontal axis of the contingency goes from 20 percent,

18 percent, 16 percent, etc. in equal jumps of 2 percent. This is typically the way the contingencies are represented because the changes from one value to another on the indicator are usually about equal in meaning. However, it is possible to have unequal intervals. This occurs when the unit wants more precise information about some values of the indicator than others. This most typically occurs at the extremes of the indicator. For example, in one delivery unit the indicator for average delivery time had a lowest possible value of 60 minutes and a highest possible of 10 minutes. However, unit personnel felt most deliveries would be in the 10–30 minute range. The contingency was drawn so that from 10 minutes to 30 minutes the intervals were 5 minutes, but for more than 30 minutes they were in 15–minute jumps. This had the effect of making the contingency quite precise from 30 minutes to 10 minutes, but less detailed for more than 30 minutes.

Is there an issue about the size of the increase in determining priorities?

One issue that comes up in dealing with the calculation of priorities for the feedback report is the size of the increase to be used in the calculations. Recall that to determine priorities, the change in effectiveness that would occur with an increase in each indicator is calculated. This requires some thought, because the size of the increase that is used to calculate the change in effectiveness will be important. If the size of the change in one indicator is smaller than another, the one with the smaller sized increase will be shown as less important to improve even when the two contingencies are exactly the same.

The idea is that each contingency has the values of the indicator on the horizontal axis ranging from minimum possible to maximum possible. There could be many different values between these extremes or only a few.

The way to deal with this problem is to make the number of intervals in each of the contingencies roughly the same. The logic is that if the maximums and minimums are defined as the same degree of positive or the same degree of negative for each indicator, the range of possible values represents a sort of standard range. Thus, dividing it into the same number of intervals for each of the contingencies is appropriate. Typically, the number of intervals selected is 5–7. However, it is usually not possible to make the same number of intervals for each contingency, so just try to get as close as possible.

Is aggregation a problem when units have different numbers of indicators?

The process of rescaling the contingencies of the units to be aggregated is aimed at making the contributions of each unit to the total effectiveness score be equal to the importance of each unit's contribution. A unit with more people doing more critical work would make more of a contribution to the total organization than a unit with fewer people doing less critical work. The process of rescaling the contingencies is done to account for this differential contribution.

A problem comes up, however, when the units to be aggregated have very different numbers of indicators. A unit which is not so important could have a large number of indicators, while a unit which is more important has fewer. In such a case, the unit with more indicators can have a higher overall effectiveness score when the two units are actually doing equally well. The percent of maximum score will account for this since it reflects productivity relative to maximum possible productivity. Thus, different numbers of indicators are not a problem when percent of maximum is used.

However, in aggregation there is still a problem. Even after rescaling, it could happen that the less important unit, because it has more indicators, could be accounting for more of the total combined effectiveness score than its importance merits. For example, a less important unit could have twelve indicators and be at 50 percent of maximum and have an overall effectiveness score of 400, while a more important unit could have six indicators and be at 50 percent of their maximum and have an overall effectiveness score of 300. Thus, the less important unit is accounting for more of the combined total than the more important unit, even when their relative productivity is the same. While this situation should not be common, there is no clear solution when it occurs. Techniques for correcting for it mathematically make the system more complex, which has the negative consequence of reducing the understandability of the system.

This problem is actually a fairly technical issue that usually has little importance in the practical use of the system. This is because the major use of the total score is to see how well the overall, combined organization is doing over time. If the number goes up or down, this is perfectly interpretable, whether the problem exists or not. It is also quite easy to see which of the units in the organization caused the increase or decrease by looking at the overall effectiveness scores for each unit over time. Thus, in practical use, it is not a problem that is very important. However, if the problem is present, it would be valuable to instruct the users of the feedback reports of this issue and to tell them to interpret the total combined effectiveness score accordingly.

17

Questions and Answers About ProMES: Questions About Feedback Reports and Meetings

The last chapter in this section deals with questions and answers about (1) developing the feedback reports and (2) using them in the feedback meetings after the system is operational.

DEVELOPING THE FEEDBACK REPORTS

How many levels up the organization should feedback reports be given?
Feedback reports should be given to all members of the unit or at least made available by posting them in an accessible location. The reports should also be given to all supervisors of the unit. How high up the organizational hierarchy to go is a matter of judgment. Certainly all the managers who participated in the approval of the system should be included in the distribution list. These managers could then be asked who else should be included.

Who should do the data collection and preparation of the feedback reports?
There are several steps in working with the feedback reports. The indicator data must be collected, the effectiveness values calculated, the report assembled and distributed, and the graphs of the unit's productivity updated.

These different steps in feedback report generation should be clearly and formally assigned to whoever is most appropriate. It should be seen as a regular, permanent part of the job of these personnel and this should be formally communicated by their supervisor. Without someone formally responsible for each step, preparation of the reports can be delayed. The longer the reports are delayed, the less useful the information is to the unit.

One issue comes up when facilitators are used who are not part of the organization. Since the facilitators have the most familiarity with the system, it is tempting for them to do the work of preparing the reports. There is a danger in this, because the organization may become dependent on the external facilitators to get the reports out. If it seems necessary for the external facilitators to do the work to get the reports out at the start of the process, this is probably acceptable as long as the facilitators very soon turn the process over to organizational personnel. A firm commitment to doing the work to collect the data and get the reports prepared should be seen as part of the commitment to do the project.

Can I automate or computerize the feedback reports?

It is an excellent idea to computerize the preparation of the feedback reports. The idea is to have a program where indicator data can be entered and the effectiveness calculations are done along with the other elements for the feedback report, such as changes in productivity from the last month and priority data. This greatly reduces the time needed to prepare the reports.

A software package that does this is available from the author. Details are presented in Appendix F.

Should information that is not part of the system ever be put into the feedback reports?

It is sometimes useful to put data in the reports that are not formally part of the system. This comes up most frequently when there is some information that will help in the interpretation of the indicator data. For example, in one unit it was felt that some of the indicators would be affected by the number of personnel on vacation. There was no easy way to include this factor in the measures, so it was decided simply to list vacations somewhere on the report. In that way, vacations could be noted in deciding the significance of changes in indicator measures. For example, if an indicator that was sensitive to number of personnel available showed a marked drop, but the number of personnel on vacation was unusually high, the drop would not be taken as a negative reflection on the unit.

Including such information can also be a useful way to achieve compromises in designing measures. For example, if incumbents feel a measure could reflect on them negatively due to factors beyond their control, including such a measure in the feedback report to help make correct attributions will sometimes help resolve conflicts about whether to use the measure. The vacations measure described above is an example of such a situation. Another example is where the work depends on the weather. Here the number of "rainouts" could be included in the report.

Does the percent of maximum measure used in feedback depend on the standards used for the different groups?

The percent of maximum measure is the most effective way to compare the productivity of different units. Recall that it is calculated by determining the maximum possible overall effectiveness score that a unit could obtain and then expressing their actual overall effectiveness as a percentage of this maximum possible. If one unit is at 75 percent of their maximum and another is at 85 percent, the second unit has higher productivity.

This method works very well as long as the standards used for determining the maximums for the different units are the same. That is, what the maximum possible indicator values are must be defined the same for all the units. If Unit A uses maximums that are easier to obtain than Unit B, it will be easier for Unit A to get a high percent of maximum. Thus, the comparison would be distorted.

Clearly, then, the maximums must be defined in the same way for different units. The best way to do this is to have the maximums carefully reviewed by someone who is a supervisor of all the groups that will be combined. The idea is to have someone who is very familiar with the functioning of both units judge whether the maximums are equally high. If there is no one who is totally familiar with all the units, knowledgeable supervisors should be brought together and the issue explained. They should then review the maximums of the units together and make their best judgment.

USING THE FEEDBACK REPORTS

How can I overcome a negative or evaluative tone in the feedback meetings?

It can happen that the feedback meetings become a negative experience, if the supervisor runs the meetings improperly. For example, the places where the unit has improved are quickly noted and the rest of the meeting focuses on the areas where the unit has decreased. There can be a search for blame or even a negative evaluation of the unit by the supervisor in the areas where productivity has decreased. This makes the feedback meetings a negative experience. It is especially frustrating to the unit members if their overall productivity has improved substantially and they get largely negative feedback in the meetings.

This should be dealt with first by the facilitators training the supervisors in how to conduct the feedback meetings. The issues of blame finding and focusing only on the decreases should be explained and the negative consequences of this discussed with the supervisor. If the facilitators see this happening in the feedback meetings, they should tactfully point it out to the supervisor, usually in private, and help him/her improve.

How important is competition in such a system?

Constructive competition can be a healthy way to increase motivation. The competition must, however, be constructive. It is possible to have competition that interferes with needed cooperation. For example, different sections of a personnel department must cooperate with each other in hiring, doing payroll, keeping records updated, etc. If a system creates extreme competition, this needed cooperation could suffer.

The best way to avoid destructive competition is to design the measurement system so that cooperation is supported where it is important. This means having indicators where cooperation leads to each unit looking good when they cooperate. Examples of this issue were discussed in the last chapter, about dealing with interdependent units.

In general, whether competition is a sensitive issue depends on the amount of cooperation needed to get the work done. When cooperation is not necessary, competition is unlikely to lead to problems. If cooperation is needed, competition should be considered with care.

How do you insure you are getting accurate indicator data?

It is important that the indicator data be accurate. Unit members and personnel outside the unit will not take a measurement system seriously if the data are known to be flawed. This means designing good measures, which has been discussed at length in earlier chapters. It also means making sure the data collection process is accurate. If there is any doubt about the accuracy of some of the data, steps should be taken to check it and to make any necessary changes in its collection.

A particular concern is when the unit is collecting the data that will be the basis of their own feedback reports. This opens the door to possible distortion of the data. Even if the unit is totally objective, it is possible that personnel outside the unit may *perceive* there to be problems with such self-collected data. To avoid these potential problems, it is best to have the data collected by sources outside the unit where possible. This adds objectivity.

It is also possible to design the system so that even if the unit collects its own data, there is some outside check that will eventually detect distortion. This could be another source of data dealing with the same indicator or a method of periodically checking the accuracy of the data gathering. Another possibility is to have a built-in checking mechanism. For example, in one unit an indicator was the number of items not inspected by Friday afternoon at three o'clock. Unit personnel did their own counting each Friday, so the potential for distortion was present. However, if the unit continually underestimated the number of items not inspected, they would eventually build up a large number of items that had not been inspected. This would become obvious to other members of the organization. Thus, a kind of built-in check was present.

How do you prevent personnel from "gaming" the system?

Any feedback system can be "gamed." That is, the unit personnel can find a way to distort the information in order to make themselves look good. While it is desirable to have mechanisms that will reduce distortion, it is impossible to design a system where none of the measures can be distorted. The secret to controlling gaming is to design the system in such a way that the unit members do not want to distort it.

ProMES attempts to accomplish this by insuring personnel involvement in all aspects of the system. If they perceive it as "their system," they will be much less likely to distort it. Equally important is that the system be a valid one. If unit personnel see the system as valid, they will be much less likely to distort it.

PART IV

Using ProMES with Other Productivity Improvement Techniques

ProMES can easily be used with other productivity enhancing techniques, such as goal setting, incentives, gainsharing, quality circles, etc. This section explores how this is done and gives concrete suggestions for such use. Chapter 18 briefly discusses these interventions, then focuses on feedback, goal-setting, and incentives. Chapter 19 gives practical suggestions on the design and implementation of goal-setting programs and Chapter 20 does this for incentive programs.

18

Other Interventions with ProMES: An Overview

The focus of this book is primarily how to design and implement ProMES in organizations. The ProMES system consists of two parts, a productivity measurement system and, secondly, a feedback system. However, there are many other methods of improving productivity besides formal feedback systems. Examples include goal setting, incentives, quality circles and gainsharing. Reviews of these and other techniques have been published (Bullock & Lawler, 1984; Guzzo, 1988; Guzzo, Jette, & Katzell, 1985; Hamner, 1988; Ilgen & Klein, 1988; Katzell & Guzzo, 1983; Lawler, 1971; Ledford, Lawler, & Mohrman, 1988; Locke & Latham, 1984; Locke, Shaw, Saari, & Latham, 1981; O'Dell, 1981, 1986; Thierry, 1987; Woodman & Sherwood, 1980). Many of these techniques can be very successful when implemented properly and serve as effective additions to ProMES. For example, goal setting and incentives are much easier to work with when there is a single index of productivity such as is provided by ProMES.

As successful as these techniques may be, there is little published information offering practical guidance in using such systems. Most of the literature is either very technical in nature or describes the success a single organization had with a particular program. Neither is especially useful to people who want to utilize such programs in their organizations. The purpose of these three chapters is to offer information for the application of two of these systems: goal setting and incentives. To do this, these systems will be compared to feedback, and then suggestions for the implementation of the three systems will be offered. This material is adapted from Pritchard, Stuebing, Jones, Roth, and Ekeberg (1987); Pritchard, Roth, Jones, and Galgay (1989); and Pritchard, Roth, Jones, Galgay, and Watson (1988); and Pritchard, Roth, Roth, Watson and Jones (1989).

FEEDBACK, GOAL SETTING, AND INCENTIVES

The section first presents definitions of feedback, goal setting, and incentives. Next, reasons why each of these systems work are discussed. The three systems are then compared.

Definitions

Feedback, goal setting, and incentives may be best defined by indicating the key characteristics of each technique.

A Feedback System Is:

Formal: A feedback system for collecting and presenting information uses procedures that have been discussed, planned, and agreed upon by job incumbents, supervisors, and management in advance. A feedback *system* is different from the type of feedback where the boss occasionally tells personnel that they are doing a good or poor job. This occasional information is *informal* feedback and is not what is meant here.

Based on quantitative information about productivity: Information fed back is in the form of numerical data that describe how well a job is being done.

Used with individuals or groups: The feedback system can be used with individuals, groups, or larger organizational units such as entire departments or divisions.

Presented in written form: Feedback information is presented in a written feedback report that can be studied and discussed.

Done on a regular, recurring basis: Feedback information is given on a regular basis that is known in advance and expected, such as at the end of each month.

ProMES is an example of a formal feedback system; it meets all these requirements.

A Goal-Setting System Is:

Formal: A goal-setting system uses procedures that have been discussed and agreed upon in advance by job incumbents, supervisors, and management.

Based on quantitative goals for productivity: Goals are set in terms of specific, numerical values that reflect how the individual or group does the job, rather than in vague terms such as "do as well as possible."

Used with individuals or groups: Goal setting can be used with individuals, groups, or larger organizational units.

Based on goals set in face-to-face sessions between incumbents and managers: The goals are set jointly by the people doing the work and their supervisors.

Done on a regular, recurring basis: Goals are set regularly on an expected, prearranged schedule; such as once a month.

Reviewed and reset after each performance period: At the end of each performance period (e.g., a month), productivity is reviewed and a new goal is set for the next period.

An Incentive System Is:

Formal: An incentive system uses procedures that have been discussed and agreed upon in advance by job incumbents, supervisors, and management. This is in contrast to an informal incentive program in which the manager gives an incentive when he/she thinks it appropriate.

Composed of regularly occurring awards and benefits: Attractive awards and benefits determined in advance are awarded on a regular, predictable basis, such as once a month.

Used with individuals or groups: Incentives can be used with individuals, groups, or larger organizational units.

Used to enhance productivity: The awards or benefits are based on how well the job is done.

Based on predefined rules known to all in advance: What it takes to earn incentives and what these incentives will be are known in advance by everyone involved.

Why Does Each System Work?

In order to implement feedback, goal-setting, and incentive systems effectively, it is helpful to understand why they affect people and increase their productivity.

Feedback works for a variety of reasons. Many of these reasons have been discussed throughout earlier sections of the book, especially in Chapter 7. A formal feedback system gives personnel a great deal of regular feedback. This allows them to work smarter; that is, they know where to focus their efforts, they can correct mistakes, they can diagnose reasons for problems, and they know when a problem is fixed. In addition, they are held more accountable for their work and they know it. Feedback indicates that management cares about what they are doing. When they are doing a good job, the feedback gives them concrete recognition for this. Finally, feedback encourages pride in accomplishment and permits constructive competition.

Goal setting works for all the same reasons as feedback, since feedback must be present to conduct goal setting. Goal setting also works because personnel know the level of performance that is expected of them. In addition, having something to shoot for is motivating, as is the public commitment to attain the goal.

Incentive systems work for all the reasons given above for feedback and goal setting, because feedback is always present in an incentive system and because some sort of goal setting is frequently used as well. In addition, incentive systems work because of the attractiveness of the incentive. This attractiveness is not only from the inherent value of the incentive, but also because receiving the incentive provides recognition. Getting an incentive carries with it public recognition for a job well done. Finally, incentives show that a worker's efforts are appreciated.

Productivity Measurement is Critical

Before discussing expected effects of feedback, goal setting, and incentives, we need to address the importance of productivity measurement. Productivity measurement is the foundation for each of these three systems. It is productivity data that is fed back, used to set goals, and forms the basis for awarding incentives.

The quality of the productivity measurement system directly affects the quality of the resulting feedback, goal-setting, or incentive system. If the productivity measurement system is a good one, the systems based on it will most likely be effective. If the productivity measurement system is weak, the subsequent systems will be weak. ProMES is an example of an effective approach to developing a productivity measurement system. A productivity measurement system like ProMES is essential for the successful application of other improvement systems.

FEEDBACK, GOAL-SETTING, AND INCENTIVE SYSTEMS COMPARED

Organizational personnel considering the use of feedback, goal-setting, and incentive programs are frequently unclear about what to expect from their use. It is difficult to say exactly what will happen in a given organization since the effects of these systems depend so much on how they are designed and on the unique characteristics of the organization. However, it is possible to identify what to expect in the average application. This information is summarized in Table 18–1. These comparative results show what one might expect in general for each system in terms of such factors as ease of design, cost of operation, etc.

Ease of Design

In Table 18–1, the first factor for comparison is ease of design. As was discussed above, the most difficult part of designing any of these three systems is developing a good measure of productivity. In fact, once a good measure of productivity is completed, much of the work to develop any of these three systems is completed. The comparison of the three systems assumes that a good measure of productivity has been developed.

Table 18–1
Comparison of Feedback, Goal
Setting, and Incentive Systems

Factors	Feedback	Goal Setting	Incentives
Ease of design	Easy	Moderate	Difficult
Cost of operation	Low	Low	Mod.- High
Supervisory time needed to operate	Low	Low	Moderate
Expected supervisory reactions	Positive	Mixed	Mixed
Expected incumbent reactions	Positive	Positive	Mixed
Ease of changing system once it is operational	Easy	Moderate	Difficult
Effects on personnel not in the system	Neutral	Neutral	Negative
Incremental effects on productivity	Strong	Moderate	Variable

Since many of the design issues in developing feedback systems will have been dealt with in the development of the productivity measurement system, doing the additional work to turn the productivity measurement system into a feedback system is not particularly difficult. Therefore, a feedback system is relatively easy to design. Goal setting is somewhat more difficult to design since the issues involved are more complex, particularly the issues of how difficult the goals should be and setting goals that are equally difficult for different units.

Incentive systems are substantially more difficult to design than the others because so many important and hard-to-resolve issues must be addressed. One such issue is the identification of incentives that are powerful yet cost-effective. It is difficult to make this determination in advance. Also, setting the levels of productivity needed to obtain the incentives such that they are equitable across units is always a problem. Finally, there are a series of logistical issues, such as timing of the incentives, time period to use for awarding incentives, and what size group or unit should earn incentives that all need to be worked out.

The issues involved in actually designing goal-setting and incentive systems are addressed in the next two chapters.

Cost of Operation

The cost of operating feedback and goal-setting systems is fairly low. Preparing feedback reports and keeping track of goals are usually fairly easy to do and require little personnel time. This does not, however, include the cost of developing and maintaining a productivity measurement system, which is necessary for the implementation of all three systems. Collecting and processing data to measure productivity can be time-consuming. The cost of incentive systems varies, depending on the nature of the incentives involved, but it can be substantially more than that of either of the other two systems. Using financial incentives or time off from work can be costly, whereas other incentives, such as formal congratulations by senior managers, are not costly.

Supervisory Time Needed to Operate

The amount of supervisory time needed to run a feedback or goal-setting system is fairly low once the system is operational. Supervisory time is required to make sure measurement data are being collected and processed and to meet with unit personnel to review feedback reports and/or set goals. These activities should not be very time-consuming. The only exception to this is if goals are set with individuals. This requires the supervisor to meet with each individual for each performance period (e.g., each month). In general, however, such individual goal setting is not recommended, at least for lower level personnel. Such programs take up too much supervisory time and, except for very simple jobs or jobs where everyone does the same work, objective measurement of individual productivity is typically too difficult to be done well. Incentive systems take more supervisory time to operate because there is usually more administrative time required.

Expected Supervisory Reactions

Supervisors can be expected to have positive reactions to feedback and goal-setting programs that are done well. One aspect of being done well that is critical to supervisory acceptance is that they participate heavily in the development of the productivity measurement system and the feedback system. Supervisors like feedback because it increases productivity. Feedback also makes it easier to see where problems exist and to allocate resources on a more objective basis. Feedback can also be used to determine the effects of any improvements made. In addition, having a formal feedback system helps supervisors counsel problem personnel, because having solid data and agreed-upon standards makes the difficult task of giving corrective feedback much easier.

Supervisors like goal setting for the same reasons they like feedback. In addition, goal setting provides them with a tool for motivating personnel. One thing supervisors do not like about goals is that they are held accountable for reaching these goals. This is especially true if they feel they do not have direct control over accomplishing the goals or if they believe goals are set too high. Another problem with goal setting is that over time there can be a tendency for the goals to be set as low as possible to insure that they will be met. This process defeats the purpose of goal setting and results in a negative reaction to the goal-setting program.

Supervisor reactions to incentives are mixed, at best. Some supervisors feel that incentives are unnecessary, that personnel should want to do a good job without incentives. Supervisors may resent the incentives if they do not get them as well. In addition, they may find incentives difficult to administer and feel that they create problems in units which do not get them. They may also feel that a formal incentive system decreases their power to award an incentive informally when they judge it appropriate. This is not to say that all supervisors are negative toward incentives; some are quite positive. However, one should expect as much negative supervisory reaction as positive reaction. The negative reaction is lessened when incentives are limited to forms of recognition such as plaques, public commendation, or other formal recognition.

Expected Incumbent Reactions

The reactions of incumbents to well-designed feedback and goal-setting programs will typically be quite positive, usually more positive than the reactions of supervisors. Such systems let incumbents know where they stand and add variety to their work. These systems also make both recognition and reprimands more accurate and fair. Incumbents will be mixed in their reactions to incentives, but overall will be more positive than supervisors. They like being formally recognized for working hard, and like the incentives themselves. High-productivity individuals or units that get the incentives will typically like the incentive system, whereas lower-productivity individuals or units not getting the incentives will not. Usually, individuals or groups not getting the incentives will attribute this to faults in the system rather than to their own lower productivity. As with supervisors, some incumbents feel that personnel should not need incentives to do a good job, but the percentage of incumbents who feel this way is much smaller than for supervisors. Finally, no matter how carefully the incentive system is designed, some perceptions of inequity in the awarding of incentives are unavoidable.

Ease of Changing the System Once Operational

Another point of comparison is the ease of changing the program after it is operational. It is almost always necessary to modify and "fine-tune" an operational system. This is because all the possible problems cannot be anticipated. The question is how difficult it is to make these changes once the system is operational. For feedback, such changes are made fairly easily and will generally be accepted by unit personnel because they see the need for the changes. Goal-setting systems are somewhat more difficult to change, especially if the change involves changing the difficulty of the goal. Changes in incentive systems are much more difficult to make, especially if the change increases the difficulty of getting an incentive or alters the type of incentive to be awarded. It is almost impossible to make such changes in incentives without some individuals feeling the change is unfair. Even if the change is to make it easier to get the incentive or to increase the incentive, units whose system is not also changed will tend to resent the modification. Thus, changing an incentive system will usually increase the negative reaction to it.

Effects on Personnel Not in the System

Implementing feedback, goal-setting, and incentive systems also affects individuals or units not included in the program. If such a program is implemented in one unit, other units in the organization will most likely become aware of it. For a feedback or goal-setting system, this effect will most likely be neutral. That is, the other units may be interested in what is being done, how it works, and its effects, but they will probably not be overly concerned that they do not have such a program themselves. If they feel it is a good program, they may express a desire to have it in their unit, but will typically be patient if it is understood that they will receive it later. In contrast, the effects of an incentive program on units not included in the system will most likely be negative. Personnel in the other units will generally feel resentful that they do not have the opportunity to earn the incentives. They will probably feel this way even though they have mixed feelings about incentives themselves.

Incremental Effects on Productivity

The final point of comparison is the effects of the three programs on productivity. This comparison is the most difficult, because it depends on so many factors, such as the quality of the measurement system, the quality of the program, the initial level of productivity of the units, etc. However, some *average, relative* effects can be described. The best way to express the expected effects of the three systems on productivity is to indicate the size of the increase that would occur if each were added to the next. Specifically, it can be said that adding a good feedback system to a unit will generally result in a strong increase in productivity. Adding a goal-setting program to the feedback program will sometimes produce a further increase in productivity, but not as large as the initial increase due to feedback. Adding an incentives program to feedback plus goal setting could result in incremental effects ranging from none to large, depending on the system and the situation.

Recommended Implementation Strategy

If one wants to use feedback, goal-setting, and incentive systems, a question that must be addressed is the way these programs should be implemented. Specifically, in what order should they be done, and what combinations should be used? While this issue was discussed in an earlier section, some comments are also in order here. The order of implementation should be first to develop the measurement system, and then to institute the feedback system. The feedback system should be allowed to operate for at least a few months. This allows time for the inevitable changes in the system to be made before the more complex systems of goal-setting and incentives are instituted. In addition, this provides productivity data so that more realistic goals can be set, and provides the information needed to determine what productivity levels should be required for awarding incentives.

Once feedback has been operational for enough time to make necessary revisions to the system, goal setting can be added. Adding goal setting would be done if it is reasonable to expect additional increases in productivity and it is judged to be worth the additional effort to develop the system. After that, incentives could be added to feedback and goal setting if they seemed warranted.

19

Designing Goal-Setting Systems

With this comparison of the three approaches in mind, we now turn to a discussion of how to design and implement each of the systems. The design and implementation of feedback has been extensively covered in the discussion of ProMES throughout the body of the book. This chapter focuses on goal setting. Incentives will be addressed in Chapter 20.

ISSUES FOR GOAL SETTING

Extensive research has indicated that productivity can be improved through the use of goal setting (e.g., Locke, Shaw, Saari, & Latham, 1981). Consequently, a series of questions will be presented to guide individuals through the process of designing a goal-setting system. Many of these issues are similar to questions raised during the development of a feedback system.

It is important first to establish a design team that will design as well as implement the system. The structure and function of this group is basically the same as the type of design team that would develop ProMES, as discussed in Chapter 9. This design team should review the questions raised here, examine the information provided, and decide how to apply it to their specific organization.

What should goal setting be based on?

Good measures of performance should be the foundation for the goal-setting system. Employees will work to maximize their performance on the *things that are measured*. Therefore, if performance information is fed back on low quality measures, problems can result. If the measures do not accurately reflect organizational objectives, they will cause personnel to concentrate on doing things that are not helpful to the organization. If the measures do not cover the entire job, unmeasured things will often be ignored.

Consistency between the measurement system, the feedback system, and the goal-setting system is also very important. This means that what is measured must relate to what is fed back, and what is fed back must relate to the goals that are set. The system designers must develop a thorough plan in advance of the implementation to insure that this consistency occurs. If they know that goals are to be set in specific productivity areas, these activities must be measured separately; the feedback for them must also be consistent with the goal-setting plan. For example, if the manager wants each section of a manufacturing department to set goals on quality, the measurement and feedback systems must be designed to allow quality to be measured separately from the other aspects of work. The contribution of each individual section must also be identified separately. If these issues are not addressed from the beginning, a considerable amount of effort could be wasted.

What type of goal-setting system should be used?

Another important question the design team must answer is which factors are going to provide the basis for goal setting, since goals can be set on many different aspects of work. Two distinct approaches are available. The first, *targeted goal setting*, focuses on a specific aspect of the work that needs improvement and must be given special attention. For example, suppose an equipment repair unit developed a backlog of repairs. After studying the situation, it appeared that the problem was a lack of trained personnel. A targeted goal-setting system would focus on how effectively the unit trained their personnel to perform these repairs.

Overall goal setting, the second type of system, uses goals to improve the general performance of the unit, rather than to address specific problems. Although many of the issues and principles to be discussed can be applied to a targeted goal-setting system, it is the overall system that is the primary focus of the chapter.

How should the goal-setting system be constructed?

Two issues that must be addressed in constructing a goal-setting system are (1) whether the performance system uses a single index of performance; and (2) whether unit personnel have control over the performance being measured.

We recommend using a single index of performance that measures all relevant aspects of performance and weights the more important aspects of performance accordingly. A system such as ProMES incorporates both of these factors. Once the system has been developed, goal setting is simply a matter of specifying the level of the overall index for which the unit will strive.

Although having a single index of productivity is desirable, goal-setting can be accomplished without one. There are two basic options available. First, goals can be set on the important aspects of the unit's work; the unit would then track how many of the goals have been met. For instance, if there were ten measures that covered the unit's work, there would be ten goals set. A record would then be made of how many of the ten goals were met. While this approach is feasible, it can become somewhat cumbersome to administer. For example, it may be hard to set accurate goals for that many different areas. More importantly, if some of the goals are achieved but not others, it is difficult to assess overall performance. This is particularly hard when it's necessary to compare performance across periods. If the unit made eight of the ten goals last month but only six of the ten this month, it would seem that they did worse this month. However, this assessment would depend on the importance and difficulty of the goals that were met.

The second alternative to a single index is a system where each area of the unit's work is assigned points for different levels of output. For example, if one measure for a quality control unit was the number of items not inspected by the end of the week, and none were left to be inspected, the unit would receive 50 points. If one to five items were left, the unit would receive 40 points; if six to ten were left, 30 points; etc. A similar point system would be developed for each productivity measure. To perform at the realistic maximum in every area might result in a total score of 550 points. Once this point system is designed, the unit's goal would be the total number of points to be earned for a given time period. The unit might, for example, set a goal of 350 points for a given month. With this method, only one goal is set, and it is clear whether the goal has been met and whether the unit is improving.

In essence, this is a simplified version of doing contingencies in ProMES. Different levels of output are given point values analogous to effectiveness points. The approach here is much simpler than the ProMES system, but this simplicity is at the cost of many of the desirable features that ProMES has.

Employee control over measures of performance is the second issue to address in constructing a goal-setting system. If a specific goal is set on a measure of performance and the goal cannot be met due to factors beyond the unit's control, the goal loses its ability to motivate and, hence, its effectiveness. Controllability in goal-setting is the same issue as has been discussed for feedback throughout the book, and the same issues that have been discussed for feedback under ProMES apply to goal-setting.

Who should participate in setting the goals?

Both incumbents and supervisors of the unit should be deeply involved in setting goals, either setting them on their own or setting them and clarifying them with higher management.

While there is some controversy in the goal-setting literature as to whether or not participation in setting goals by those who will do the work is necessary, there are two reasons why we would argue for participation. First, since the incumbents and supervisors know the specific factors they must face on a day-to-day basis, their participation will result in more appropriate goals. Second, participation in the goal-setting process will increase acceptance of the goal-setting system, which will improve the effectiveness of the system.

How difficult should the goals be?

Goals that are difficult but attainable should be the aim of the goal-setting system. Since it is important that personnel accept the goals, they should not be so difficult that unit members will not accept them.

The meaning attached to the goals is another factor to consider in determining how difficult the goals should be. In some systems, the unit is expected to achieve the goals; in this case, the goals are the minimum acceptable performance and if the goals are not met, unit members must explain why. This is very different from the approach where the goals are seen as a challenge to shoot for and failure to achieve them is not seen as negative.

These two different approaches create systems with very different effects. If the goals are set as the minimally acceptable performance, the goals can be seen as fairly aversive; if personnel exceed the minimally acceptable goals, nothing happens, but if they fall below them, they are criticized. Units often respond to this type of system by setting goals as low as possible and avoid raising them, even if they have been exceeding them for some time.

In contrast, if the goals are seen as a challenge and the unit is not criticized for failure to achieve the goals, unit personnel set more difficult goals and increase them when appropriate. The goals then become a source of pride and positive outcomes rather than as a trigger for criticism.

The determination of which approach to use must be made by the design team in conjunction with management. It is clear from the above presentation that the challenging goal approach is preferable, but organizational realities may prevent the use of this approach. Once the approach has been selected, setting the difficulty of the goal becomes a matter of judgment.

Should the goals be public or private?

The decision to make goals public (i.e., both the unit and higher-level management know what the goals are) or private (i.e., set by the unit and not communicated to anyone else) should depend upon the goal-setting system desired and the circumstances involved.

There are several reasons for using public goals. First, they often increase the motivation and awareness levels of the individuals involved. Consequently, personnel work harder to achieve them. Second, public recognition is possible, which can also be highly motivating. Finally, public goals can have a motivating effect on the rest of the organization because competition may result between the various units who are participating in the system.

Although the private goals approach may seem unusual, it has definite advantages in certain situations. Specifically, if unit personnel assume that any goal they set will become the minimum level of acceptable performance, they will be reluctant to set challenging goals. Instead, they will set goals they know they can exceed. One way to eliminate this problem is to keep the goals private. In this approach, the unit sets challenging goals but does not communicate them to the managers above them in the organizational hierarchy. Thus, the unit is not held formally accountable for achieving their goals, but unit personnel are still motivated because they know when they have achieved their goal.

The rationale underlying this approach is that the ultimate objective is to increase productivity, not to achieve a specific goal. Consequently, focusing on the achievement of goals rather than the level of unit performance is really not appropriate; whether the unit makes its goals is often largely a function of the difficulty of the goal, not of excellent performance. In the private approach, the unit is held accountable only for its level of performance, not whether it has achieved any particular goal.

The design team should consider the potential positive and negative effects of each system before choosing which to use. The public system should be used if the goals will not be treated as minimally acceptable performance. If, however, goals will become minimums, the private system should certainly be considered. In any event, the incumbents and supervisors who will be doing the work and setting the goals should have a strong voice in the decision.

For what period of time should goals be set?

When establishing the time period for goal setting, the same factors should be considered as have been discussed for the time period for feedback. That is, both the job cycle and the availability of performance measures should be considered. These are discussed in Chapter 12.

Should goals be reviewed each period?

It is important that goals be reviewed each period (e.g., monthly), in terms of both goal attainment and goal difficulty. A goal-attainment meeting should be held to discuss reasons for reaching or not reaching a goal. Unit members should address potential changes in operations that would improve performance and goal attainment as well as plan how to implement these changes. These meetings need to be managed so that they are constructive, fact-finding, idea generation exercises, rather than sources of criticism for not reaching goals. If goals are not met, the reasons should be outlined in a constructive, problem-solving fashion rather than in a blaming manner. Put another way, the process of using goal meetings to review productivity should proceed in a way similar to that described for the feedback meetings under ProMES in Chapter 12.

Additionally, this meeting should be used to assess how difficult the goal is. The goal system should be designed with the expectation that goals can be easily changed. In other words, those who set the goals should be able to change them if they feel it is necessary. This is important because situations rarely remain the same. The unit's performance could be improving or declining in a particular area, indicating the need to set a different goal; or perhaps personnel simply want to experiment with using different goals for a period of time.

Thus, units may want to change their goals frequently and they should be allowed to do so. This emphasizes the fact that the system belongs to them and is responsive to their needs, which can greatly increase acceptance of the system. As stated above, unit members should be accountable for their *performance*, not what goals they set or whether the goals are achieved.

One word of caution concerning changing goals is necessary. Changes in goals should only be made with the approval of the unit personnel. Should upper management decide to increase goals without the support of the incumbents, morale can be weakened and acceptance of the program decreased.

Should supervisors be trained to do goal setting?

The individuals who set up goal-setting systems should be familiar with the following, either through prior experience with the system or through appropriate training:

1. What goal-setting is and why it works.
2. How the system was designed and why certain decisions were made (e.g., why there is an overall measure of performance, the use of public vs. private goal setting, how participation will be handled, etc.).
3. The importance of participation in the goal-setting process.
4. How to address the possible problem of the unit wanting to set either unrealistically high or low goals.

5. The importance of a positive approach when discussing performance levels with unit personnel.

Any supervisors who have assisted in the implementation of the measurement system, the feedback system or the goal-setting system should have gained familiarity with at least some of these concepts. However, if the supervisors are not familiar with these issues, at least minimal training will be necessary.

How should the goal-setting system be introduced to the unit?

Once the system is designed it must be implemented. The nature of the system should be reviewed with all the incumbents before the goal-setting system is activated. This review should include the type of goal-setting system being used (i.e., targeted or overall), whether goals are public or private, the frequency of setting the goals, etc. Incumbents should be asked to think about and discuss amongst themselves what goal(s) should be set for the first period. A few days later, the first formal goal-setting meeting should be held with all incumbents or, if this is not practical, a representative group of incumbents. From then on, the goal setting and review are done for each period.

20

Designing Incentive Systems

This chapter focuses on issues that need to be addressed in designing incentive systems. Generally, all of the issues that are important in designing feedback and goal-setting systems must also be addressed for incentives, since to use incentives, one must first have a feedback system. This is because giving incentives requires that a method be available for determining whether performance has reached the level necessary to receive the incentives. Thus, to design an incentive system, the issues about designing feedback must first be addressed. Additionally, it is typical that the issues associated with goal setting must be addressed, since incentives are usually based on achieving a specific level of productivity, or goal. Thus, issues of goal setting also become important.

ISSUES FOR INCENTIVES

There are a number of issues directly pertinent to designing incentive systems which must be addressed.

Should the incentives in the system be individual or group incentives?

Either individuals or groups can receive incentives or other forms of recognition, such as being given paid time off, being recognized by a senior manager, or being relieved of unpleasant tasks. The choice of which to use depends on the measurement and feedback systems. If individual productivity is being measured and fed back, the incentives should be for individuals, and given to individuals. If the measurement and feedback systems are based on group productivity, the incentives should be group based.

What productivity measures should be used as the basis for awarding incentives?

In the discussion of feedback and goal setting, it was stressed that all important aspects of the unit's work should be included in the measurement system. This is even more important for incentive systems, since the more powerful they are, the more their design flaws are magnified. If an important aspect of the work is omitted from measurement and a powerful incentive program is used, it is particularly likely that the unmeasured portion of the work will suffer. The more powerful the incentive program, the more serious the problem. Thus, when using powerful incentives, all important aspects of the work must be included in the measurement system.

Although having a single index of productivity has been important for each system discussed so far, it is particularly useful if incentives are to be used. When multiple aspects of the work are measured and not combined, it is extremely difficult to award incentives. The difficulty is determining the point at which the unit should receive the incentive. In contrast, when there is a single index, the incentive is based on that index; if a unit exceeds a specified value in overall productivity, it is awarded the incentive.

Although the single index is preferable, there are two other approaches that can be considered. One alternative is the point system described in the goal setting section. With this approach, if the unit achieves a specified number of points, it receives the incentive. The second alternative involves using incentives with multiple measures and is based on achieving a certain percentage of the goals. If, for example, the unit had eight measures of their work, a goal level could be established for each area. If the unit exceeded the goal in some specified number of these areas (e.g., six of the eight areas), it would receive the incentive.

How many levels of productivity should be defined for incentives?

Although some of the previous questions have related to all three types of systems, feedback, goal setting, and incentives, this question is relevant only to incentive systems. The issue is whether there should be a single level of productivity that results in award of an incentive, or multiple levels of productivity that result in differential incentives. The first option is to define a single level of productivity, and if the unit reaches it, members get the incentive(s). For example, personnel could get a paid day off if the unit's overall monthly productivity exceeded 650 on an overall measure of productivity. The other alternative is to have more than one level defined such that at one level of productivity they get one incentive, but at higher levels of productivity they get more or larger incentives. An example of this approach would be that personnel could get one hour off if the monthly productivity index exceeded 500, two hours off if it exceeded 525, three hours if it exceeded 550, etc. A middle ground would be a half day off for exceeding 600, and a full day off for exceeding 650. The extreme of this approach would be a piece-rate or commission system where for each unit completed a specific amount of the incentive (usually money) is awarded.

The primary advantage of the multiple-level approach is its continuing ability to motivate; if the unit exceeds the first level necessary to earn the incentive, unit members are still motivated to perform at higher levels in order to earn the next level of incentive. With the single-level approach, once they exceed the level necessary to earn the incentive, there is no motivation for better performance. The primary disadvantage of the multiple-level approach is that it is more complex to administer. More levels must be set so the system becomes more complex and it is more difficult to retain equity across different units.

A recommendation that fits many situations is to use a system that has two to three productivity and incentive levels, with the highest incentive level reflecting very high productivity. In this way, the unit always has a very difficult goal to aim for, and there is no problem with the unit stopping improvement efforts when they reach the incentive level.

How much influence should unit personnel have in setting the productivity levels necessary to earn the incentives?

Incumbents and supervisors should be heavily involved in the design of the incentive system and in the setting of incentive levels. Higher level management will, however, need to be directly involved as well. Since powerful incentives tend to be costly, management should have a major involvement in approving those incentives. Although we recommend discussing incentive levels with representative incumbents and supervisors, the ultimate decision needs to be made at the management level that can authorize implementation. It can be disastrous to allow supervisors and incumbents to make the decision without sufficient authority to award the incentives. Supervisors can also be placed in an awkward conflict-of-interest situation. If they set the needed productivity levels too low, the unit receives too many incentives. If they set the levels too high, their people are not rewarded.

How can productivity levels be set so that they are equitable across units?

If an incentive system is used for more than one unit, the productivity level needed to obtain the incentives should be comparable across the units. If it is much easier for one unit to get the incentive than it is for another, inequity and serious morale problems can result.

Unfortunately, this problem is not easily solved. What is equitable depends on one's view of the situation. For example, it could be argued that it should be equally difficult for each unit to receive the incentives. This point of view implies that if each unit increases its productivity by an equal amount, each should get the incentives. A different position is that this strategy penalizes the higher productivity units. If a unit has been high in productivity, it will be more difficult for that unit to improve the same amount as a unit that began at a lower level of productivity. Thus, it would be unfair for both units to have to improve the same amount to get the incentive. Since both of these positions are logical, it is easy to see how conflicts can develop over the equitable determination of incentive levels.

The best way to deal with this issue is for individual(s) chosen as facilitators and/or higher-level management to discuss it openly with representative incumbents and supervisors. It should be acknowledged that this is a serious issue, and that there is no ideal solution. The only solution is to discuss the different opinions about what is fair and equitable and have the group reach consensus on how to handle it. This approach may not remove all feelings of inequity once the system is operational, but having unit personnel participate in the decisions will minimize the problem.

How can an incentive system be designed so that it is powerful?

An incentive system is made powerful by several features. The most obvious is that the incentives themselves must be desirable to unit members. If the incentives are not highly attractive, the system will be weak. Managers frequently assume that they know what incentives are most attractive to their personnel. However, it is a good idea to discuss possible incentives with the personnel who will be under the incentive system during the design phase. This participation in selecting incentives will help the power of the resulting system.

Several less obvious features are also needed to make an incentive system powerful. For instance, a clear connection is required between productivity and obtaining the incentive. This means that the rules for awarding incentives must be clear and understood by all. For example, suppose that a unit is told that superior performance will lead to being excused from doing a particularly unpleasant task for a month. If "superior performance" is not clearly defined, the system will be weakened.

Furthermore, the rules for awarding incentives must be consistently applied. One example of inconsistency would be where a unit reached the performance level to earn an incentive (avoiding an unpleasant task), but due to an unexpected influx of work, personnel had to work on the unpleasant task anyway. There might be no other choice than to have the unit work on that task. However, if arrangements are not made for the unit to get time off from the unpleasant task very soon, the system will again be weakened. Thus, the rules for incentives must be clear and applied as consistently as possible.

Increasing the levels of productivity needed to get incentives after the system is implemented is probably the greatest threat to the strength of an incentive system. For example, suppose that a delivery unit has determined that the incentive (a picnic for unit personnel and their families) is to be earned when its average delivery time is less than 20 minutes, and that the unit improves its productivity so that it meets this goal each month. If management decides at this point that the goal was too easy and changes it to an average delivery time of 15 minutes, this would seriously weaken the system. In fact, it would probably lead to a serious loss of morale, and could easily lead to a backlash where the unit's productivity sharply decreases.

Management must realize that once a set of rules for incentives is agreed upon, this is a serious commitment that should be changed only for the strongest of reasons. Consequently, it is advisable to have a feedback and/or goal-setting system in place for some time before implementing incentives. This allows management to get a clear picture of what the incentive levels should be before the system is begun.

Is there a difference between incentives and forms of recognition?

Incentives are considerably different from forms of recognition, and they produce different effects. The primary differences between the two are that (1) incentives can be given to everyone; and (2) they are repeatable. This is not true for forms of recognition.

Repeatability means that the incentive will remain powerful even if it is given again and again. Paid time off from work or financial incentives will be as valuable the tenth time as the first time. Having a photograph of the unit taken with a senior manager may be highly valued the first time it occurs, but it decreases in value after that. Thus, money or time off would be classified as incentives, whereas the photo would be a form of recognition.

The second factor that differentiates incentives from forms of recognition is that incentives can be given to everyone. Generally speaking, all personnel can earn an incentive at the same time, but not all can get recognition. For example, getting a financial bonus, getting time off from work, or attending a conference in a desirable location are all things that everyone could receive in the same month. Being chosen as the "Employee of the Month," the one to represent the work group in a formal meeting, or the one to meet a visiting dignitary are all things designed for one person. Even if an award is given as a group outcome (such as a "Top Unit" award), only one group can receive it at a time.

Very different effects arise from incentives and forms of recognition, so the distinction between the two is very important. If the system is properly designed, incentives will improve motivation, while forms of recognition will not. Because recognition is usually given to only one person or one unit out of many, most individuals see little connection between his/her efforts and receiving the recognition. In other words, the probability of getting the recognition is so low that it does not impact most people's day-to-day behavior. If the person does actually receive the recognition, it soon loses its power to motivate since additional instances of getting it are less valuable. In contrast, incentives are available to all, and will be equally valuable each time they are awarded. This means that everyone can see a chance to obtain the incentive, and day-to-day motivation is increased.

This is not to say that forms of recognition are not valuable. Individuals and groups place great value on receiving forms of recognition. They are concrete manifestations that productivity is appreciated; they generate a feeling of pride, and therefore can have a positive effect on morale. However, the manager and design team should not confuse the expected effects of incentives with the expected effects of forms of recognition. In general, well developed incentives change behavior, while forms of recognition only change attitudes.

In conclusion, feedback, goal-setting, and incentive systems can be powerful tools. When based on a sound productivity measurement system, they are feasible and have positive effects on both productivity and attitudes. They vary considerably, however, in their ease of use and expected effects. Organizations considering their implementation should be sensitive to these expected differences so that a more informed decision can be made about their use.

PART V

Evaluating the Effects of a Productivity Improvement Program

The last part of this book is a single chapter that describes how to go about doing a formal evaluation of a productivity improvement program.

21

How to Evaluate the Effects of a Productivity Improvement System

It is frequently desirable to document the effects of a system designed to increase productivity. Documentation allows for an unambiguous evaluation of the program that goes beyond subjective impressions. Such an evaluation can be useful to convince higher management of the success of the program. It can also be useful in deciding whether to implement the program more broadly. Finally, such information makes for impressive presentations to organizational visitors and clients. This chapter describes how to conduct such an evaluation.

DESIRABLE FEATURES OF AN EVALUATION

Use of a Baseline Period

In order to evaluate a program properly, three features are highly desirable. The first is the presence of what is called a baseline. This is a time period when data from the measurement of productivity are being collected, but no feedback is being given. It serves as a basis of comparison against which to evaluate the effects of the feedback. Typically, three to four months of baseline data are sufficient, as long as the baseline period occurs during a typical period for the unit. If this is not a typical period, the baseline should be longer. For example, if the baseline falls during a period where there are substantial vacations or during a time of very high or very low work load, the baseline should be extended so that a proper comparison period is available.

The problem with having a baseline is that the unit will not want one. Once they have done all the work to develop the system and have begun collection of the data to put into the system, they will want to see the results. It will be frustrating to have to wait for several months.

Several strategies are possible for dealing with this. First, it should be explained from the start of the project that a baseline will be used. Its importance should be explained and the fact that this can be frustrating should be noted. Just prior to when the time for the baseline arrives, the design team and unit personnel should be reminded of the baseline and its importance.

Another strategy can be used to shorten the apparent length of time for the baseline. The normal procedure is once the system has been finally approved and the feedback report designed, the process of collecting the indicator data is started. It takes some time to work out the procedures for doing this, such as how to get access to the data, who will be responsible for collecting the data, etc. A different ordering would be to work out this data-gathering strategy as soon as products and indicators are developed.

Using this strategy, the indicator data could be collected while the contingencies are developed and the feedback report is being designed. These data would not be given to the unit personnel, but the explanation that the system is not yet finished will help make this more acceptable. By the time the contingencies are finished and the feedback report is designed, there will be a period of time where some indicator data are available that can be use to calculate effectiveness scores. This becomes part of the baseline. It may still be necessary to have some additional period of baseline, but it will be substantially shorter.

An example of a full evaluation of a productivity improvement program is described in Pritchard, et al. (1989) in their evaluation of ProMES. In this article, a design using a baseline and the other features described here is presented.

Comparison Groups

The second essential feature for a proper evaluation is the use of comparison groups. Comparison groups are units which are similar to the units doing ProMES, but which receive no interventions themselves. The evaluation of ProMES should include collecting data on the productivity of these comparison units during the same time periods as the baseline and implementation periods. It is not necessary or even desirable to develop a formal productivity measurement system for these comparison units. These units should be left to function in their normal way. It is necessary only to collect readily available measures of some important aspects of their work.

The purpose of these comparison units is to be able to show that any changes in the productivity of the target units were due to ProMES and not some broader organizational change. Someone could look at data that showed that the units in the program increased in productivity and remain unconvinced that it was due to ProMES. He/she could argue that what accounted for the increase was that all units in that part of the organization were improving because of overall management practices, and so the change was not due to the system. The comparison group data provide evidence on this issue. If the comparison units did not increase, or did not increase as much as the target units, this is evidence that ProMES increased productivity in the target units.

Ideally, several comparison units (3–6) should be selected from the same part of the organization, and for which some productivity data could be readily collected. If the system is being tried with several units from different parts of the organization, there should be one set of three to six comparison groups for the units in each different part of the organization.

Monitoring Personnel Time

The third highly desirable feature is to keep track of available personnel time for the units where the system is used and in the comparison units. This should be done from the start of the baseline until the end of the evaluation period. Having such data helps evaluate the effects of the system. One could argue that the productivity of the units under ProMES increased because the number of personnel increased or the hours worked increased. Having the data available on personnel time would enable this question to be answered. If productivity went up over the evaluation period and number of personnel or hours worked did not appreciably change, this would deal with the point. It could also be that productivity went up and personnel went down. This would be very useful information to have available since it makes the effects of the system even more powerful. If both personnel and productivity went up, it would be useful to compare the increase in productivity with changes in productivity for comparison groups whose personnel also changed, if such comparison groups are available.

OTHER EVALUATION ISSUES

The Hawthorne Effect

One criticism of the evaluation that could be raised is that any positive effects after the system is implemented are due to what is known as a "Hawthorne effect," as mentioned in Chapter 6. This is a phenomenon that when a unit is given special attention of some sort, their performance or productivity can improve simply because they are getting such special attention. In other words, no matter what you do, the added attention will lead to improvements. Thus, the improvement is not due to ProMES, but due to a Hawthorne effect.

The answer to this criticism is that the special attention that can produce such an effect would occur while the system is being developed. The system is being developed and the unit is getting the special attention for some time before any measurement during baseline occurs. The attention is occurring all through the development of products and indicators. Thus, any such effect that occurs will happen prior to the start of baseline and should not be influencing the results.

Attitude Data

In addition to these highly desirable features, it is worthwhile to supplement the evaluation with data on subjective reactions to the system. Asking incumbents and supervisors to indicate how well they like the system aids in system evaluation. It can identify areas where the system could be improved. It also makes a more convincing argument that users saw the system as valuable, rather than just a subjective impression given by someone familiar with the operation.

Questionnaire items that can be used to make such an evaluation can be found in Table 6–2 in Chapter 6. This is a questionnaire used by Pritchard, et al. (1989) in their evaluation of ProMES.

Another desirable feature is to measure the effects of the system on overall work attitudes such as job satisfaction and morale. Attitude measures can be taken prior to the implementation of the system and again after three or four months of experience with feedback from the system. Scores on the attitude measures can be compared from the first administration to the second. This will give a measure of any changes in attitudes that have occurred. Some measures that could be used are presented in Appendix G. These questionnaires were also used by Pritchard, et al. (1989) in their evaluation of ProMES.

Concluding Statement

Improving organizational productivity is an important topic. It is tied to the success of national economies, industries, and individual firms. It is important for the conservation of our planetary resources and for the quality of our lives.

This book offers a practical method for improving productivity that has been successful in a variety of settings. The method is feasible to implement, is well accepted, and works well in improving productivity.

It is my hope that ProMES will be tried in many settings, and that it will continue to be successful. I will be very interested in hearing from people who have tried it in new settings.

Appendices

Products and
Indicators from Actual Units

EXAMPLE 1. COMM/NAV PRODUCTS AND INDICATORS

Description of the unit: These are the actual products and indicators for the Comm/Nav unit from which the example in Chapter 11 was taken, about the unit doing repairs on aircraft electronic equipment. The example in Chapter 11 is hypothetical, but based on this unit. The information in Appendices A, B, and D is based on the actual results of the system for that unit. The unit's primary responsibility is to repair items as quickly and as accurately as possible. If a repaired item does not function properly when installed in the aircraft, it is returned to them to redo the repair. The unit is periodically inspected by a Quality Control function, which determines whether maintenance personnel are accurately following the procedures for repair that are detailed in the repair manuals. The maintenance unit also has responsibility for conducting on-the-job training, and a technician can repair a piece of equipment only if he/she has passed the training certification required for that piece of equipment. Thus, it is important that a sufficient number of people be qualified through training so that all the items can be repaired in a timely manner.

The indicators for each product are shown below that product.

Product 1. Keep Equipment Repaired

Bounces: Percentage of repaired equipment that did not function immediately after installation.

Percent QA (Quality Assurance) inspections passed.

AWM: Number of units awaiting maintenance.

AWP: Number of units awaiting parts.

Demand Met: Percentage of equipment brought in for repairs that was actually repaired.

Product 2. Meet Training Needs

STS Tasks Completed: Mean number of standard (more basic) training tasks completed for personnel in training.

Percent Qual Tasks Completed, Comm: Mean percent of advanced
training tasks completed for personnel repairing communications
equipment.

Percent Qual Tasks Completed, Nav: Mean percent of advanced
training tasks completed for personnel repairing navigation
equipment.

Scheduled Training Tasks Overdue: Total number non-technical
(e.g., military) training requirements not met on time for all shop
personnel.

Product 3. Complete Other Duties

Mobility Equipment: Number of pieces of equipment used for
mobility exercises that were not calibrated by the shop on
schedule.

PMEL Overdue: Number of pieces of shop calibration and test
equipment that were not calibrated by the shop on schedule.

Percent 349 Errors: Percent of errors on a major manpower
documentation form.

Missed Appointments: Number of formal on-base appointments
missed.

EXAMPLE 2. MANUFACTURING UNIT

Description of the unit: This set of products and indicators is for a
small production team working for an electronics assembly plant. The
plant is responsible for producing various kinds of printed circuit
boards which are used in computer-related equipment. Boards are
assembled and tested by a series of teams that work on the boards in
a serial fashion. Thus, a given team cannot finish more boards than
the previous team has ready for them. The team in the example is
composed of technicians who are responsible for the final steps in the
production process. The team is also responsible for a series of maintenance and housekeeping/safety procedures that are checked with a
regular inspection. A team itself is composed of five technicians who
are responsible for the final steps in the production process. They
insure that the numbers on the board are still legible after assembly,
the wires have not been jarred loose, the boards are clean, the boards
have not been contaminated, and the final touches have been applied.
Once this team is finished with the boards, they are sent to inspection

and then to shipping. This unit was the basis for the example in Chapter 4.

Product 1. Maintain High Level of Production

Actual Productivity: Number of boards completed divided by number of boards received from other units, expressed as a percent.

Percent of Mix Demand Met: Number of high priority boards completed divided by number of high priority boards needed, expressed as a percentage.

Product 2. Make Highest Quality Boards Possible

Percent of Boards Passing Inspection: Number of boards passing inspection divided by number of boards sent to inspection, expressed as a percentage.

Product 3. Maintain High Attendance

Daily Attendance: Total hours worked divided by total hours available (total hours available equals 40 hours per week per employee, minus holidays and extended sick leave), expressed as a percentage.

Occurrences: Number of occurrences divided by number of technicians (an occurrence is being late to work or being absent for less than half a day).

Product 4. Optimal Use of Work Hours

The work is done under a Department of Defense contract with a fairly complex payment system. There are two categories of work hours: budget hours (those used in accomplishing company business such as meetings, training, etc.) and billable hours (those the customer will pay for). There are three types of billable hours: standard (predetermined hours that reflect how long it should take to complete each type of board), rework (time spent in correcting mistakes on boards), and engineering changes (time spent in making corrections to boards requested by the customer).

Billable Hours (NAH): Number of hours billed to the customer divided by number of technicians.

Charging Efficiency: Number of hours actually billed to the customer divided by number of hours available to be billed (hours available to be billed includes total work hours minus budget hours).

Realization Factor: Number of hours available to be billed to the customer divided by standard hours for the work done. The denominator does not include hours due to rework or engineering changes.

Product 5. Follow Housekeeping and Maintenance Procedures

Audit Violations: Number of violations on a general audit of housekeeping and maintenance procedures.

EXAMPLE 3. WAREHOUSE UNITS

There are two units in this example. They are related in that they both work in a large warehouse. The Storage and Issue unit stores material in the warehouse. When material is ordered by someone in the organization, unit personnel retrieve it from its location and bring it to the delivery area. The second unit, Pickup and Delivery, delivers the material to the place it is needed in the organization. They also pick up material that is to be stored in the warehouse.

Storage and Issue Unit

Product 1. Store Items in Warehouse

Warehouse refusals later found in wrong location: A refusal is a situation where the records indicate that an item is in the warehouse, but it cannot be found. This type of refusal is caused by storing items in an incorrect location.

Total number of items found to be improperly stored: There is a monthly inspection of the warehouse. Each item found to be in violation of procedures is counted.

Product 2. Do Warehouse Maintenance

Percent of items cleared off No Location Listing each week. The No Location Listing is a record of items that have no permanent location in the warehouse. Keeping the number of items on this list low helps insure that all items have a proper location and can thus be found when needed.

Number of special inventories done per month: When a discrepancy between records and actual items in the warehouse is noticed by Storage and Issue, they may call for a special inventory to resolve the discrepancy. Doing this indicates that they are noticing problems and taking the trouble to report them.

Product 3. Issue Requested Items

Average time from receiving order to getting it to Pickup & Delivery: This is the average time to get items to the delivery unit. There were actually three indicators here, one for each of three levels of priority of item ordered.

Product 4. Respond to inspections

Number of repeat findings by an inspection unit: Storage and Issue must correct the monthly inspection findings; failure to do so results in repeat findings.

Pickup and Delivery Unit

Product 1: Pick Up Turn-ins

Number of late pickups of equipment that are to be returned to the warehouse.

Product 2: Deliver Items Properly

Average delivery time: Average time it takes from getting the item from Storage and Issue to the item being delivered to the customer. There were actually three indicators here, one for each of three levels of priority of item ordered.

Number of errors in delivery: The number of deliveries to wrong locations comes from a customer complaint form.

Product 3: Keep Vehicles in Operating Condition

Score on monthly inspection: An inspection of each vehicle is done monthly, using a standard evaluation procedure resulting in a score for the operating condition of the vehicle.

Product 4: Maintain Vehicle Safety

Number of reportable accidents: The number of accidents that result in more than $1000 of damage.

Number of non-reportable accidents: The number of accidents that result in less than $1000 damage.

Appendix B

Sample Contingencies from Actual Units

This appendix presents the actual contingencies that were developed in two units for which ProMES was developed. The first set are the contingencies for the thirteen indicators for the unit maintaining electronic communications and navigation equipment, called the Comm/Nav unit. This is the unit that was the basis for the example in Chapter 12. Their products and indicators appear in Example 1 of Appendix A. The associated feedback report which comes from them is presented as the first example in Appendix D. The second example is a unit manufacturing printed circuit boards, called the Circuit Board Manufacturing Unit. This unit was used as the basis for the example in Chapter 4. Their products and indicators appear in Example 2 of Appendix A. An example of their feedback report is shown as the second example in Appendix D.

COMM/NAV CONTINGENCIES

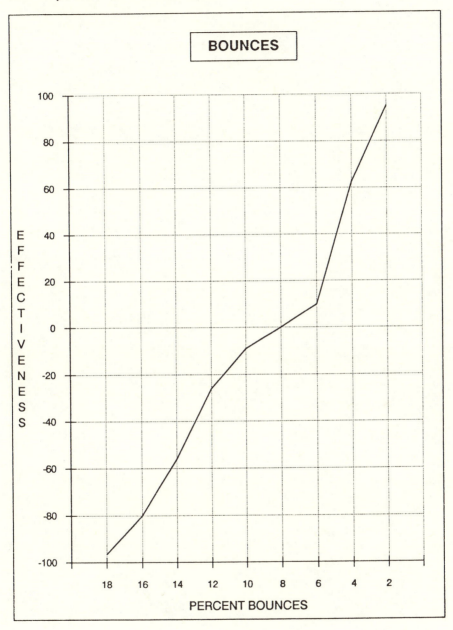

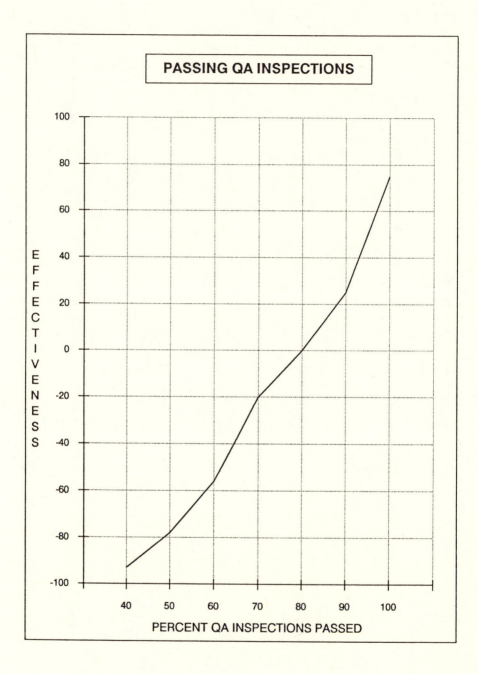

PASSING QA INSPECTIONS

EFFECTIVENESS (y-axis)

PERCENT QA INSPECTIONS PASSED

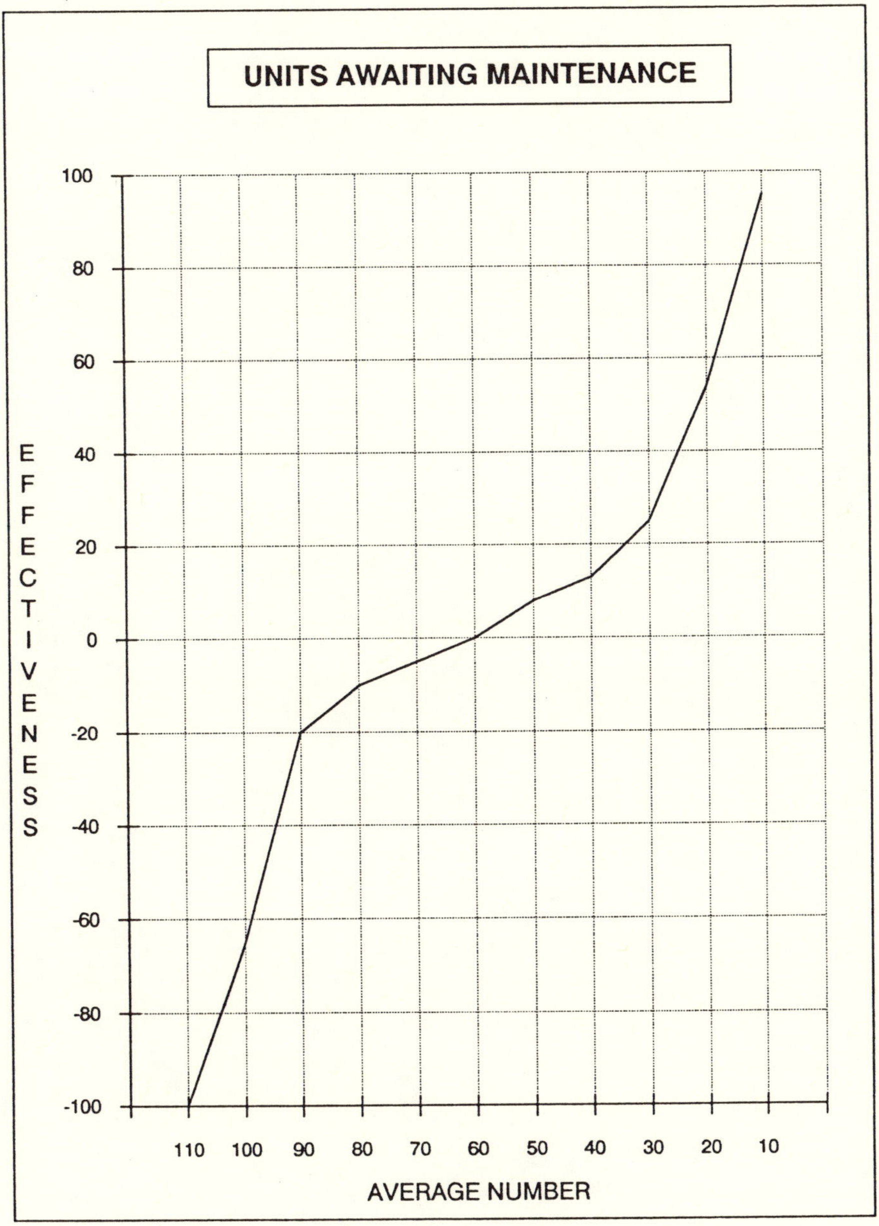
UNITS AWAITING MAINTENANCE
EFFECTIVENESS
100
80
60
40
20
0
-20
-40
-60
-80
-100
110
100
90
80
70
60
50
40
30
20
10
AVERAGE NUMBER

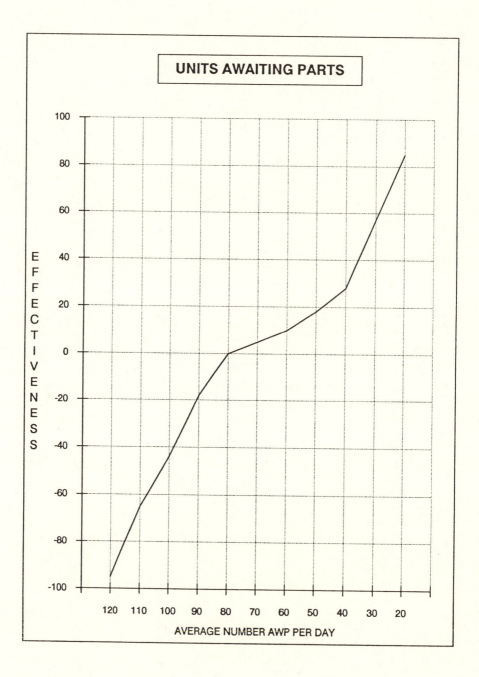

UNITS AWAITING PARTS

EFFECTIVENESS

AVERAGE NUMBER AWP PER DAY

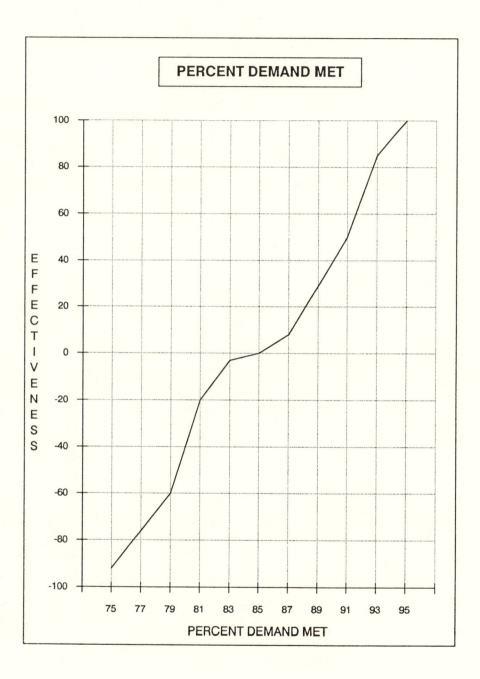

PERCENT DEMAND MET

PERCENT DEMAND MET

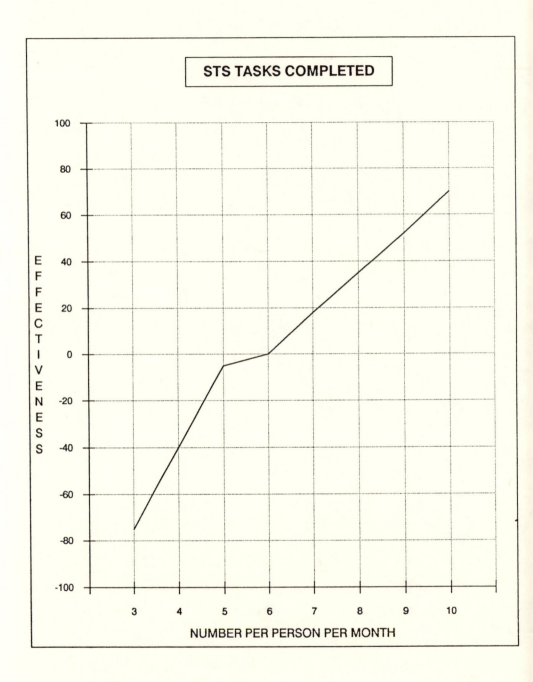

STS TASKS COMPLETED

NUMBER PER PERSON PER MONTH

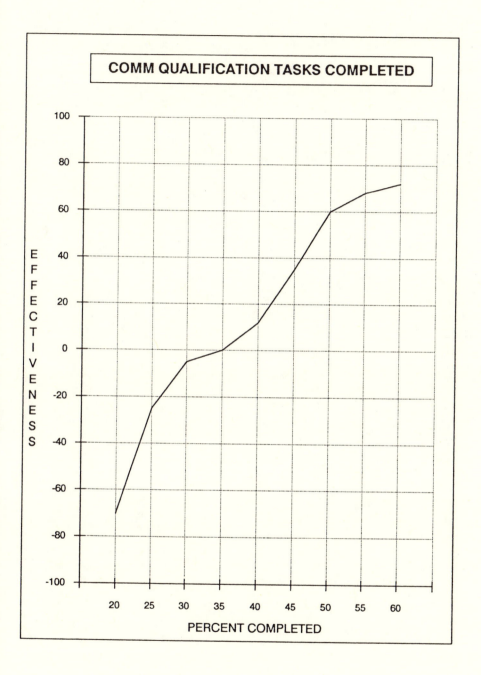

COMM QUALIFICATION TASKS COMPLETED

EFFECTIVENESS

PERCENT COMPLETED

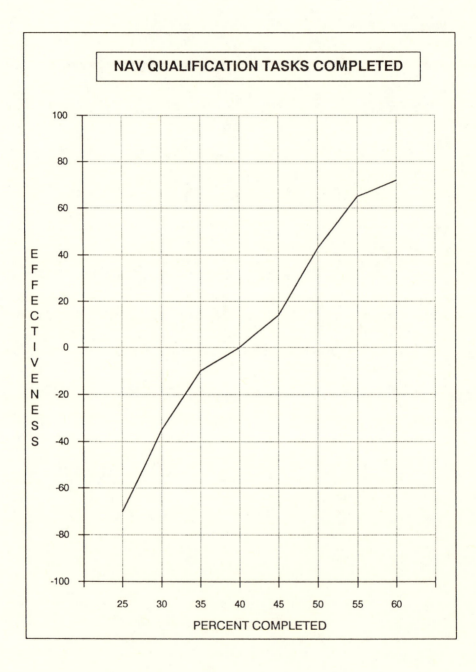

NAV QUALIFICATION TASKS COMPLETED

EFFECTIVENESS

PERCENT COMPLETED

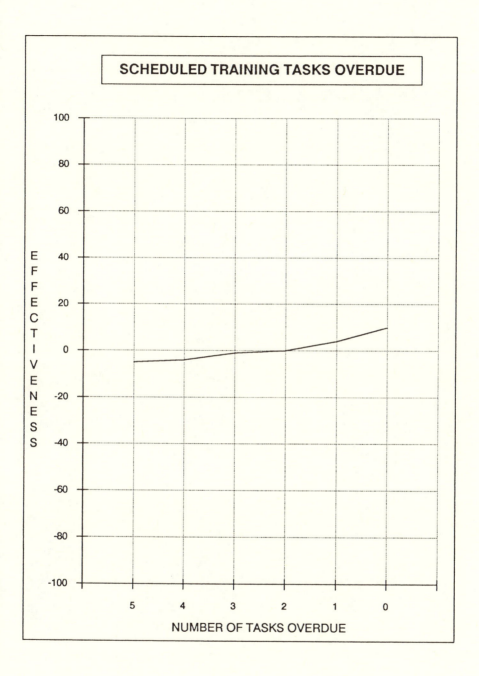

SCHEDULED TRAINING TASKS OVERDUE

EFFECTIVENESS

NUMBER OF TASKS OVERDUE

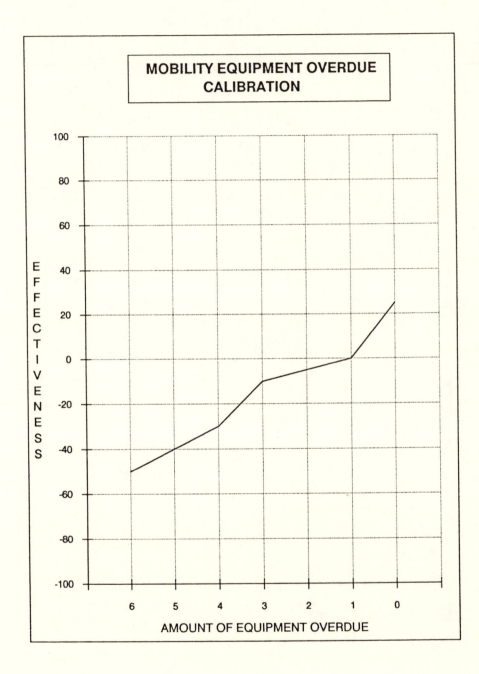

MOBILITY EQUIPMENT OVERDUE
CALIBRATION

AMOUNT OF EQUIPMENT OVERDUE

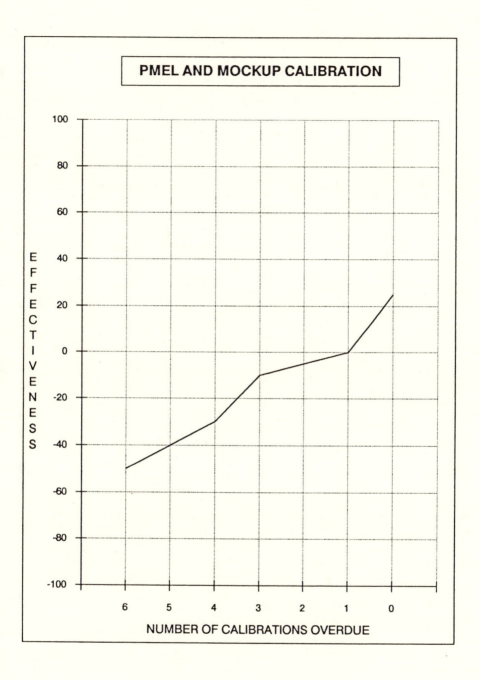

PMEL AND MOCKUP CALIBRATION

EFFECTIVENESS

NUMBER OF CALIBRATIONS OVERDUE

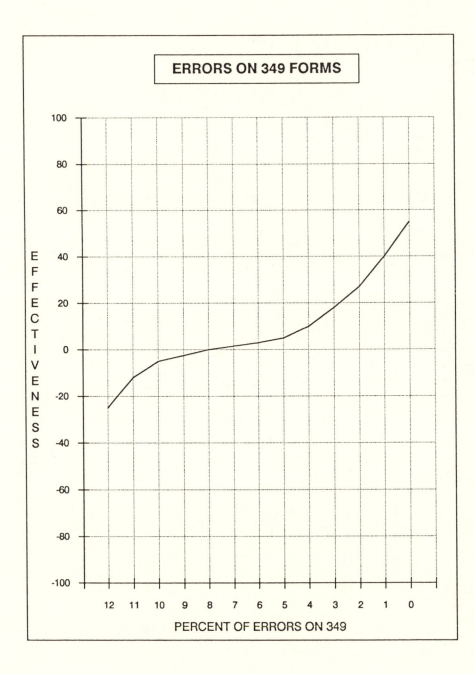

ERRORS ON 349 FORMS

EFFECTIVENESS

PERCENT OF ERRORS ON 349

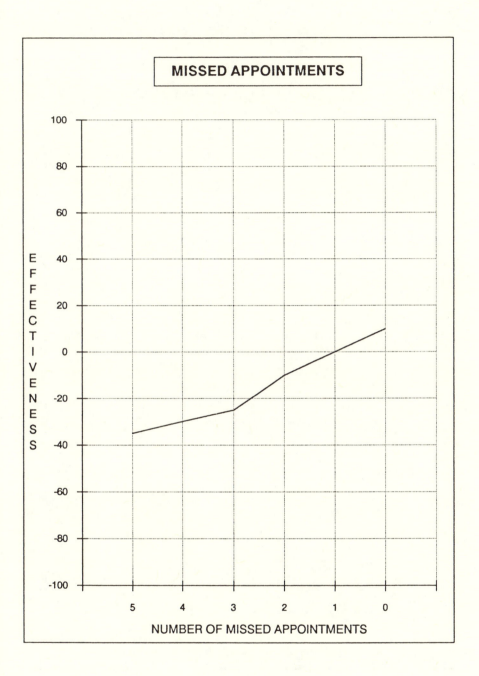

MISSED APPOINTMENTS

EFFECTIVENESS

NUMBER OF MISSED APPOINTMENTS

211

CIRCUIT BOARD MANUFACTURING UNIT CONTINGENCIES

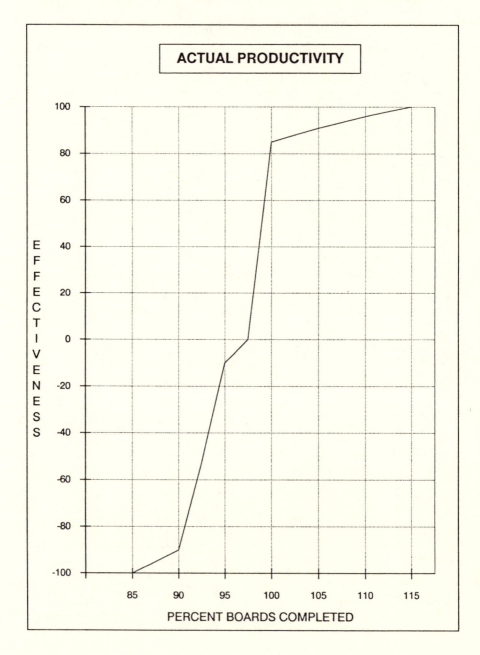

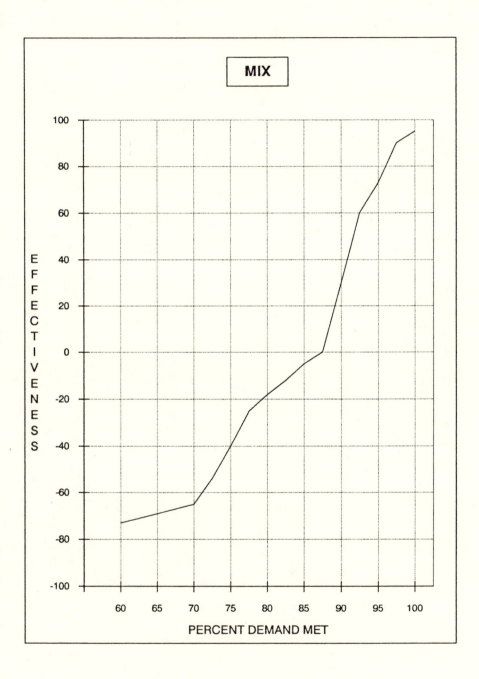

MIX

PERCENT DEMAND MET

EFFECTIVENESS

213

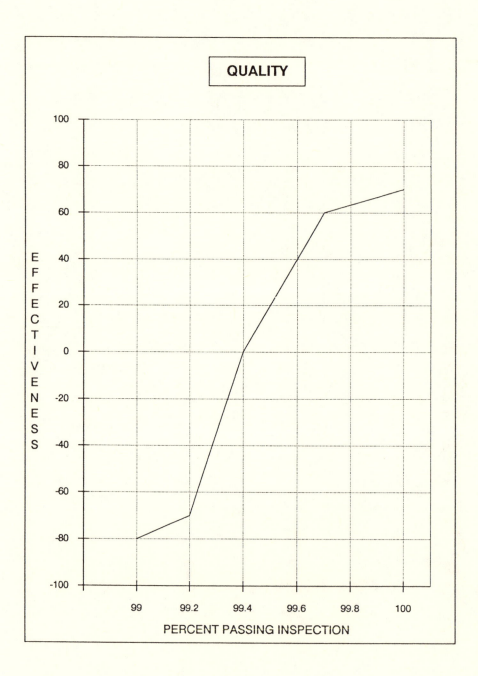

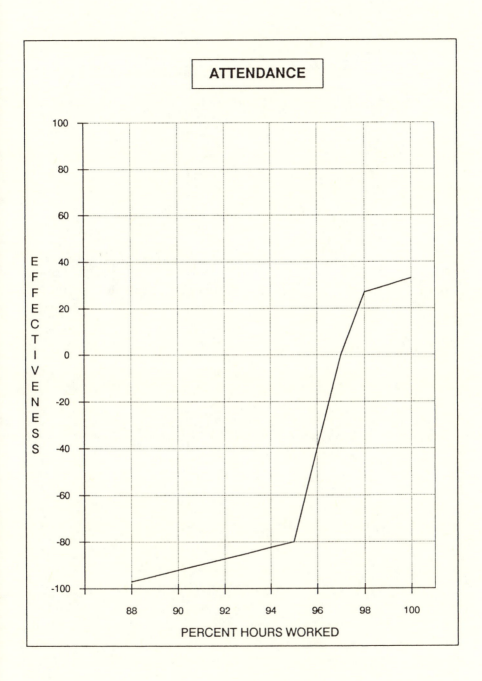

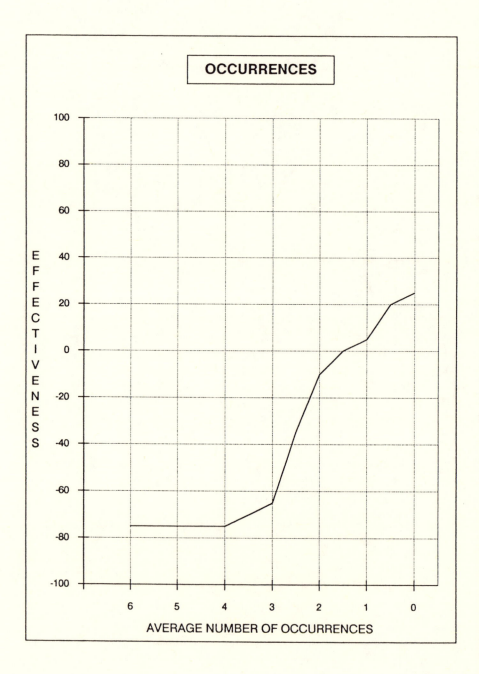

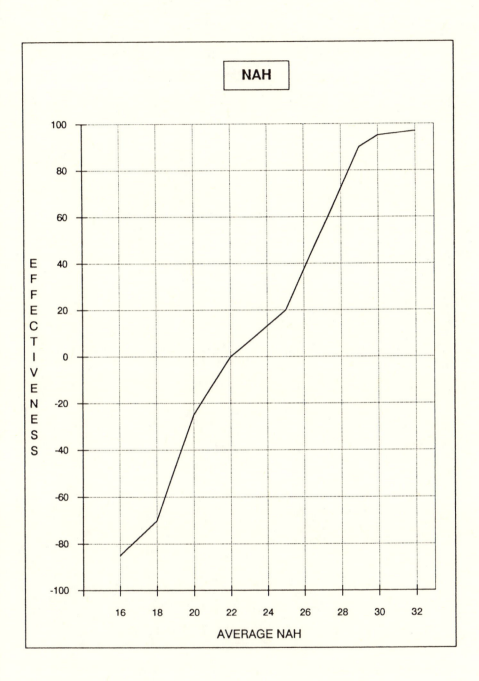

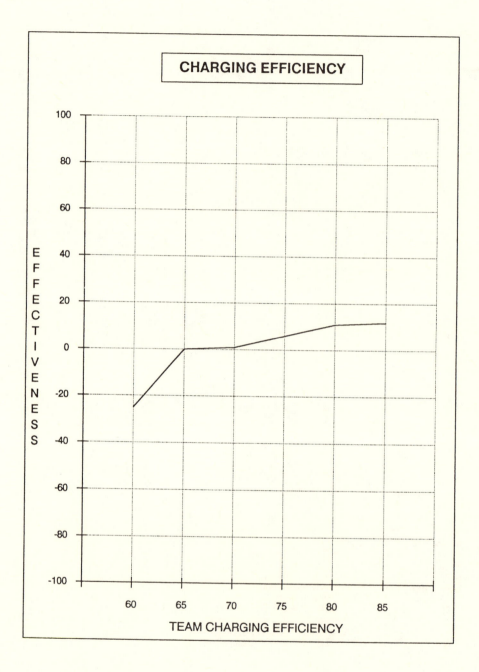

CHARGING EFFICIENCY

EFFECTIVENESS

TEAM CHARGING EFFICIENCY

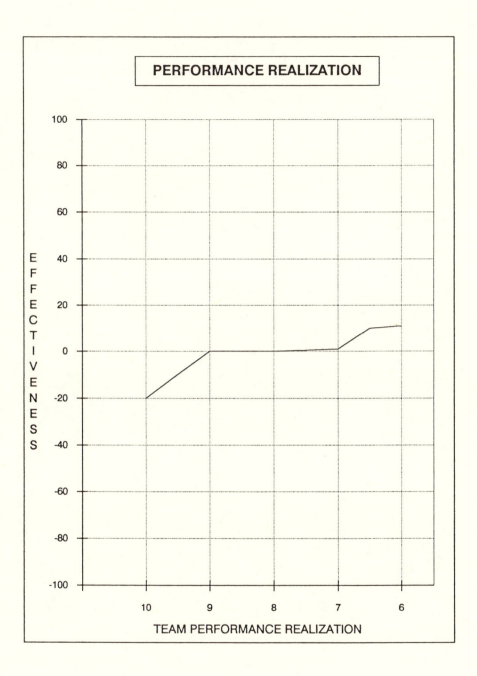

PERFORMANCE REALIZATION

TEAM PERFORMANCE REALIZATION

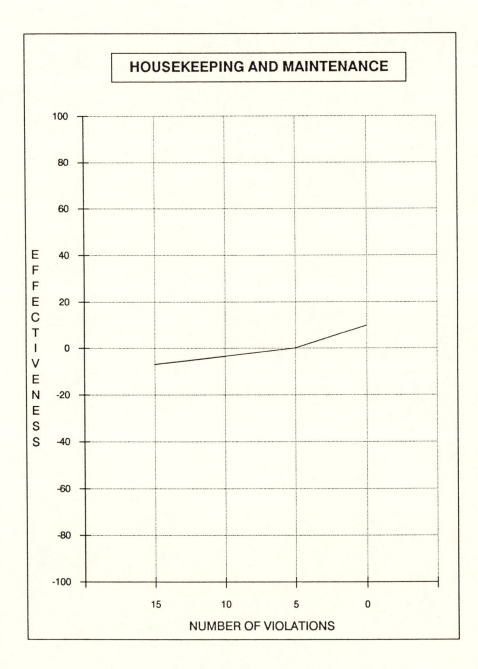

HOUSEKEEPING AND MAINTENANCE

NUMBER OF VIOLATIONS

Appendix C

Template for Developing Contingencies

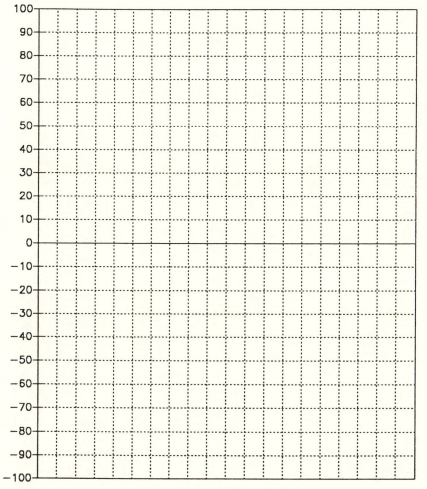

INDICATOR VALUES

Sample Feedback Reports

EXAMPLE 1. COMM/NAV UNIT

The first page of the report provides the basic productivity data. It shows the products and indicators, the indicator data for that month, and the effectiveness score associated with that level of each indicator. The full description of the indicators can be found in the first example in Appendix A. The lower portion of the page shows the total effectiveness for each of the products and finally, the overall effectiveness for the unit. The second page of the report adds information to the basic data. The top half of the page shows the change in productivity from the previous month to the current month. The indicator data and effectiveness scores for both the previous month and the current month are shown, as are the changes in effectiveness from last month to the current month.

The bottom half of the page is the information on priorities for increasing productivity. For each indicator there is a column labeled FROM, TO, and GAIN. The FROM column is the amount of the indicator for the current month. The TO column is the amount of the indicator that represents an increase of one unit on the contingency and the GAIN column indicates the gain in effectiveness that would be achieved by such an increase. For example, if Demand Met went from the March level of 91.7 percent to 95.2 percent in April, effectiveness would increase by 37 points. Examination of the GAIN column indicates that for the next month, the unit would increase their productivity most effectively by focusing on Quality Assurance Inspections and the number of units Awaiting Parts (AWP). These show potential gains in effectiveness of 45 and 48 respectively. It would not be useful to devote attention to training in Comm Qualification Tasks, trying to further decrease Overdue Scheduled Training Tasks, or any of the other indicators that have a gain value of zero or near zero. This information can therefore serve as a basis for determining priorities for the next month. The unit should focus on those areas where the maximum gain in effectiveness could be produced.

The calculation of the GAIN amount is based on the amount of increase in effectiveness that would occur with an increase of "one unit" of the indicator. The size of a one unit increase was determined from the indicator values used in the contingencies. If the indicator values in a contingency were 2 percent, 4 percent, 6 percent, 8 percent, etc., the size of a one-unit increase for that indicator was 2 percent. If the indicator values were 50, 60, 70, 80, etc., the size of a one-unit increase was 10. The contingencies were originally developed so that the number of increments for the different contingencies was as equal as possible so that a one-unit increment was roughly comparable across the different contingencies. Once the size of the one-unit increase was determined for each contingency, the TO figure was calculated by adding the one-unit increase to the actual value of the indicator for the preceding month. If the last month's indicator level was 83.6 and the size of one unit was 10, the FROM value would be 83.6, the TO value would be 93.6, and the GAIN value would be determined by what the contingency indicated as the gain in effectiveness if the unit went from 83.6 to 93.6 on that indicator.

There was one special circumstance that had to be considered. It was possible for the TO value to be higher than the maximum value of the indicator. This occurred when the unit was already high on that indicator and increasing one unit would put them over the maximum. It also occurred occasionally if the unit was already over the maximum on that indicator. This was dealt with by using the maximum possible effectiveness value for the indicator as the upper limit in effectiveness. In other words, if the effectiveness value for being at the maximum of the indicator was +75, this was the maximum effectiveness score that was used for that indicator. If the unit was near the maximum already with, for example, a past month's indicator level which yielded an effectiveness score of +73, the most they could improve would be to the value of the ceiling, +75, for a maximum gain of only +2.

PRODUCTIVITY REPORT
COMM/NAV UNIT

INDICATOR AND EFFECTIVENESS DATA FOR MARCH

INDICATOR	INDICATOR DATA	EFFECTIVENESS SCORE
EQUIPMENT REPAIR		
BOUNCES	3.1	76
% QA INSPECTIONS PASSED	90.9	30
AWM	13.5	80
AWP	39.6	29
DEMAND MET	91.7	63
TRAINING		
STS TASKS COMPLETED	8	35
% QUAL TASKS COMPLETED: COM	69.5	72
% QUAL TASKS COMPLETED: NAV	56.8	68
SCHED TRAINING TASKS OVERDUE	0	10
OTHER DUTIES		
MOBILITY EQUIPMENT OVERDUE	0	25
PMEL OVERDUE	0	25
% 349 ERRORS	1	40
MISSED APPOINTMENTS	0	10

TOTALS	EFFECTIVENESS SCORE
EQUIPMENT REPAIR	278
TRAINING	185
OTHER DUTIES	100
OVERALL EFFECTIVENESS	563

EFFECTIVENESS CHANGE FROM FEBRUARY TO MARCH

	INDICATOR DATA: FEBRUARY	EFF. SCORE	INDICATOR DATA: MARCH	EFF. SCORE	CHANGE IN EFFECT.
BOUNCES	2.8	81	3.1	76	-5
% QA INSPECTIONS	91.7	34	90.9	30	-4
AWM	15.58	72	13.5	80	8
AWP	40.6	27	39.6	29	2
DEMAND MET	91.5	59	91.7	63	4
STS TASKS COMPLETED	9	52	8	35	-17
%QUAL TASKS-COMM	68.6	72	69.5	72	0
%QUAL TASKS-NAV	59.5	71	56.8	68	-3
SCHEDULED TRAINING TASKS OVERDUE	0	10	0	10	0
MOBILITY EQUIPMENT OVERDUE	0	25	0	25	0
PMEL OVERDUE	0	25	0	25	0
% 349 ERRORS	2	27	1	40	13
MISSED APPOINTMENTS	0	10	0	10	0

CHANGE TOTALS		
	EQUIPMENT REPAIR	5
	TRAINING	-20
	OTHER DUTIES	13
	OVERALL EFFECTIVENESS	-2

POTENTIAL EFFECTIVENESS GAINS FOR NEXT MONTH

	FROM	TO	GAIN
BOUNCES	3.1	0.4	17
QA INSPECTIONS	90.9	100	45
AWM	13.5	0	15
AWP	39.6	22.6	48
DEMAND MET	91.7	95.2	37
STS TASKS COMPLETED	8	9	17
%QUAL TASKS COMP: COMM	69.5	76	0
%QUAL TASKS COMP: NAV	56.8	62.8	4
SCHED TRNING TSKS OVERDUE	0	0	0
MOBILITY EQ OVERDUE	0	0	0
PMEL OVERDUE	0	0	0
349 ERRORS	1	0	15
MISSED APPOINTMENTS	0	0	0

EXAMPLE 2. CIRCUIT BOARD MANUFACTURING UNIT

INDICATOR AND EFFECTIVENESS DATA FOR JUNE

INDICATOR	INDICATOR DATA	EFFECTIVENESS SCORE
PRODUCTION		
ACTUAL PRODUCTIVITY	101	86
% MIX	96	80
QUALITY		
% QUALITY	100	70
ATTENDANCE		
% ATTENDANCE	97.5	10
AVERAGE OCCURRENCES	1.5	0
CHARGING OF HOURS		
NAH	25	20
CHARGING EFFICIENCY	73	4
REALIZATION FACTOR	6.2	11
HOUSEKEEPING AND MAINTENANCE		
AUDIT VIOLATIONS	4	2

EFFECTIVENESS TOTALS

PRODUCT	PRODUCT EFFECTIVENESS	OVERALL EFFECTIVENESS
PRODUCTION	166	283
QUALITY	70	
ATTENDANCE	10	
CHARGING	35	
MAINTENANCE	2	

EFFECTIVENESS CHANGE FROM LAST PERIOD TO CURRENT PE-RIOD

| | LAST PERIOD | | CURRENT PERIOD | | |
	INDICATOR DATA	EFF. SCORE	INDICATOR DATA	EFF. SCORE	CHANGE IN EFFECT.
INDICATOR					
ACTUAL PROD.	99	57	101	86	29
% MIX	98	91	96	80	-11
% QUALITY	99.95	68	100	70	2
% ATTENDANCE	97	0	97.5	10	10
AVG. OCCURRENCES	1	5	1.5	0	-5
NAH	27	55	25	20	-35
CHARGING EFF.	69	1	73	4	3
REALIZATION	6	11	6.2	11	0
AUDIT VIOLATIONS	2	6	4	2	-4

POTENTIAL EFFECTIVENESS GAINS FOR NEXT PERIOD

| | INDICATOR DATA | | CHANGE IN EFFECT. |
	FROM	TO	
INDICATOR			
ACTUAL PRODUCTIVITY	101	107	6
% MIX	96	104	15
% QUALITY	100	100.2	0
% ATTENDANCE	97.5	99.9	23
AVERAGE OCCURRENCES	1.5	0.3	22
NAH	25	28	53
CHARGING EFFICIENCY	73	78	5
REALIZATION FACTOR	6.2	5.4	0
AUDIT VIOLATIONS	4	1	6

Appendix E

Additional Sources of Productivity Information

For general discussions about the conceptualization and measurement of productivity:

Alluisi, E. A., & Meigs, D. K. (1983). Potentials for productivity enhancement from psychological research and development. *American Psychologist*, 38(4), 487–493.

American Productivity Center. (1981). *Productivity perspectives*. Houston, TX: Author.

American Productivity Center. (1986). *White collar productivity improvement*. Houston, TX: Author.

Balk, W. L. (1975). Technological trends in productivity measurement. *Public Personnel Management*, March-April, 128–133.

Brief, A. P. (ed.) (1984). *Productivity research in the behavioral and social sciences*. New York: Praeger Publishers.

Campbell, J. C., & Campbell, R. J. (eds.) (1988). *Productivity in organizations*. San Francisco: Jossey-Bass.

Duerr, E. C. (1974). The effect of misdirected incentives on employee behavior. *Personnel Journal*, 53(12), 890–893.

Dunnette, M. D., & Fleishman, E. A. (eds.). (1982). *Human performance and productivity: Vol. 1. Human capability assessment*. Hillsdale, NJ: Erlbaum Associates.

Guzzo, R. A. (1988). Productivity research: Reviewing psychological and economic perspectives. In J. C. Campbell & R. J. Campbell (eds.), *Productivity in organizations* (pp. 63–81). San Francisco: Jossey-Bass.

Guzzo, R. A., Jette, R. D., & Katzell, R. A. (1985). The effects of psychologically based intervention programs on worker productivity: A meta-analysis. *Personnel Psychology*, 38, 275–291.

Katzell, R. A., & Guzzo, R. A. (1983). Psychological approaches to productivity improvement. *American Psychologist*, 38(4), 468–472.

Kendrick, J. W. (1984). *Improving company productivity*. Baltimore, MD: Johns Hopkins University Press.

Kopelman, R. E. (1986). *Managing productivity in organizations: A practical, people-oriented perspective.* New York: McGraw-Hill.

Mahoney, T. A. (1988). Productivity defined: The relativity of efficiency, effectiveness and change. In J. C. Campbell & R. J. Campbell (eds.), *Productivity in organizations* (pp. 13–38). San Francisco: Jossey-Bass.

Mali, P. (1978). *Improving total productivity.* New York: Wiley and Sons.

Miller, S. (1982). *Productivity: The state of the art, a review for mental health service providers.* Denver: Colorado Division of Mental Health, Human Resources Department.

Muckler, F. A. (1982). Evaluating productivity. In M.D. Dunnette & E. A. Fleishman (eds.), *Human performance and productivity: Vol. 1. Human capability assessment* (pp. 13–47). Hillsdale, NJ: Erlbaum Associates.

National Center for Productivity and Quality of Working Life. (1977). *The future of productivity.* Washington, DC: Author.

National Center for Productivity and Quality of Working Life. (1978). *Total performance management: Some pointers for action* (NTIS No. PB300249). Washington, DC: Author.

Pritchard, R. D. (1990). Organizational productivity. In M. D. Dunnette (ed.), *Handbook of Industrial/Organizational Psychology* (2nd ed.) Vol. 4. Palo Alto, CA: Consulting Psychologists Press.

Riggs, J. L., & Felix, G. H. (1983). *Productivity by objectives.* Englewood Cliffs, NJ: Prentice-Hall.

Sink, D. S. (1985). *Productivity management: Planning, measurement and evaluation, control and improvement.* New York: Wiley and Sons.

Tuttle, T. C. (1981). *Productivity measurement methods: Classification, critique, and implications for the Air Force* (AFHRL-TR-81–9). Brooks AFB, TX: Manpower and Personnel Division, Air Force Human Resources Laboratory.

White House Conference on Productivity. (1984). *Productivity growth: A better life for America* (NTIS #PB 84–159136). Washington D.C.: Author.

For more of the theoretical background about ProMES:

Pritchard, R. D., Jones, S. D., Roth, P.L., Stuebing, K. K., & Ekeberg, S. E. (1986). *Organizational productivity measurement: The development and evaluation of an integrated approach.* Air Force Human Resources Laboratory Technical Report, AFHRL-TR-86-64.

Pritchard, R. D., Jones, S.D., Roth, P. L., Stuebing, K. K., & Ekeberg, S. E. (1987). *Feedback, goal setting, and incentives effects on organizational productivity.* Air Force Human Resources Laboratory Technical Report, AFHRL-TR-87-3.

Pritchard, R. D., Jones, S. D., Roth, P. L., Stuebing, K. K., & Ekeberg, S. E. (1988). The effects of feedback, goal setting, and incentives on organizational productivity. *Journal of Applied Psychology Monograph Series, 73*(2), 337–358.

Pritchard, R. D., Jones, S. D., Roth, P. L., Stuebing, K. K., & Ekeberg, S. E. (1989). The evaluation of an integrated approach to measuring organizational productivity. *Personnel Psychology, 42*(1), 69–115.

Descriptions of other productivity measurement systems:

American Productivity Center. (1981). *Productivity perspectives*. Houston, TX: Author.

American Productivity Center. (1986). *White collar productivity improvement*. Houston, TX: Author.

Craig, C. E., & Harris, R. C. (1973). "Total productivity measurement at the firm level." *Sloan Management Review, 14*(3), 13–28.

Deming, W. E. (1982). "Improvement of quality and productivity through action by management." *National Productivity Review*, Winter, 12–22.

Deming, W. E. (1986). *Out of the crisis*. Cambridge, MA: Massachusetts Institute of Technology.

Joint Financial Management Improvement Program. (1976). *Productivity programs in the Federal government: Vol. 1. Productivity trends and current efforts*. Washington DC: Author.

Kendrick, J. W. (1984). *Improving company productivity*. Baltimore: Johns Hopkins University Press.

Mali, P. (1978). *Improving total productivity*. New York: Wiley and Sons.

Peeples, D. E. (1978). "Measure for productivity." *Datamation, 24*(5), 222–230.

Riggs, J. L., & Felix, G. H. (1983). *Productivity by objectives*. Englewood Cliffs, NJ: Prentice-Hall.

Rowe, D. L. (1981). "How Westinghouse measures white collar productivity." *Management Review*, November, 42–47.

Sink, D. S. (1985). *Productivity management: Planning, measurement and evaluation, control and improvement*. New York: Wiley and Sons.

Tuttle, T. C., & Weaver, C. N. (1986a). *Methodology for generating efficiency and effectiveness measures (MGEEM): A guide for commanders, managers, and supervisors* (AFHRL Technical Paper 86–26). Brooks AFB, TX: Manpower and Personnel Division, Air Force Human Resources Laboratory.

Tuttle, T. C., & Weaver, C. N. (1986b). *Methodology for generating efficiency and effectiveness measures (MGEEM): A guide for Air Force measurement facilitators* (AFHRL-TP-86–36, AD-A174 547). Brooks AFB, TX: Manpower and Personnel Division, Air Force Human Resources Laboratory.

Appendix F

Software for
Computerizing ProMES

The process of developing feedback reports from ProMES can be done by hand with no special skills or equipment. However, it is much easier to computerize the process. A program for doing this has been written and is available from the author.

To use the program, first the product, indicator, and contingency information for a given unit are entered. After this step, the program can generate the feedback reports. To get an actual feedback report, indicator data for a given period are entered and the ProMES data for that period are calculated and the feedback report is generated.

The program generates information for the feedback report such as:

1. The name of the unit.
2. The time period for which the data apply.
3. The name of each indicator.
4. The data for each indicator for the period.
5. The effectiveness score for each indicator for the period.
6. The product to which each indicator belongs.
7. The total effectiveness for each product.
8. Overall effectiveness.
9. Indicator and effectiveness scores from the last period.
10. Indicator and effectiveness scores for the current period.
11. The change in effectiveness between the last period and the current period, by indicator.
12. The change in effectiveness that would occur if each indicator were increased (priorities information).
13. Also included is the percent of maximum for the period and the change in percent of maximum from last period to the current period.

14. The program will also very conveniently do the rescaling of contingencies that is necessary when aggregation of the system across multiple units is done.

At the time of this writing (January 1990), the program requires an IBM compatible machine and DOS 2.0 or higher.

Information, prices and ordering information can be obtained by writing to:

Robert D. Pritchard
Department of Psychology
Texas A&M University
College Station, Texas 77843

Instruments for Measuring Attitudes

Items for these questionnaires came from the following sources. Job satisfaction was measured by seven items adapted from the Minnesota Satisfaction Questionnaire (Weiss, Dawis, England, & Loftquist, 1967). The items for the morale scale were adapted from ISR instruments (Seashore, Lawler, Mirvis, & Cammann, 1983). Items for turnover intentions, clarity of objectives, and evaluation clarity were developed by the author. Items for individual role clarity were adapted from the Rizzo, House, and Lirtzman (1970) instrument.

JOB SATISFACTION

Response format: Five-point format with anchors of Very Dissatisfied, Dissatisfied, Not Sure, Satisfied, and Very Satisfied.
Items:
1. The chance to do something that makes use of my abilities.
2. The way organizational policies are put into practice.
3. The freedom to use my own judgment.
4. The chance to try my own methods of doing the work.
5. The working conditions.
6. The praise I get for doing a good job.
7. The feeling of accomplishment I get from the job.

MORALE

Response format: Five-point format with anchors of Strongly Disagree, Disagree, Neutral, Agree, and Strongly Agree.
Items:

1. A spirit of teamwork exists between the people in my unit.
2. The people in the unit work together to accomplish the unit's objectives.
3. I feel a sense of pride at being a member of this unit.

TURNOVER INTENTIONS

Response format: Five-point format with anchors of Strongly Disagree, Disagree, Neutral, Agree, and Strongly Agree.
Items:
1. My current plans are to stay in this organization.
2. I would like to leave this organization within the next year.
3. I have started to look around for another job.

ROLE CLARITY

Response format: Five-point format with anchors of Strongly Disagree, Disagree, Neutral, Agree, and Strongly Agree.
Items:
1. I know what my responsibilities are.
2. I know exactly what is expected of me.
3. Explanation is clear of what has to be done.

CLARITY OF OBJECTIVES

Response format: Five-point format with anchors of Strongly Disagree, Disagree, Neutral, Agree, and Strongly Agree.
Items:
1. I understand which of my work objectives are more important than others.
2. The work objectives of my section are clear and specific.
3. I understand which of my section's objectives are more important than others.

References

Algera, J. A. (1989). Feedback systems in organizations. In C. L. Cooper & I. Robertson (eds.), *International review of industrial and organizational psychology: 1990*. Chichester: John Wiley & Sons.

Alluisi, E. A., & Meigs, D. K. (1983). Potentials for productivity enhancement from psychological research and development. *American Psychologist*, 38(4), 487–493.

American Productivity Center (1981). *Productivity perspectives*. Houston, TX: Author.

American Productivity Center (1986). *White collar productivity improvement*. Houston, TX: Author.

Annett, J. (1969). *Feedback and human behavior*. Baltimore, MD: Penguin.

Balk, W. L. (1975). Technological trends in productivity measurement. *Public Personnel Management*, March–April, 128–133.

Belcher, J. G., Jr. (1982). *The productivity management process*. Oxford: Planning Executives Institute.

Brief, A. P. (ed.) (1984). *Productivity research in the behavioral and social sciences*. New York: Praeger Publishers.

Bullock, R. J., & Batten, D. B. (1983). *Organizational productivity: A measurement review*. Paper presented at the meeting of the Southwest Division of the Academy of Management, Houston, TX.

Bullock, R. J., & Lawler, E. E. (1984). Gainsharing: A few questions and fewer answers. *Human Resources Management*, 23 (1), 23–40.

Campbell, J. P. (1977). On the nature of organizational effectiveness. In P. S. Goodman, J. M. Pennings, & Associates (eds.), *New perspectives on organizational effectiveness* (pp. 13–55). San Francisco: Jossey-Bass.

Campbell, J. C., & Campbell, R. J. (eds.) (1988a). *Productivity in organizations*. San Francisco: Jossey-Bass.

Campbell, J. C., & Campbell, R. J. (1988b). What industrial-organizational psychology has to say about productivity. In J. C. Campbell & R. J. Campbell (eds.), *Productivity in organizations* (pp. 1–10). San Francisco: Jossey-Bass.

Campbell, J. C., & Campbell, R. J. (1988c). Industrial-organizational psychology and productivity: The goodness of fit. In J. C. Campbell & R. J. Campbell (eds.), *Productivity in organizations* (pp. 82–94). San Francisco: Jossey-Bass.

Craig, C. E., & Harris, R. C. (1973). Total productivity measurement at the firm level. *Sloan Management Review,* 14(3), 13–28.

Deming, W. E. (1982). Improvement of quality and productivity through action by management. *National Productivity Review,* Winter, 12–22.

Deming, W. E. (1986). *Out of the crisis.* Cambridge, MA: Massachusetts Institute of Technology.

Dockstader, S. L., Nebeker, D. M., & Shumate, E. C. (1977). *The effects of feedback and an implied standard on work performance* (NPRDC TR 77–45). San Diego, CA: Navy Personnel Research and Development Center.

Duerr, E. C. (1974). The effect of misdirected incentives on employee behavior. *Personnel Journal,* 53(12), 890–893.

Dunnette, M. D., & Fleishman, E. A. (eds.). (1982). *Human performance and productivity: Vol. 1. Human capability assessment* (pp. 13–47). Hillsdale, NJ: Erlbaum Associates.

Feather, N. T. (1968). Change in confidence following success or failure as a predictor of subsequent performance. *Journal of Personality and Social Psychology,* 9, 38–46.

Fleishman, E. A. (1982). Introduction. In M. D. Dunnette & E. A. Fleishman (eds.), *Human performance and productivity:* Vol. 1. *Human capability assessment* (pp. xv–xix). Hillsdale, NJ: Erlbaum Associates.

Galgay, P. J. & Pritchard, R. D. (1989). Non-linearities in measures of productivity: An unanswered question. Presented at the Society for Industrial/Organizational Psychology Meetings, Boston, MA, April 1989.

Guzzo, R. A. (1988). Productivity research: Reviewing psychological and economic perspectives. In J. C. Campbell & R. J. Campbell (eds.), *Productivity in organizations* (pp. 63–81). San Francisco: Jossey-Bass.

Guzzo, R. A., Jette, R. D., & Katzell, R. A. (1985). The effects of psychologically based intervention programs on worker productivity: A meta-analysis. *Personnel Psychology,* 38, 275–291.

Hammond, K. R., & Summers, D. A. (1972). Cognitive control. *Psychological Review,* 79, 58–67.

Hamner, T. H. (1988). New developments in profit sharing, gainsharing, and employee ownership. In J. C. Campbell & R. J. Campbell (eds.), *Productivity in organizations* (pp. 328–366). San Francisco: Jossey-Bass.

Hurst, E. G. (1980). Attributes of performance measures. *Public Productivity Review,* 4(1), 43–50.

Ilgen, D. R., Fisher, C. D., & Taylor, M. S. (1979). Consequences of individual feedback on behavior in organizations. *Journal of Applied Psychology,* 64, 349–371.

Ilgen, D. R., & Hamstra, B. W. (1972). Performance satisfaction as a function of the difference between expected and reported performance at five levels of reported performance. *Organizational Behavior and Human Performance,* 7, 359–370.

Ilgen, D. R., & Klein, H. J. (1988). Individual motivation and performance: Cognitive influences on effort and choice. In J. C. Campbell & R. J. Campbell (eds.), *Productivity in organizations* (pp. 143–176). San Francisco: Jossey-Bass.

Ivancevich, J. M., Donnelly, J. N., & Lyon, J. L. (1970). A study of the impact of management by objectives on perceived need satisfaction. *Personnel Psychology*, 23, 139–151.

Ivancevich, J. M., & McMahon, J. T. (1982). The effects of goal-setting, external feedback, and self-generated feedback on outcome variables: A field experiment. *Academy of Management Journal*, 25(2), 359–372.

Joint Financial Management Improvement Program (1976). *Productivity programs in the Federal government: Vol. 1. Productivity trends and current efforts*. Washington DC: Author.

Kahn, R. L. (1977). Organizational effectiveness: An overview. In P. S. Goodman, J. M. Pennings, & Associates (eds.), *New perspectives in organizational effectiveness* (pp. 235–248). San Francisco: Jossey-Bass.

Katzell, R. A., & Guzzo, R. A. (1983). Psychological approaches to productivity improvement. *American Psychologist*, 38(4), 468–472.

Kendrick, J. W. (1977). *Understanding productivity*. Baltimore: Johns Hopkins University Press.

Kendrick, J. W. (1984). *Improving company productivity*. Baltimore: Johns Hopkins University Press.

Kim, J. E. (1980). Cost-effectiveness/benefit analysis of post-secondary occupational programs: A conceptual framework. *Planning and Changing*, 11(3), 150–165.

Kopelman, R. E. (1986). *Managing productivity in organizations: A practical, people-oriented perspective*. New York: McGraw-Hill.

Latham, G. P., & Yukl, G. A. (1975). A review of research on the application of goal-setting in organizations. *Academy of Management Journal*, 18, 824–845.

Lawler, E. E., III. (1971). *Pay and organizational effectiveness: A psychological view*. New York: McGraw-Hill.

Ledford, G. E. Jr., Lawler, E. E. III, & Mohrman, S. G. (1988). The quality circle and its variations. In J. C. Campbell & R. J. Campbell (eds.), *Productivity in organizations* (pp. 255–295). San Francisco: Jossey-Bass.

Locke, E. A., & Latham, G. P. (1984). *Goal-setting: A motivational technique that works*. Englewood Cliffs, NJ: Prentice-Hall.

Locke, E. A., Shaw, K. N., Saari, L. M., & Latham, G. P. (1981). Goal-setting and task performance: 1969–1980. *Psychological Bulletin*, 90(1), 125–152.

Mahoney, T. A. (1988). Productivity defined: The relativity of efficiency, effectiveness and change. In J. C. Campbell & R. J. Campbell (eds.), *Productivity in organizations* (pp. 13–38). San Francisco: Jossey-Bass.

Mali, P. (1978). *Improving total productivity*. New York: John Wiley & Sons.

Miller, S. (1982). *Productivity: The state of the art, a review for mental health service providers*. Denver: Colorado Division of Mental Health, Human Resources Department.

Muckler, F. A. (1982). Evaluating productivity. In M. D. Dunnette & E. A. Fleishman (eds.), *Human performance and productivity: Vol. 1. Human capability assessment* (pp. 13–47). Hillsdale, NJ: Erlbaum Associates.

National Broadcasting Company (1980). *If Japan can, why can't we?* NBC White Paper. New York: Author.

National Center for Productivity and Quality of Working Life (1977). *The future of productivity*. Washington, DC: Author.

National Center for Productivity and Quality of Working Life (1978). *Total performance management: Some pointers for action* (NTIS No. PB300249). Washington, DC: Author.

Naylor, J. C., Pritchard, R. D., & Ilgen, D. R. (1980). *A theory of behavior in organizations*. New York: Academic Press.

O'Dell, C. S. (1981). *Gainsharing: Incentives, involvement, and productivity*. New York: American Management Associations.

O'Dell, C. S. (1986). *Major findings from people, performance, and pay*. Houston, TX: American Productivity Center.

Peeples, D. E. (1978). Measure for productivity. *Datamation, 24*(5), 222–230.

Pritchard, R. D. (1990). Organizational productivity. In M. D. Dunnette (ed.), *Handbook of Industrial/Organizational Psychology (2nd ed.). Vol. 4.* Palo Alto, CA: Consulting Psychologists Press.

Pritchard, R. D., Bigby, D. G., Beiting, M., Coverdale, S., & Morgan, C. (1981). Enhancing productivity through feedback and goal-setting. *Air Force Human Resources Laboratory Technical Report*, AFHRL-TR-81-7.

Pritchard, R. D., Jones, S. D., Roth, P. L., Stuebing, K. K., & Ekeberg, S. E. (1986). Organizational productivity measurement: The development and evaluation of an integrated approach. *Air Force Human Resources Laboratory Technical Report*, AFHRL-TR-86-64.

Pritchard, R. D., Jones, S. D., Roth, P. L., Stuebing, K. K., & Ekeberg, S. E. (1987). The feedback, goal-setting, and incentives effects on organizational productivity. *Air Force Human Resources Laboratory Technical Report*, AFHRL-TR-87-3.

Pritchard, R. D., Jones, S. D., Roth, P. L., Stuebing, K. K., & Ekeberg, S. E. (1988). The effects of feedback, goal-setting, and incentives on organizational productivity. *Journal of Applied Psychology Monograph Series, 73*(2), 337–358.

Pritchard, R. D., Jones, S. D., Roth, P. L., Stuebing, K. K., & Ekeberg, S. E. (1989). The evaluation of an integrated approach to measuring organizational productivity. *Personnel Psychology, 42*(1), 69–115.

Pritchard, R. D., & Montagno, R. V. (1978). The effects of specific vs. nonspecific, and absolute vs. comparative feedback on performance and satisfaction. *Air Force Human Resources Laboratory Technical Report*, AFHRL-TR-78-12.

Pritchard, R. D., Montagno, R. V., & Moore, J. R. (1978). Enhancing productivity through feedback and job design. *Air Force Human Resources Laboratory Technical Report*, AFHRL-TR-78-44.

Pritchard, R. D., & Roth, P. G. (1989). *Accounting for non-linearities in measures of productivity*. Unpublished manuscript, Texas A&M University.

Pritchard, R. D., Roth, P. L., Jones, S. D., & Galgay, P. J. (1989). *Implementing feedback systems to enhance performance: A practical guide.* Unpublished manuscript, Texas A&M University.

Pritchard, R. D., Roth, P. L., Jones, S. D., Galgay, P. J., & Watson, M. D. (1988). Designing a goal-setting system to enhance performance: A practical guide. *Organizational Dynamics,* Summer, 69–78.

Pritchard, R. D., Roth, P. L., Roth, P. G., Watson, M. D., & Jones, S. D. (1989). Incentive systems: Success by design. *Personnel,* May, 63–68.

Pritchard, R. D., Stuebing, K. K., Jones, S. D., Roth, P. L., & Ekeberg, S. E. (1987). Manager's guide to the implementation of feedback, goal-setting, and incentive systems. *Air Force Human Resources Laboratory Technical Report,* AFHRL-TR-87-4.

Riggs, J. L., & Felix, G. H. (1983). *Productivity by objectives.* Englewood Cliffs, NJ: Prentice-Hall.

Rizzo, J. R., House, R. J., & Lirtzman, S.I. (1970). Role conflict and ambiguity in complex organizations. *Administrative Science Quarterly,* 15, 150–163.

Rowe, D. L. (1981). How Westinghouse measures white-collar productivity. *Management Review,* November, 42–47.

Seashore, S. E. (1972). *The measurement of organizational effectiveness.* Paper presented at the University of Minnesota, Minneapolis.

Seashore, S. E., Lawler, E. E., Mirvis, P. H., & Cammann, C. (1983). *A guide to methods, measures, and practices.* New York: John Wiley & Sons.

Sink, D. S. (1985). *Productivity management: Planning, measurement and evaluation, control and improvement.* New York: John Wiley & Sons.

Taira, K. (1988). Productivity assessment: Japanese perceptions and practices. In J. C. Campbell & R. J. Campbell (eds.), *Productivity in organizations* (pp. 40–62). San Francisco: Jossey-Bass.

Thierry, H. (1987). Payment by results systems: A review of research 1945–1985. *Applied Psychology: An International Review,* 36(1), 91–108.

Tubbs, M. E. (1986). Goal setting: A meta-analytic examination of the empirical evidence. *Journal of Applied Psychology,* 71, 474–483.

Tuttle, T. C. (1981). *Productivity measurement methods: Classification, critique, and implications for the Air Force* (AFHRL-TR-81-9). Brooks AFB, TX: Manpower and Personnel Division, Air Force Human Resources Laboratory.

Tuttle, T. C. (1983). Organizational productivity: A challenge for psychologists. *American Psychologist,* 38, 479–486.

Tuttle, T. C., & Sink, D. S. (1984). Taking the threat out of productivity measurement. *National Productivity Review,* Winter, 24–32.

Tuttle, T. C., & Weaver, C. N. (1986a). *Methodology for generating efficiency and effectiveness measures (MGEEM): A guide for commanders, managers, and supervisors* (AFHRL Technical Paper 86–26). Brooks AFB, TX: Manpower and Personnel Division, Air Force Human Resources Laboratory.

Tuttle, T. C., & Weaver, C. N. (1986b). *Methodology for generating efficiency and effectiveness measures (MGEEM): A guide for Air Force measurement facilitators* (AFHRL-TP-86–36, AD-A174 547). Brooks AFB, TX: Manpower and Personnel Division, Air Force Human Resources Laboratory.

Tuttle, T. C., Wilkinson, R. E., & Matthews, M. D. (1985). *Field test of the methodology for generating efficiency and effectiveness measures* (AFHRL-TR-84-54, AD-A158 183). Brooks AFB, TX: Manpower and Personnel Division, Air Force Human Resources Laboratory.

Weiss, D. J., Dawis, R. V., England, G. W., & Loftquist, L. H. (1967). *Manual for the Minnesota Satisfaction Questionnaire.* Minnesota Studies in Vocational Rehabilitation: Vol. XXII.

White House Conference on Productivity. (1984). *Productivity growth: A better life for America* (NTIS #PB 84-159136). Washington D.C.: Author.

Woodman, R. W., & Sherwood, J. J. (1980). The role of team development in organizational effectiveness: A critical review. *Psychological Bulletin, 88*(1), 166–186.

Index

244 Index

ABOUT THE AUTHOR

Robert D. Pritchard is a Professor and Director of the Industrial/Organizational Psychology Program at Texas A&M University. He works primarily in the area of measuring and improving organizational productivity. He has published one book and over sixty articles in the area of motivation and organizational productivity. He has also worked with many organizations in the United States and abroad in the area of productivity.